It's My Time: The A to Z of Property and Financial Terms

Brian McNicol

Muthu Pannirselvam

This book contains some 2000 terms with concise definitions and with simple, easy-to-understand explanations arranged alphabetically. It is a quick reference guide for buyers, vendors, real estate professionals and investors. It has over 100 graphs, charts and tables that apply to all aspects of real estate, both residential and commercial.

Disclaimer

The information contained in this book is given in good faith and has been derived from sources believed to be accurate at the time of writing. No liability will be accepted by the authors or publishers for actions taken by any person on the strength of this information alone. It is recommended that professional independent advice be sought.

Editors

Anthony Skinner
John Bone
Samantha Boholt

First published in November 2019 by Arthur Phillip Books

Cover designed by Brian McNicol and Muthu Pannirselvam

Dedicated to:
The Platinum Family

Contents

A word from author Brian McNicol

In 2010, I included on my vision board, and in my five year plan, the desire of becoming an author. I had started researching and had written some chapters, had the title for the book, but then other aspects of life intervened which meant that the book writing was no longer a priority. The desire to write was still there but finding the time was more difficult.

I first met Muthu in 2016 when we both attended a property coaching course. We spoke on a few occasions over the course of the year and I presented on a couple of occasions on commercial property: a topic that Muthu was interested in 2016 ended and we both went back to doing what we had been doing. I was in Melbourne in early 2017 and Muthu asked to meet me for coffee and it was at that meeting that Muthu broke the news that we would be writing a book together.

We both come from different backgrounds but both believe strongly in education, in giving back to our community and providing a legacy for our children; so what better way than to write a book? This book in its final form has little resemblance to its original format as Muthu and I believe that, after several rewrites, it has ended up a book that people will find very useful as a reference. Having been investing for over 40 years, I had forgotten the basics. (That is not that I would go close to saying that I knew everything or even a fraction of what you need to know). But Muthu explained that he would have found a book covering property terminology very useful when he started his property journey. I then remembered living in New Zealand for a couple of years and getting used to the different terminology over there and – no - it is not just the way words are pronounced.

As we started to write this book the different terminology also became apparent across the different states in Australia. So, whether you are just buying your first house to live in (or as an investment), undertaking renovations, looking at developing, or buying commercial property, then this book has many terms and illustrations that you will find useful. This book is being translated into Mandarin for our growing Chinese audience in the hope that it will help our Chinese investors to understand the terminology used in Australia.

I could see the benefit of this book but it was only the start of one person's journey. Somewhere along the line, I might have suggested to Muthu that we needed another book or two to be written so we have identified six-book series. I know some people will be saying why do we need another six books on property? Our bookshops previously had shelves full of property and investing books and at home, I have quite a library. We have set out from the start to write books that are relevant to today. Yes, we will cover the basics but we also want to cover topics that are relevant to today's property investor, developer and people in retirement or planning retirement. The series of books is a meaningful attempt to provide useful resources to those who on the journey with us in property and looking forward to a long and healthy retirement free of money worries.

Neither Muthu, nor I, is a JK Rowling or a Robert Kiyosaki so we do not expect to give up our day jobs to live off the royalties of the books. We do hope that we will both be able to contribute, from each book sold, to two very special and worthwhile charities that we support. Firstly, the Destiny Rescue, an Australian initiative that is touching many lives across the world. Destiny Rescue is a non-profit organisation that is striving hard to end child sexual exploitation and slavery. Secondly, Opportunity International exists to bring about a measure of justice, dignity and purpose for families living in poverty. They do this by supporting local microfinance organisations that provide innovative financial solutions to empower people, create small businesses and build vibrant communities.

Please discourage any form of illegal downloads of this book that defeats the purpose of the series published by Arthur Phillip Books. We wish you the best of luck on your property journey and may your dreams come true in near and far future! Visit our website for recent updates, blogs and other interesting information on properties www.arthurphillipbooks.com.

Acknowledgements

To my co-author, Muthu Pannirselvam, for approaching me to write this book, for the hours spent in following up on definitions, then organising, editing and publishing of this book. Originally our ideas may have been a little different but the end result is good. For believing in my thoughts that we could write six books (one is complete, number two is well on the way) and broad outlines for the other three are complete).

To the various authors and teachers that have influenced my life over many years: Dymphna Boholt, Stephen Covey, Hans Jakobi, Robert Kiyosaki, Steve McKnight and Michael Yardney to name but a few.

Networking is important particularly in the property industry and I have been fortunate to belong to a number of property groups that meet regularly to have a meal and talk about property. It is good to have mates in the game that can assist you with questions and keep you focused when things don't always go according to plan.

Chapter 1

Real estate

A

Absolute Title
The registered proprietor of land registered with absolute title has a State guaranteed title that there is no other person that has a better right to the land.

Abut
To touch, or border on. For example, a property abutting a highway or sharing a common boundary with another property.

Acceptance
A consent, by someone receiving an offer, to its terms and conditions

Access rights
The right of ingress to, and egress from, a property which abuts an existing street or property. It is an easement in the street which is appurtenant to abutting property and is a private right as distinguishable from rights to the public.

Accommodation
Accommodation is a room, group of rooms, or a building in which someone may live or stay.

Short-term accommodation refers to the average length of stay well below the stipulated 28 days. (Example: bed and breakfast type rooms for rentals, AirBNBs)

Long term accommodation refers to a property where 80 % of guests stay longer than 28 days (Example: a rooming house and boarding house, caravan park). The 28 day period is a period used for taxation purposes: for example Goods and Services Tax (GST) by the Australian Taxation Office.

Acreage
A term which usually refers to an area of agricultural land. Strangely, such land is not necessarily measured in acres. The terminology remains despite Australia going metric in 1974.

Acreage conversion
One acre is approximately 4000 m^2. (Remember the great Australian dream that speaks of a 'quarter acre block').

Example: A land survey shows that Adam owns land that measures 300 m x 20 m. To calculate the area in square metres and in acres. (Note:1 acre = 4,046.86 m^2)

$$Total\ area = 300m \times 20m = 6000\ m^2$$

$$Total\ area\ in\ acres = \frac{6000}{4046.86} = 1.483\ acres$$

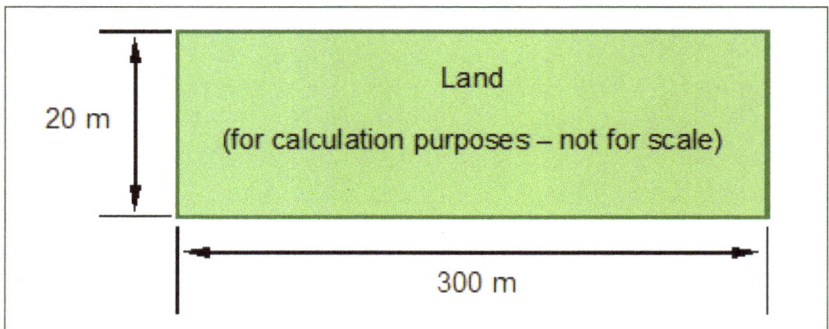

Land

(for calculation purposes – not for scale)

20 m

300 m

Figure 1: Rectangular piece of land

Acquisition cost

Acquisition costs to all fees required to obtain a property. This includes the purchase price of a property, solicitor fees, loan fees, valuation costs and other fees. (See *Holding costs* and *Blockchain*)

Acts

Are a type of law passed by a legislative body (government body). Some acts related to properties are: the Estate Agent's Act, Residential Tenancies Act, Landlord and Tenancies Act, Anti-discrimination Act, Stamp Duties Act, Dividing Fences Act, Local Government Act, Subdivision of Land Act, Trade Practices Act, Companies Act, Environment Protection Act, Occupational Health and Safety Act. The actual names of the acts will vary from state to state and after the name of the act, the year it was enacted provides the correct name of the act: for example Residential Tenancies Act 2010 in New South Wales and Residential Tenancies and Rooming Accommodation Act 2008 in Queensland.

Adjoining

This is used to indicate that two pieces of land have a common boundary.

Adjustments

This is a term primarily associated with apportionments made to council rates and water rates at the time of settlement of the Contract of Sale. It can also apply to the termination of leases, both residential and commercial, where there may be an apportionment of rent. An example is an adjustment to rates at settlement. Council rates are paid in advance, either quarterly, half yearly or yearly depending upon the local council. The solicitors for both the purchaser and seller will agree upon the amount of rates that the vendor has paid in advance and should have paid up until the date of settlement. The purchaser will refund the vendor the agreed amount on settlement.

Alignment

This term is commonly used in relationship to the boundaries of property. For example, a requirement that the building must be set back six metres from the front alignment. Property professionals will also talk of a realignment of boundaries. This might mean council realigning a road or footpath, or a property developer realigning the boundaries of a property when subdividing to ensure that the new subdivision conforms to council requirements.

Amenities

Amenities mean the 'attractiveness' of a place. This is more often used for commercial property and used in reference to service buildings such as toilets.

Anchor tenant

The main, and usually the largest, tenant who attracts other tenants and customers to a shopping centre (also called key tenant).

Annexure

This is an attachment to a Contract of Sale. An attachment may be used if there are additional clauses to the contract and they don't fit on the contract document, or there is an inventory such as chattels or covenant conditions.

Appraisal

The term used by real estate agents when giving an opinion on the approximate value and the saleability of a property, based on the past sales. Whilst appearing similar to a valuation, valuations can only be given by licensed valuers.

Appurtenance

Something that is external to the property itself but is considered a part of the property. An easement and right of way (ROW) are examples of appurtenances.

Arrears

Debts not paid by the due date including rent, mortgage repayments, utility payments, etc.

Asking price

Asking price is the price at which the owner is willing to sell a property (also called an offer price). It is the listed price of a property which may be negotiated.

Assessed value

A property valuation created for taxation purposes.

Assignment

By a Deed of Assignment, one party (assignor) will assign or transfer their interest to another (assignee). An example of this is in commercial real estate where there is a transfer by the original tenant (the assignor) of his or her rights to a sub-tenant (the assignee) to use the leased property. However, the assignor remains liable under the original lease contract unless expressly released by the landlord.

Attractive nuisance

An appealing yet potentially hazardous feature or characteristic of part of a property which may attract trespassers who could suffer harm. Examples: swimming pool, 'Pokemon Go' feature

Auction

This is a public sale in which goods or properties are sold to the highest bidder. The price is neither set nor arrived at by negotiation, but is arrived at through the process of competitive and open bidding. An auction is complete (and a binding contract is created) when a bid is accepted by the seller. Auctions are claimed to bring the highest price possible for the vendor on a particular property. It can be counter claimed that the highest bid is just one bid higher than what others were prepared to bid and may be well below what the winning bidder was prepared to pay.

Avigation easement

This is similar to an electrical easement across a property. It cedes the right to use the airspace above the property in return for a monetary payment by an airport to the property owner. This easement allows certain rights: right of flight, noise and dust. This is very topical in recent times when drones are slowly creeping into our daily lives. (Read our book "*It's My Time: Commercial Investment*" for further details on the impact of technology on the property market).

B

Battle-axe block

This refers to a lot that has been created at the rear of an existing lot. It derives its name from the shape created by the lot. It can also be called a hammerhead block. If a house is located in the front of a large block to be subdivided, then the owner may consider renting the house at the front and building a new house behind the existing property. One drawback is that the long driveway takes up valuable square metres of land. In the following image, the properties 344 and 348 are battle axe (or hammerhead type subdivisions). See *subdivision* for more types.

Figure 2: **Aerial view of battle axe blocks (adjacent to the red coloured roof)**

Bill of Sale

A written instrument given to pass from a seller to the buyer stating that the seller transfers the legal title of the item to the buyer for a certain price.

Blockchain

A blockchain can be regarded as an open, distributed ledger for recording transactions between parties in an efficient manner. It can be verified and is permanent. As a distributed ledger it is typically managed by a peer-to-peer network that adheres to a specific protocol. Once recorded, the data cannot be altered retroactively without altering subsequent data and with the cooperation of others in the network.

- For example, blockchain would make title deeds transparent and would make any manipulation virtually impossible as it is based on a distributed database. Blockchain may potentially remove legal costs, title related costs, title insurance, and legal fees associated with property transfer. Blockchain is one of the products that will be extensively used in the real estate industry in the future and will make real estate transactions cheaper, faster and safer than ever before.

Currently the buyer, bank, conveyancing agent, and all involved in a property transaction, have their private ledger of transactions. Each can neither see other's ledgers, nor verify that everything is accurate among all involved. In simple terms, blockchain technology will allow all parties to look at the same ledger. This technology will create complete transparency in all transactions and hence no fraudulent transactions can occur.

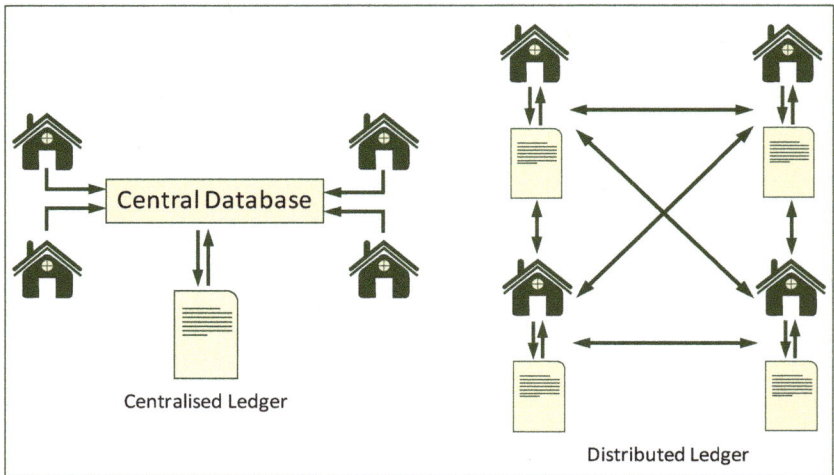

Figure 3: Conceptual image of centralised ledger and distributed ledger (blockchain)

Body Corporate *(now known as Owner's Corporation in some states)*

This is a legal entity created when land is subdivided and registered to establish a community title scheme. It is a corporation of the owners in a strata title building which serves to manage the building and common areas. It can cover duplexes, residential unit blocks, high rise apartments, shopping complexes and entire residential suburbs.

It is run by a council, or committee, consisting of unit owners (or sometimes a tenant as a current resident of the property) that manage a strata or unit development including the buildings and common property. In some properties, common areas could be a pool, a parking area, a park or other amenities that are public to all. If you are the owner, or resident, of a property managed by an Owner's Corporation, you are entitled to vote on decisions during annual general meetings, propose to develop or repair common areas, or even upgrade from the sinking fund normally available to cover the expenses. The properties in these estates are usually at higher prices than the neighbouring ones that are not managed by an Owner's Corporation.

Body corporate fee

A body corporate fee, or levy, is collected periodically from the owners, after the annual budget is set. The levy normally comprises contributions and a sinking fund. Contributions cover the normal running costs for the particular body corporate such as maintenance and lighting of common areas, building and public liability insurances and manager's fees. (See *repairs, maintenance*)

Sinking fund provides a fund for future maintenance such as repainting off the building. If there are insufficient funds in the sinking fund then a special levy may be raised to cover the costs of works to the building. (See *sinking fund*)

- Anybody considering purchasing strata titled unit would be wise to get a copy of the Body Corporate Disclosure Statement. This will provide some indication as to whether the current strata levy is sufficient to carry out the required maintenance or whether the strata levies are likely to be increased in the near future.

Body corporate insurance

Body corporate insurance, also called strata insurance, is more suited to a strata-titled investment unit. An owner has rights to the common areas of the building along with any associated liabilities through the body corporate. The body corporate insurance usually covers building, common contents, workers compensation, machinery or plant breakdown, office bearer's liability and fidelity guarantee, and public liability.

Bond

This is money paid by a tenant prior to taking up a tenancy and held until after the tenant has vacated the premises and the property has been inspected to ensure that it is clean and tidy and there is no damage to the property. The bond is held by the Rental Bond Authority, or equivalent, and there are strict guidelines to be followed. Normally a bond is equivalent to four weeks rent but differs depending on the state or territories in Australia.

The rental manager collects the bond money from the tenant and, at the end of the lease, applies to the Rental Bond Authority to have the money refunded. In Queensland the tenant is also able to apply for the bond to be refunded.

Building process (residential)

It is normally a three step process in residential projects. These steps may vary depending on the builder; however the volume builder would like to follow the steps methodically as the system is in place for such a process. (See *construction stages, contract, warranty, life time warranty*)

Step 1 Pre-site	Design of home, colour, electrical selection, contract sign off and site preparation
Step 2 Construction stages	Site, Base, frame, lock-up, fixing, completion
Step 3 Warranty	Settlement, inspection, completion of works including defective items

'Bundle of rights' theory

The theory that ownership of a property implies a group of rights such as occupation, use, enjoyment, sale, bequeathment, giving, or lease of all or part of these rights. Such rights in the property can be split.

Buy-back agreement

A clause in a contract under which the seller agrees to repurchase the property at a set price upon the occurrence of a specified event within a specified time period.

Buyer's agent or advocate

This is a licensed real estate professional who works on behalf of the buyer (their client) to secure property matching as close as possible to the requirements their client has provided. A buyer's agent saves the buyer time and money. The buyer pays the buyer's agent a fee normally up to about three percent of the purchase price for finding the property. Buyer's agents are very common overseas and are becoming more common in Australia. In simple terms, it is the person who acts on behalf of a buyer.

Buyer's market

This terminology is often used when market prices are around what is deemed reasonable or even below market expectations. There is generally a good number of properties for sale and not as many buyers hence buyers have a larger choice of properties and can negotiate good deals when purchasing property. It is related to supply and demand with an oversupply of properties causing prices to decline.

Buying 'off-the-plan'

This is when the purchaser signs a contract to purchase a property that is yet to be built or subdivided (based on viewing the design, building plans and a schedule of finishes) but there is no physical property to see or inspect.

- The developer will normally use words such as 'or similar' when indicating the types of inclusions because they cannot guarantee what type of products may be available in the time that it takes to complete the building.
- During this time, there can be delays in completion of the project, interest rate increases and the builder could go into liquidation. Drawbacks are that many people cannot visualise room size from a set of plans and the quality of construction and finishes may not be as expected.

There are a number of reasons why people buy off-the-plan.

- Firstly, they may have first choice of which apartment they can purchase. They may also be able to choose colour schemes and floor coverings. In some states in Australia, there may be stamp duty concessions.
- Finally, for property speculators, there is the hope the property will be worth more when it is completed than what they sign the contract for in today's prices. For the speculator, this will depend on the mix of purchasers and the surrounding buildings that may be completed around a similar time.

The speculator is hoping to on-sell the apartment prior to the apartments being completed or shortly thereafter and makes a capital gain during that period of time. There is a risk attached to finance for the purchase of the apartment in the future as lending criteria can change between signing of the contract, and paying the deposit, to completion of the apartments. Our next book entitled *"It's My Time: Successful Residential Investing. Fundamentals and emerging trends in today's property market"* looks further at supply and demand for buying off the plan and completed properties.

C

Caveat

This is a legal document lodged at the Titles Office and noted against the Title Deed of a particular property that another party has an interest or claim on that property. It is a warning or proviso to a prospective buyer that there is a requirement that must be observed, or someone has an interest in the land, or there is some condition or limitation. The caveat could be as a result of a dispute or an agreed form of security if money is lent. Until the caveat is lifted, either by settlement of the dispute or agreement, a property transfer cannot occur.

The three types of caveats are:

- Registrable caveat
- Hostile caveat
- Mutually agreeable caveat

Caveat Emptor

A Latin phrase literally meaning "let the buyer beware". This places the onus upon the purchaser to ensure that he/she is satisfied with the property and all conditions of the sale. Potential buyers must examine or conduct due diligence on goods or property at their own risk. (See *due diligence*)

Certificate of Title

A copy of title to land held under the Torrens system. It shows when the certificate was created, ownership, details of the land, as well as any caveats, covenants, etc. The original is held at the Land Titles office and a copy is held by the registered proprietor or, if the land is mortgaged, by the lending organisation.

Chattels

This is a legal term referring to personal property in a dwelling that is moveable such as clothing, furniture, tools, crockery and cutlery. Conversely, items such as carpets and curtains (that are fixed) are known as fittings. (See *real property and personal property*).

Collateral

Collateral is an addition, asset or security pledged by a person that borrows money for a mortgage in order to guarantee the principal security. Whilst it can be anything of value that a lender can use as security should the borrower default on repaying the loan, real property is the preferred security. Lenders may also consider motor vehicles, boats and business equipment and leasehold businesses as collateral. Most often you hear the term cross collateralising the properties.

Example: Suppose you have a house (principal place of residence) that is worth $500,000 of which you have an outstanding loan for an amount $320,000. There is an equity in this principal place of residence (PPR). You go to your bank and express your interest to purchase another property without knowing that you are cross collateralising your principal place of residence (PPR) to purchase an investment. The bank will be happy to use the equity from your PPR and cross collateralise with your investment property. This is a typical situation of many avarice investors. (See *Equity*)

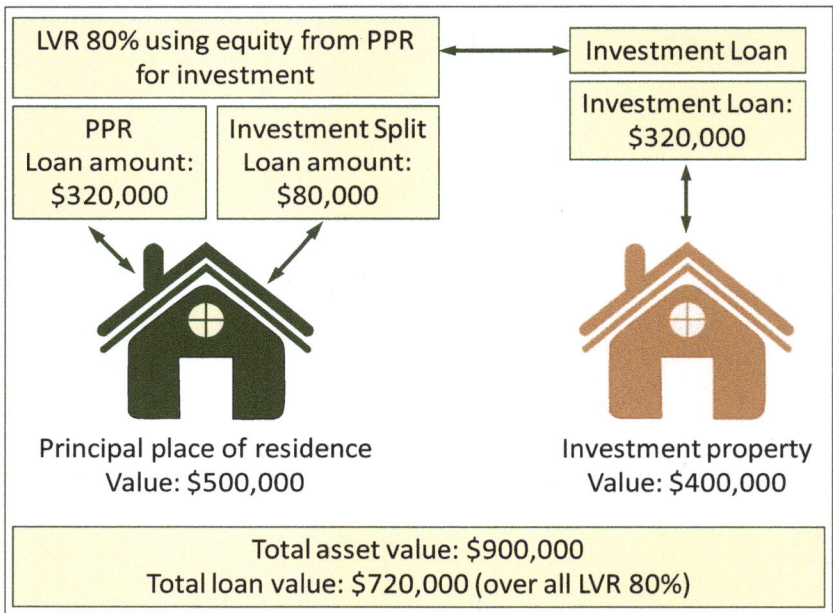

Figure 4: Example showing cross collaterising an investment with the principal place of residence

Common Property

This is property commonly owned within a strata scheme that is shared by tenants such as the grounds, gardens and external facilities, driveways and visitor car parking, stairwells, lifts and foyers. An exception to the grounds and common property is where a particular apartment has been granted exclusive use such as a private courtyard area or a dedicated parking space and this is normally shown on the property title.

Commission
It is a mutually agreed (or fixed by custom or law) fee accruing to an agent, broker, or salesperson for facilitating, initiating, and/or executing a commercial transaction. For example a real estate agent will be paid a commission by the vendor for selling a property and a finance broker will receive a commission from the lending institution for arranging a loan. It is a fee payable as an incentive to a salesperson, usually based on the value of the goods or services sold.

Community title
Generally relates to retirement villages where the properties are not individually titled but each "Owner has an exclusive use". This is when a parcel of land is subdivided into smaller lots and there is a shared or common space among all owners of that subdivided parcel of land.

Company title
This is a form of ownership for apartment blocks and commercial buildings before strata titles. Owners purchase shares in a company which owns the land and buildings. This form of ownership can be difficult to finance.

Concurrent lien
Two or more liens over the same property. (See lien)

Continuing authority period
In a sales agreement with a real estate agent, a continuing authority period is that period beyond the exclusive authority period during which the agent still has the authority to sell.

Contract of Sale
A legal agreement between the vendor and purchaser relating to the sale of property that sets out the terms and conditions of the sale. Depending upon the state or territory, the sale contract or contract of sale is prepared by the vendor's solicitor or real estate agent. It contains information and certificates from relevant authorities and outlines the terms and conditions of the sale and includes the details of fittings and plant (air conditioners, antennae).

Conversion
The act of changing a property from one use to another.

Conveyancing
This is the process whereby the ownership of a property passes from one person or company to another lawfully. Vendors and buyers normally engage a solicitor or conveyancer for this transfer although it is not mandatory. This process generally involves checking if the seller has full and proper legal title and is registering the transfer of ownership of land with no encumbrance. The latter will be flagged by solicitors should such exist. (See *Blockchain on how the conveyancing process will be simplified in the future*).

Cooling-off period
A period, normally 3 – 5 days, during which time somebody who is about to enter into an agreement may reflect on all aspects of the arrangement and change their mind if necessary.

Corner blocks
Corner lots in some subdivisions are preferred because they may have a larger land area and access to both streets. This is particularly beneficial for multi-unit developments and may provide flexibility in design for houses. However, traffic might be an issue on busy intersections especially at night with the intrusion of headlights. Also, development costs might be higher because councils tend to be more strict about presentation due to their

prominence and, without front fencing, locals may be tempted to take a 'shortcut' across the property.

Cost-plus contract

A contract where the builder obtains materials and services at each stage of the building process and passes the actual cost to the customer by adding an agreed margin to cover overheads and profits (see *overheads*).

Council contributions

A council or development contribution is a levy paid to council either by payments or in-kind works, facilities or services provided by developers towards the supply of infrastructure such as water, sewer and parks required to meet the future needs of the community.

D

Date of settlement

In relation to real estate transaction, it is the day, on which, under the terms of the contract, the vendor is required to transfer their interest in property to the purchaser.

Developer

The person who transforms raw land into a site and then improves the property by the use of capital, labour and entrepreneurial skills. (See *net income*).

Deposit

It is the amount that the purchaser pays as part of the sale price to the vendor at the time of entering into a contract and is normally 5 to 10 % of the agreed sale price. The purchaser must ensure that the Contract of Sale contains appropriate clauses to protect the deposit or it may be forfeited. For example, if the purchaser has not yet received approval for finance from a lender, then the purchaser must ensure that the contract is conditional upon this occurring. It is also common to make the sale subject to a satisfactory building and pest inspection (See *mortgage broker*).

Development approval

This is normally the first step in the development process. An application is submitted to the council specifying such things as building plans, various reports by professionals such as engineers. Council then assesses the application against the town planning requirements.

- If approved the plans are stamped and a formal document is issued detailing the terms and conditions of the Development Approval (DA).
- Some councils have streamlined approval processes and allow 'fast-track' if certain conditions are met. For example, single storey construction and location within a specified 'foot print'.

Types of developments approval include: self-assessable, code assessable and impact assessable. (See *Engineers*)

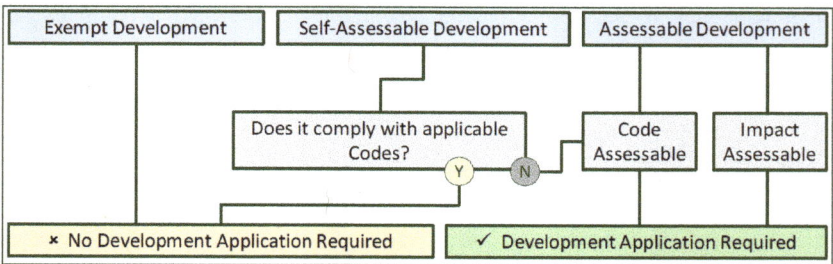

Figure 5: **Flow diagram showing various types of development approvals**

(Our book entitled "*It's My Time: Successful Residential Investing. Fundamentals and emerging trends in today's property market*" contains further details on types of consent and specifications of development application).

Distressed property
A property that is under foreclosure, or imminent foreclosure, due to insufficient income generation.

Double-dip
A broker or an intermediary that takes a percentage of commission from both the buyer and the vendor. The vendor and the buyer both believe that only one of them is paying the commission.

Dutch auction
A bidding process in which the asking price is lowered slowly until someone places a qualifying bid.

Dummy bidding
An unethical practice whereby a person makes a 'fake' bid at an auction in an attempt to deceive genuine bidders into making a higher bid. It is illegal in most states and territories.

E

Earnest money
A deposit made to a vendor showing the buyer's good faith in a transaction.

Easement
An easement is a strip of land granting access over property for use by another party.

- For example, an access easement allows the owner of a rear property access to that property by an easement over part of the front property.
- Another example are utility easements created in favour of councils and other authorities for the provision of water, sewerage and drainage.

These service easements allow for the construction of these services as well as the right of access to inspect or repair these services at any time. Depending upon the council and the type of service provided, no one can build over these easements. Generally, most service easements run along the rear or side boundaries and can be about three metres wide so will likely have little impact upon the construction of a standard residential house.

In the following plan, E1 and E2 are sewer easements.

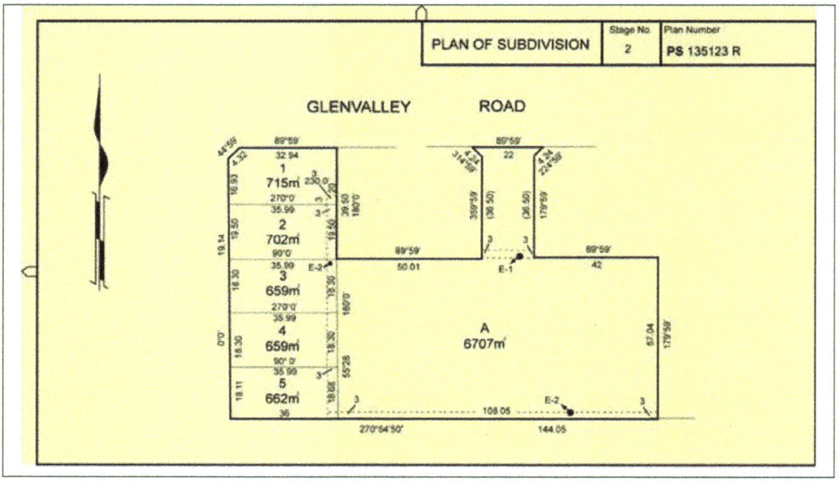

Figure 6: Schematic of plan of subdivision that shows easements

Encumbrances

This is an interest in a piece of land by someone other than the registered owner and places limitations on the property. Examples include mortgages, easements, leases and restrictive covenants.

It is a burden on a property giving legally enforceable rights to someone that is not the owner of the property. A solicitor or conveyancer should search for encumbrances on a property and report to their client (buyer or lender or mortgagee) on their meaning and impact. The presence of the encumbrance will be revealed by a search of the title documents.

Englobo

Vacant land that is able to be subdivided. Englobo is defined as "an undeveloped lot, group of lots or parcel of land that is zoned to allow for, and capable of significant subdivision into smaller parcels under existing land use provisions".

Entry condition report

This is a form filled out by the property manager and given to the tenant prior to or on the day of occupation showing the condition of the premises at the start of the tenancy. The tenant should inspect and report to the property manager any discrepancies that the tenant notes.

Entry notice

The notice required to be given to the tenant about entry by the lessor, the property manager, sales agent or maintenance contractors.

Estate at sufferance

The wrongful occupancy of a property by a tenant after the lease has expired

Exclusive agency

This agreement gives one real estate agent the exclusive right to sell a property. Even if some other person, including the vendor, sells the property, the real estate agent is still entitled to be paid commission. It differs from a sole agency in that the vendor retains the right to sell the property under a sole agency.

Exit Condition report

It is compared to the entry condition report. It shows the condition of the property and any inclusions when the tenant leaves.

F

Fair market value

Fair market value is the value of a property in today's dollars if it were placed on the market for sale. It is based on what a buyer is willing to pay and a seller is willing to accept when both are on equal terms of being knowledgeable, willing and unpressured in the marketplace.

If an insured property is damaged and is not in a liveable condition, then the owner is compensated based on the fair market value. A property valuation once every two years is recommended and the fair market value registered on the bank's system.

Fair Trading Department (or regulatory services or consumer affairs or consumer protection)

This department, in some states, is responsible for the receipt and management of residential tenancy bonds and is the regulatory and licensing body for real estate agents.

Fee simple

Fee simple is the highest form of ownership. It is a legal interest in property or estate capable of being inherited without limitation. (See free hold property).

First Home Owner Grant

The First Home Owner Grant (FHOG) scheme was introduced on 1 July 2000 to offset the effect of the GST on home ownership. It is a national scheme funded by the states and territories and administered under their own legislation. The grant is made via electronic funds transfer (EFT) at settlement (when purchasing an existing home), on the first draw down of the loan (in case of a contract to build) or after sighting of the Certificate of Occupancy (for owner builders).

First Mortgage Security

A loan where the lender holds a first registered mortgage which is registered with the government agency responsible for land ownership such as the Department of Natural Resources Mines and Energy.

Fittings

Fittings may be personal property installed by the landlord or tenant and may be removed without causing irreparable damage to the property or land. In simple terms, they are non-fixed items. (See *real property, personal property, chattel, land* and *site*).

Fixed-rate lease

A fixed-rate lease is when the tenant or business pays a fixed rent per month over the life of the lease. This is used for community or neighbourhood centres on a peppercorn rent type. (See *graduate lease*).

Fixtures

These are items which are fixed to the property and which could not be removed from the property without causing serious damage to either the fixture or the property it is attached to.

Final inspection

Final inspection of a property is made during the week before a new owner takes possession. The purpose is to ensure that the property is in much the same condition as it was at the time the contract of sale was signed, with due allowance for wear and tear during the settlement period. The purchaser might take this opportunity to discuss the vendor's intentions regarding removal of rubbish.

Folio

Under the Torrens system, land is given a unique identification number known as the folio. The folio consists of land dimensions, its boundaries, the name of the registered owner and other encumbrances that affect the title of the land.

Forfeit

This means a fine or penalty for a wrong-doing. In real estate, forfeit generally means the buyer has breached a clause of the contract and hence forfeits the deposit money to the vendor (See *deposit, subject to finance approval, notice to complete* for more details).

Frontage

This is the width of a property measured along its abutment with the street. It is an important factor when considering subdivision as all properties must have a minimum frontage per lot.

G

Gage

This is a deposit made in good faith to ensure fulfilment of an agreement.

- Historically, live gage was a method of transaction whereby a borrower would physically deliver real property, capable of generating revenue, as a gage. It was 'live' because the revenue was self-redeeming (it could pay off the debt).
- Dead gage was a loan where the deposit was unable to generate funds and hence did not reduce the debt. Combining the French word for 'dead' – mort – with gage gives us the common term MORTGAGE.

Goodwill

It is an asset of a business created mainly by customer and stakeholder relations. It is considered to be of intangible value though, upon sale of the business, a valuer may attach a value.

Gift deed

This allows a person to give away assets, or transfer ownership of property, without an exchange of funds.

Graduated lease

This is a lease that provides for a certain rent for an initial period, followed by an increase or decrease in rent over a specified period. This is typically applicable for a commercial property lease in which the payments are variable and adjusted periodically to reflect changes in the property's appraised value or Consumer Price Index (CPI). (See *fixed rate lease*).

Granny flat

A granny flat is a smaller home for an ageing parent, built on the same land where a single-family home is already located. Local council regulations and compliance determine the maximum size of a granny flat. They are suited to offspring that are moving out of home for the first time and also suitable as an investment strategy to generate additional income. (Our book entitled *"It's My Time: Successful Residential Investing. Fundamentals and emerging trends in today's property market"* will have more details).

H

Habitable

A formal certification through local building codes that a dwelling is suitable for human habitation.

Hard landing

The resulting economic pull-back after a government steps in to slow an economy.

Hedge funds

These are offshore investment funds which are speculative and use borrowed capital.

Hereditament
An item of property, tangible (land, property) or intangible (rent) that may be inherited.

High density development
High density developments mostly fall within residential and resi-mercial zones that occur in locations of intense activity with excellent connectivity (public transport, amenities, access). These high density developments are located mostly within central business districts and immediate suburbs in the metropolitan cities of Australia.

Highest and best use of land
The use most likely to generate the highest net return on the land and/or building over a given period. (Refer to *Questions to ask a town planner* in the Appendix VIII).

Holding costs
Costs such as loan repayments, council rates, water rates and insurance expenses incurred while waiting for resale of a property.

Holding deposit
A sum of money given to register interest before a full deposit is made.

Holding over
Holding over is a clause in a commercial lease that allows the lessee (tenant) to remain in possession of the property after the lease has expired, on similar terms as before. At the end of the lease term, the lease rolls over to a month-to-month basis. Landlords are wise to ensure that the security deposit or bank guarantee extends to any default of payment that may occur during the holding over period.

Home ownership
Home ownership is considered a key cultural icon, and part of the Australian tradition known as the Great Australian Dream.

Of all the states and territories in Australia, Tasmania has the largest home ownership percentage (70%) and Northern Territory the lowest (46%). ABS data as of September 2016 shows that there is a total of 9.76 million residential dwellings in Australia for a population of 24.1 million. This equates to 2.47 occupants per residential dwelling.

Housing Industry Association (HIA)
The Housing Industry Association is a national association for building trades and professionals in the building and construction industries. The association supports residential builders, trade contractors, developers, design professionals, kitchen and bathroom specialists, manufacturers and suppliers.

I

Impact assessable
When a proposed development does not meet the (planning) code assessable requirements of the local council, it is deemed impact assessable and is evaluated based on its merit and ability to satisfy specific council needs.

Industrial zone
A zone or area where businesses/ factories are located

K

Key tenant
The major tenant in an office block or shopping centre. (See anchor tenant).

L

Landlord
Also known as the lessor, the landlord is the owner of leased property who leases to a lessee.

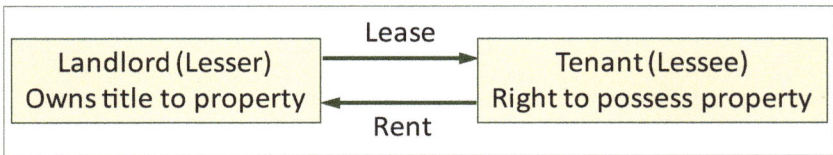

Figure 7: **Relationship between the landlord and a tenant**

Land tax

A state based tax, payable annually with respect to the ownership of land valued at more than a set threshold. The value of the land tax payable is determined from the assessed valuation of the property, the entity the property is owned by and any threshold that is applicable. It is levied by the state government and is assessed on the unimproved value of the land. The tax is levied when a person or company owns land valued at more than a set threshold. This threshold varies between states and territories. Any land tax paid is generally a tax deduction. The principal place of residence is usually excluded from the calculation of the value of the land that one owns.

Land Titles Office

The Land Titles Office is responsible for registration of all land-related transactions pertaining to the purchase and sale of land and properties in the state and territories, and maintaining the land titles register under the relevant acts. The Land Titles Office holds land title information and property information, valuation surveying, geodesy and place names.

Lease

A lease is a document that creates a leasehold interest. The lease terms are binding on both the landlord and tenant. The lease is a contractual agreement that will "set out the terms upon which the tenant will hold the interest and the landholder will then be restricted in his/her activities on the land by those terms". An investor should carefully peruse the leasing documentation to ensure that there are no existing leases to the property. Any undesirable provisions may be used for negotiating the purchase price of the property if they are not already reflected in the asking price.

Lease agreement
This is a legal contract between a landlord and a tenant setting out all the terms and conditions of the lease in regard to the property.

Leaseback
A property sale where the vendor stays on as a tenant.

Leasehold
The right to use real estate for a certain time as set out in an agreement. Leasehold is when the property is held other than in absolute ownership. For example a property in the Australian Capital Territory (ACT) is a leasehold with generally a 99 year lease to the government. (See *free hold, fee simple*).

Leasehold improvement
This is the expenditure made by the lessee to alter or improve leased property.

Lessee
The person leasing a property.

Lessee fixtures
In commercial properties, the lessor provides only the space and the lessee is to attach and detach the fixtures, fittings, plant and equipment at the start of the lease and on expiration of the lease. A separate clause is normally added in the lease regarding the obligation of attachment and removal of fixtures.

This clause transfers any liability for damage to the property incurred as an outcome of installing or removing these fixtures to the lessee. If the lessee did not remove the fixtures after the expiry of lease, then the lessor may have the right to the fixtures remaining and to carry out the required work to make good any damage, at the lessee's expense.

Lessor
The owner of a leased property.

Liability insurance
Liability insurance will generally cover you for any liability incurred as a result of being the owner or occupier of the property. For example, liability insurance may pay the amount the owner has to pay for an accident that happens because of a defect in the contents (assuming the contents are insured).

Lien
A type of encumbrance. A right to hold someone else's asset as security. Lien is defined "a charge upon real or personal property for the satisfaction of some debt or duty ordinarily arising by operation of law". In other words, it is a right that allows someone to keep possession of an individual's property until that person has paid back a debt owing.

Life estate
A freehold property interest that expires when someone dies.

Low density housing
Low density housing consists of single storey and double storey detached or semi-detached dwellings with small to medium setbacks to side boundaries.

Figure 8: Aerial view of low density housing

M

Management fees

Managing agents will charge a commission fee (fully tax deductable) of around 5 to 9% of the gross rent collected on a residential or commercial property. This may be higher for properties such as boarding, rooming houses and holiday properties.

Managing agent

The person appointed by the landlord of a rental property to manage that property. This person manages the property, collects the rent and pays owners corporation fees and utility bills. Depending upon negotiations, the agent may also charge a fee for lease renewal, advertising, statements, end of financial year statement, routine inspections, rent review and miscellaneous costs.

Marketing expenses

In real estate terms they represent the cost of selling a property and include advertising, display furniture, photography, etc in addition to the agent's commission.

Market feasibility study

It determines the current condition of the property market and how the market would respond to a proposed project. Market feasibility is very critical as it studies condition of the market and the ability to support a project (be it residential or commercial property). Our books entitled "It's My Time: Successful Residential Investing" and "It's My Time: Successful Residential Investing" for more details on how market feasibility determines the profitability of a particular project.

Market rent

It is the rental income that a property would most likely command on the open market as per the current rents paid by tenants that live in that area.

Market value
The estimated amount for which an asset should exchange on the date of valuation between a willing buyer and a willing seller in an arms-length transaction after proper marketing and where each party has acted knowledgeably, prudently and without compulsion.

Material Change of Use (MCU)
This is the commencement of a new use of a building or on land or the re-establishment of one that has been abandoned.

Medium density
Medium density housing usually occurs within inner and middle suburbs as redevelopment, rezoning. They are normally closer to community services, facilities and amenities. Examples are units, apartments and multi-units with small setbacks to the side boundaries and the street. There is limited private open space or living area.

Middle ring suburbs
Are the suburbs that are located within 10 – 20 kilometres of the city, although it varies with cities.

Mortgage duty
Duty charged on the amount secured by a mortgage.

N

Negative equity
When falling prices make a mortgage debt greater than the value of a property.

Net Lettable or Leasable Area (NLA)
These terms are very useful for commercial and resi-mercial properties. The net lettable or leasable area shows the floor space rented to tenants.

Example: A building contains 3 floors with each floor containing 3000 m^2 (9000 m^2) but only 7500 m^2 is available to tenants with the remaining 1500 m^2 of floor being common area (mostly lifts, lounge, common rest rooms).

Net residential density
Net residential density refers to the number of dwellings per hectare on land allocated solely for residential development. Net density does not include public roads and areas of public open space.

Notice to complete
The contract of sale of property includes a provision for a party to the contract to issue a notice to complete on another party in default to fulfil its obligation. For example, if a vendor is not ready to settle on the date specified in the contract of sale, the buyer's solicitor or conveyancer would issue a notice to complete within 14 days. If settlement still does not take place, the contract outlines the penalties which may be applicable. This might include a monetary penalty, or even loss of deposit and voiding of the sale. (See *deposit, subject to finance approval, forfeit for details*).

O

Old system title
Also called common law title. A chain of documents where the overall title holds only if every document along the way is sound.

Open listing
This is a method of selling a property whereby the vendor effectively allows any real estate agent the right to list the property.

Open Space
Land with no improvements: often required by a council in a subdivision as recreational space.

Option agreement

This is an agreement between a property owner and a developer allowing purchase of land at an agreed price. Nobody else can buy the property during the term of the agreement (normally 24 months). The agreement is secured with an option fee.

Overlay

This is a term used by planning departments when there is a particular restriction over a property. A council planning scheme map that shows the location and extent of special features such as land subject to flooding. Overlays relate to storm events and historical rainfall data. It is an additional layer of planning control that allows local government to decide upon the type of development that occurs. There are several types of overlays: special buildings overlays, land subject to inundation overlays, height overlays, mining overlays, vegetation overlays, floodway overlays, urban floodway zones and vegetation overlays.

Owner occupier

An owner occupier is an owner who uses the property owned as a principal place of residence or a commercial premise from which the owner operate his or her business. (See *small office, home office*).

P

Passed in

This is a term that refers to a property not being sold at auction because the owner's reserve price was not reached. On behalf of the owner, the real estate agent would then negotiate with the highest bidder and other bidders to purchase the property at the reserve price or a new negotiated price.

Pay As You Go (PAYG)

A system of income taxation for making regular payments towards expected annual income tax liability.

PAYG – withholding	Tax withheld from payments to others (salaries, wages)
PAYG - instalments	Tax withheld from one's own income (investment and business income)

Peppercorn rent

A token or nominal rent, or a very small payment, used to satisfy the requirements for the execution of a legal contract. When the rental contract is executed and is current, and if the owner would like the property to be rent-free, it is normal to charge a peppercorn rent. This small amount mutually binds both parties to the contract.

Peppercorn rental

This is a metaphor for a very low or nominal rental which will normally be money but can also be in the form of chattels or services. This amount is used to satisfy the requirements for the execution of a legal contract. Did you know? The Governor of Bermuda gives the annual sum of a single peppercorn on a velvet cushion atop a silver platter for renting the old state house as his residence. This ceremony has been in place since 1816.

Personal property

Personal property is an item that can be removed without serious damage either to the property or to the item itself. A portable air conditioner would be considered personal property but if a hole were cut in a wall for installation, the unit could be considered as part of real property (or fixture).

Pest inspection report

A pest inspection report will give an overview of an investigation into potential pest infestation in a property (termites, white ants, borers, spiders).

Termites can cause extensive damage to the structure of a building, as well as the fixtures, fittings and floor coverings. Local councils are able to provide a list of preferred pest inspection companies.

Plan sealing

This is the final stage of council approval for a subdivision or strata title prior to registration whereby the survey plan is endorsed with the council seal. This relates to land subdivision and building strata title or subdivision, depending upon the terminology in a particular state or territory.

Population density

Population density is a product of residential density and occupancy rate.

Pre-purchase inspections

These include building and pest inspections and, if purchasing an apartment, then a strata report as well. If purchasing a house then a survey of the land, to ensure that fences and building are as per title, might also be included in this definition.

Prime Cost (PC) method

Prime cost method is a method of calculating depreciation of chattels using the total purchase price as the basis. Items are claimed using the same amount of depreciation each year. For example, if a range hood was purchased for an investment property for $750, and the deduction rate was 20 %, then $150 is written off every year for 5 years.

If the item is not owned for a full year, a pro-rata deduction is calculated:

$$Asset\ Cost \times \frac{Days\ held}{365} \times \frac{1}{Asset's\ effective\ life}$$

The prime cost method produces the higher annual tax deduction towards the end of the effective life of the item.

Original cost $5000		
Year	Percentage	Tax deduction
1	20%	$1000
2	20%	$1000
3	20%	$1000
4	20%	$1000
5	20%	$1000

Principal Place of Residence (PPR)

A dwelling as a main residence where individuals live that is solely or jointly owned. As the name suggests, ownership of only one principal place of residence is allowed. The property nominated affects things such as the stamp duty at time of purchase and capital gains tax on the sale of the property.

Property law

Property law is the law that "governs the ownership and tenancy in real property and creates a platform for evidencing, transferring title and facilitating its use as an economic instrument". It is property law that manages the ownership of land in Australia. The fundamental of this personal property law is that no one can transfer a better title to property than they had (*Nemo dat quod non habet* - no one gives what he does not have). In Australia, land registration is based on the Torrens system of "title by registration" and is named after Sir Robert Richard Torrens, third premier of South Australia.

Public housing

Government-owned housing for those on low incomes at a nominal cost or rental.

Purchasing entity

This refers to a person, company, trust or partnership that purchases a property.

Property levy
A property levy is raised by a body corporate or owner's corporation. The committee is the managing group. If the property shares facilities or the building (common building areas), then there will be a levy to cover common expenses.

Put Option
The right, but not the obligation, to sell an asset at a set price on a set date.

Q

Qualified acceptance
The offer is accepted subject to certain conditions.

Quantity Surveyor
A person who is qualified to prepare a depreciation schedule for a property owner and may also prepare a bill of quantities for construction projects (See *Bill of Quantities*).

R

Real Estate Agent
A real estate agent is a licensed professional who acts as an intermediary between sellers and buyers of real estate. The real estate agent is acting on behalf of the seller and works in the best interest of their client. The agent is generally paid a commission for their services in selling the property.

Real property
Real estate means we can see, feel, touch and use the property. Property means it is 'proper' as it provides shelter and is also a 'proper' measure of one's wealth.

Type	Examples
Residential	Construction of new, and resale of existing, homes
Commercial	Shopping centres, hotels, offices, medical suites, apartment buildings
Industrial	Manufacturing units, warehouses
Land	Vacant land, working farms, acreages

Recreational facilities

Recreational facilities are generally found in large apartment complexes and some commercial buildings and include: spas, saunas, swimming pools, parks, tennis courts and club houses.

Redevelopment site

Redevelopment is any new construction on a site that has pre-existing uses. The site can be reused and improved by adding more marketable properties.

Registered plan

This is a plan that has been drafted and registered by the surveyor with the appropriate government land registry. The plan includes designated lots and their relation to the surrounding area. On legal documents, such as a contract of sale and mortgage documents, it may be shown as L20 on RP 123567 or lot 20 on registered plan 123567.

Relaxation

This is a term used by council to allow for exceptions to the code. A common relaxation can apply to boundary setbacks where a garage may be built on the side boundary closer than the setback specified by the code.

Relet prior to vacancy

Re-letting prior to vacancy is permitting access to properties for the purpose of showing them to prospective tenants.

Requisition On Title

Requisitions on title are questions about the property the purchaser is entitled to ask the vendor to find out if the vendor is aware of any deficiencies in relation to title.

Reserve price

Reserve price is the minimum acceptable price predetermined by the owner of a property but which is not disclosed to the bidders at the auction. It is the lowest fixed price at which an item is offered at an auction sale and (1) at which it will be sold if no higher price is bid, or (2) below which the seller is not obligated to accept the winning bid. The reserve price is a form of insurance for the vendor against the property being sold at a low price if attendance on the day of the auction is poor due to, for example, bad weather. If the reserve price has not been reached, then the highest bidder will have first right to negotiate a price with the vendor or his agent.

Residential vs commercial

The following table shows the difference between residential and commercial properties in Australia. (Our book entitled It's My Time: Successful Residential Investing" will provide more details on residential, commercial and residential vs commercial properties).

	Residential properties	Commercial properties
Returns	Between 4 to 10% depending on the location	Between 7 and 13% depending on the location
LVR (as of July 2017)	Minimum 80% (most banks)	Usually between 50% and 80 %
Median price	$50,000 to several million dollars	Up to $100 million
Lease term	Short term (1 or 2 year), even a monthly lease	3 to 15 years
Outgoings	Landlord pays	Tenant pays as per lease
Terminology for rent	Gross rent	Net rent
Price factor	Location, amenities and appearance	Yield, weighted average lease expiry (WALE) for multiple tenancies
Bond	4 weeks (rental bond board)	Bond, personal guarantors and bank guarantees
Rental	Based on bedrooms and bathrooms	Based on total floor space
Rental increase	Subject to annual review	Commercial rents goes up in increments with either CPI or a fixed rate %
Owners obligation to check and to maintain	Smoke alarm, fire alarm, security doors, alarms and other safety related items	Fire hoses, blankets, fire extinguishers, exit and entry signs, evacuation procedure signage

Residential Density

Residential density is the number of dwellings divided by the area of the land they occupy. Low density = 12.5-20 dwellings per hectare, medium density = 20-40 dw/ha and high density = 40 dw/ha. Residential density will vary across councils.

Residential Tenancies Act

Each state and territory has its own act which deals with such issues as how to manage bonds and disputes.

State / Territories	Act
Australian Capital Territory	Residential Tenancies Act 1997
Victoria	Residential Tenancy Act 1997
New South Wales	Residential Tenancy Act 1997
Northern Territory	Residential Tenancies Act 1997
Queensland	Residential Tenancies and Rooming Accommodation Act 2008
South Australia	Residential Tenancies Act 1995
Tasmania	Residential Tenancy Act 1997
Western Australia	Residential Tenancies Act 1987

Resimercial

A building that is part residential and part commercial. They are found in both new and older buildings generally with commercial (retail or office) on the ground floor and residential upstairs.

Retail leases

Retail Leases Act by state and territories:

State / territory	Retail lease act	Minimum term
Victoria	Retail Leases Act 2003	5 years unless waived (small business commissioner certificate)
New South Wales	Retail Leases Act 1994	5 years unless waived (solicitor certificate)
Queensland	Retail Shop Leases Act 1994 Retail Shop Leases Amendment Bill 2015	Not applicable
Western Australia	Commercial Tenancy (retail shops) Agreements Act 1985	5 years
Australian Capital Territory (ACT)	Leases (commercial and retail) act 2001	5 years unless waived (solicitor certificate)
Northern Territory	Business Tenancies Act 2003	5 years unless waived (solicitor or accountant certificate)
Tasmania	Fair Trading Regulations 1998	5 years unless waived (solicitor certificate)

Right of first refusal
This is part of an agreement providing a person the first opportunity to buy or lease a property. This clause gives the lessee (tenant) the right to purchase the property if the lessor (landlord) decides to sell during the current lease. The highest price that someone is willing to pay for the property is the price offered to the lessee under a right of first refusal clause.

Right of Way (RoW)
The right to access or cross a property.

Rising inflation
This means the cost of living is increasing (See *Reserve Bank of Australia* for more details).

ITEM	AVERAGE PRICE (DOLLARS)		
	JANUARY 1913	JANUARY 2013	% INCREASE
BREAD	$ 0.056	$ 1.422	2439%
FLOUR	$0.033	$0.524	1488%

Figure 9: Image showing the price difference of bread and flour in 100 years

Rooming house
A rooming house is a Class 1B building where one or more rooms is available for rent. In most rooming houses, residents share bathrooms, kitchens, laundries and other common areas. The owner and their family generally do not live on the premises and separate rental agreements may exist for different residents.

Routine inspection report
As part of an ongoing management service, a rental manager undertakes a routine inspection of the property, usually every six months, although the frequency depends upon the legislation of the state or territory.

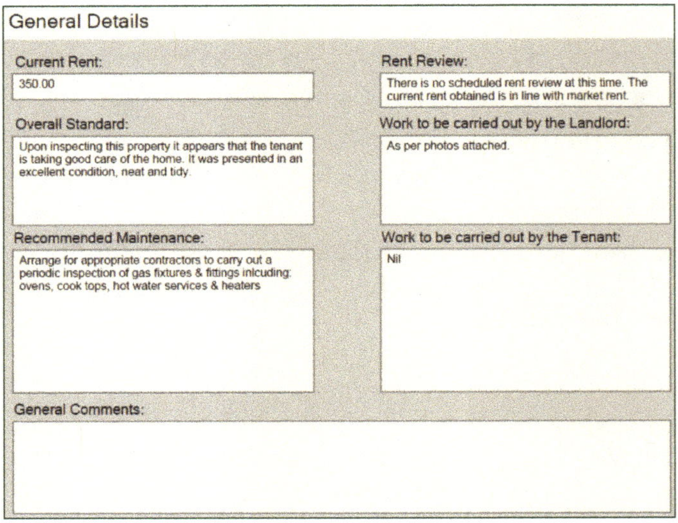

General Details

Current Rent:
350 00

Rent Review:
There is no scheduled rent review at this time. The current rent obtained is in line with market rent.

Overall Standard:
Upon inspecting this property it appears that the tenant is taking good care of the home. It was presented in an excellent condition, neat and tidy.

Work to be carried out by the Landlord:
As per photos attached.

Recommended Maintenance:
Arrange for appropriate contractors to carry out a periodic inspection of gas fixtures & fittings inlcuding: ovens, cook tops, hot water services & heaters

Work to be carried out by the Tenant:
Nil

General Comments:

Figure 10: Template of a routine inspection report of residential rental property.

S

School catchment area

A school catchment area is a geographical location where a state school's core intake of students must live. Sometimes one private school in the whole council area could lift the property values up as businesses thrive around the school catchment area.

School zone

School zones are also called residential boundaries or catchment areas in the suburbs where the schools are located.

Table 1: **Websites of school zones in metropolitan cities of Australia**

Metropolitan cities	School zones
Sydney	schoolzones.net.au/nsw/
Melbourne	melbourneschoolzones.com/
Brisbane	www.qgso.qld.gov.au/maps/edmap/
Perth	www.schoolcatchment.com.au/?page_id=1148
Adelaide	www.sa.gov.au/topics/education-and-learning/ schools/choosing-a-school/school-zones
Canberra	www.schoolcatchment.com.au/?p=1302
Hobart	www.findschoolzones.com.au/school-zone-list. php?state=TAS&region=All

Security deposit

A security deposit is the amount that the tenant (lessee) agrees to pay the lessor (landlord) before moving into a rental unit to insure the lessor against default by the tenant if the tenant (individual or company) becomes financially distressed This amount is usually equal to one month's rent. (See *bank guarantee*).

Self-assessable

A self-assessable development is one which is identified by an assessment manager as not needing a development or compliance permit. This can usually be found in the local planning scheme.

Self-assessable developments must comply with any applicable code/s under relevant legislation or planning schemes. It is an offence to carry out self-assessable development that contravenes the applicable code/s. In some circumstances, self-assessable development may require approval for building works which can be sought from a building certifier.

Sellers' market

Sellers' market prevails when there are lower interest rates, higher inflation, increased Gross Domestic Product (GDP) growth, low unemployment, and unfavourable projects (landfill or tip).

Sellers' market vs Buyers' market

Buyers' market prevails when there are higher interest rates, lower inflation, lower Gross Domestic Product (GDP) growth, rising unemployment and new amenities in the area (train stations, shopping centre and schools)

Setback

Councils will often have strict guidelines as to where new dwellings can be built, the distance between new and existing dwellings, and distance from boundaries.

Settlement

This is the process of legally transferring a property from the vendor to the buyer. It usually occurs between 30-120 days after the contract of sale is signed and is usually, but not necessarily, carried out by the conveyancers.

Settlement date

The day on which settlement occurs and payment is finalised.

Shared equity

A shared equity scheme allows a borrower to purchase a property which they would otherwise have been unable to afford due to lack of a deposit. The government will make up the shortfall and, in return, will own up to 25% of the property.

"HomesVic will take an equity share of up to 25% and eligibility will target applicants with incomes of up to $75,000 for singles, or up to $95,000 for couples or families. Buyers will need to have a 5% deposit. When the properties are sold, HomesVic will recover its share of the equity and reinvest it in other homes."

Reference: http://www.vic.gov.au/affordablehousing/buying-a-house-in-victoria/shared-equity.html

Suppose you buy a house in 2017 for $500,000. You enter into a shared equity mortgage for 20% of this home with HomeVic and borrows the remaining 80% at 5% p.a (variable) over a 30 year term.

Your loan looks like this:

Loan principal (80%)	$400,000
Monthly repayment on $400,000 at 5% on 30 year term	$2147.30
Shared equity component $100,000 (monthly repayment – nil) you save	$536 dollars per month (savings)

In 2027 a buyer is interested to purchase this property for $900,000 (See *Relationship between capital growth and rental return*).

In 2027 you sell this property for	$900,000
Your principal in 2027 would be (in 10 years' time from 2017)	$328,369 (rounded off to a dollar)
Total equity of this home in	$571,631
HomeVic gets 40 % of this equity ($571,631) and initial contribution (20 % of $500,000)	= 40 % ($571,631) + 20 % ($500,000) = $228,652.40 + $100,000 = $328,652.40
In 2027, when you sell this property that you purchased in 2027, you can keep	= $900,000 – ($328,652.40) – ($328,369) = $242,978.60

You have saved $64,418.40 as you have not paid interest at 5% for 10 years (monthly repayment is $536.82).

Interest for 10 years at 5% on 100,000 = $536.82 per month

$$= \$536.82 \times 12 \times 10$$

$$= \$64,418.40$$

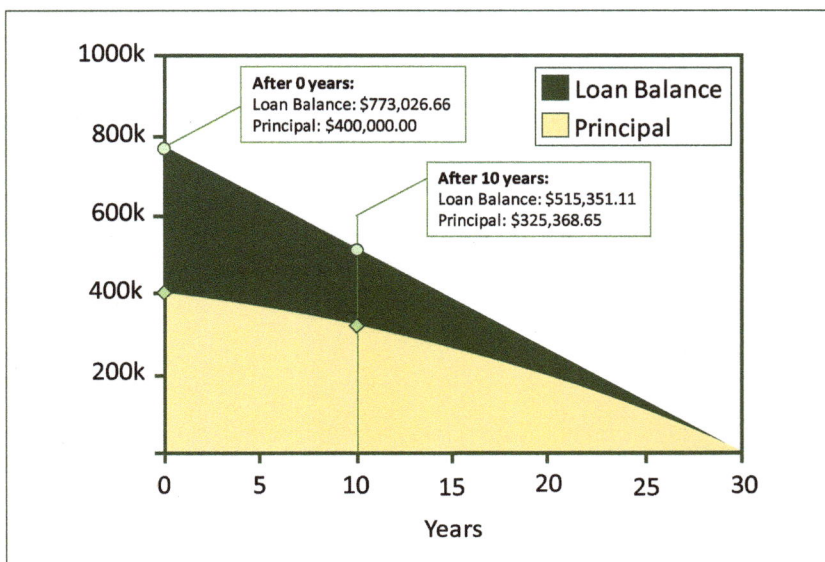

Figure 11: Example to outline the concept of shared equity

Sole agency

This is when only one real estate agent has been instructed to handle a property sale. A sole agency agreement normally applies for a specific period. The difference between the sole agency and an exclusive agency is that under a sole agency, the vendor is still able to sell their own property without paying commission to the agent.

Sole listing vs Open listing vs Multiple listing

Sole listing is when a property is listed with only one agent to conduct the marketing and sale.

Open or multiple listing is when your property is able to be marketed by any interested agent.

Sole ownership

Sole ownership occurs when one person has purchased a property in their name only.

Solicitor or conveyancer

Either of these legal professionals are responsible for facilitating the transfer of property from vendor to purchaser.

Splitter

This is a term, used more in Queensland, for a process of subdivision: dividing a vacant lot into two or more separate titles.

Staging

The process of preparing a property for sale in the market place. The aim is to make the property appealing to the highest number of potential buyers and hence selling the property quickly for higher profit margin. Staging a property is to create a fresh aesthetic and to enhance the appeal for potential buyers. (Our book entitled *"It's My Time: Successful Residential Investing"* contains more detail on property staging/styling and how it affects the purchase price).

Stamp duty

Stamp duty is also called land transfer duty. Stamp duty is a state tax imposed upon both documented and undocumented acquisitions (purchase). Stamp duty applies for real estate, vehicles, assets, gifts and insurance policies. In most instances, the stamp duty is paid by the purchaser. It varies between states and is calculated as a certain percentage of the purchase price. When a property is sold, the stamp duty paid on purchase is added to the cost base for the purpose of calculating Capital Gains Tax liability.

Stamp duty is raised at two points on the purchase of real estate:

1. Stamp duty on the transfer of property
2. Stamp duty on the mortgage. Both lots of stamp duty must be paid by the purchaser on, or before, settlement of the purchase.

Concessions may be available for those buying their first home or for people on low income. (Our book entitled *"It's My Time: Successful Residential Investing"* will provide more details on various tax breaks and a strategic approach to reducing taxable income).

Stamp duty varies between states and territories and also varies based on the type of product purchased. The example below is for the purchase of an investment property for $100,000: note how the stamp duty and other fees vary between states and territories. If the purchase is by an overseas citizen (not a permanent resident or an Australian citizen), then the purchaser is required to pay "Foreign Buyers Duty".

Table 2: Mortgage registration fee, transfer fee and stamp duty for a permanent resident or an Australian citizen (as of Nov 2017)

States and Territories	Mortgage registration fee	Transfer fee	Stamp duty on investment property	Total
Victoria	$114.90	$329	$2,150	$2,594
South Australia	$160	$677	$2,830	$3,667
Western Australia	$168.70	$178.70	$1,900	$2,247
Northern Territory	$142	$142	$2,157.14	$2,441
ACT	$140	$272	$1,400	$1,812
New South Wales	$138.80	$138.80	$1,990	$2,268
Tasmania	$132.52	$203.05	$2,435	$2,771
Queensland	$181	$181	$1,925	$2,287

Table 3: Mortgage registration fee, transfer fee and stamp duty for an overseas citizen (as of Nov 2017)

States and Territories	Mortgage registration fee	Transfer fee	Stamp duty on investment property	Total
Victoria	$114.90	$2,435	$55,000	$57,550
South Australia	$160	$7,922	$48,830	$56,912
Western Australia	$168.70	$358.70	$42,615.50	$43,143
Northern Territory	$142	$142	$49,500	$49,784
ACT	$140	$272	$40,500	$40,912
New South Wales	$138.80	$138.80	$40,490	$40,768
Tasmania	$132.52	$203.05	$40,185	$40,521
Queensland	$181	$2,969	$38,025	$41,175

Statement of Adjustments

During the settlement of the property, the buyer is required to reimburse the vendor for any water and sewerage rates, council rates, and land taxes that the vendor has paid in advance. The conveyancer will normally calculate these rates for the purchaser on a pro-rata basis. The following image shows a typical statement of adjustment.

Statement of Adjustments as at 20 Nov 2012						VENDOR	PURCHASER
15 Nov 2012							
Purchaser:							
Vendor:							
Property Flat No:							
Property Street No:							
Adjustment Description						**VENDOR**	**PURCHASER**
	City		$1,166.50				
Paid	From: 01 Jul 2012	To: 30 Jun 2013	**Purchaser Allows**	222	**Days**		$709.49
	Water		$151.88				
Paid	From: 01 Jul 2012	To: 30 Jun 2013	**Purchaser Allows**	222	**Days**		$92.38
Rent PCM			$1,473.00			$726.41	
Paid	From: 05 Nov 2012	To: 05 Dec 2012	**Vendor Allows**	15	**Days**		

Figure 12: Statement of adjustments (council rate, water rate, rent per calender month PCM)

State Revenue Office (SRO)

The State Revenue Office deals with the rate of transfer duty, what a land threshold is, how to check if land tax is owing, and other information associated with buying and owning property.

Sterling suburbs

These are the suburbs where the land values appreciate steadily.

Strata title

This is a system of property ownership based on both vertical and horizontal division entitling the owner to sell, lease or transfer a strata unit. The land and buildings are divided into parcels and common property. Each parcel or unit will have a separate strata title issued to a registered proprietor. An example is a block of home units, where each unit has a separate title and can be sold and owned independently of other units. It also allows the owner membership of the body corporate. The building insurance for strata buildings is covered in strata fees including common areas and painting of the outside of the building (see *owner's corporation*). In the following Figure 14, red represents the common areas and green represents strata titled blocks of units each with a fire rated wall.

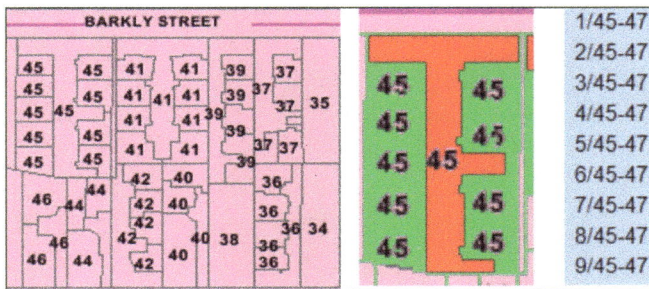

Figure 13: **Example of strata titled properties (there are nine units (green) with common areas (red))**

Strata title fees
These are fees charged to the owners of a strata titled property, generally quarterly. These fees cover such things as building insurance and public liability insurance, common electricity and water usage, repairs and maintenance of common areas, pest control, cleaning, gardening and fees paid to the management company.

Stratum title
A title which pre-dates strata title providing ownership of a freehold unit and membership of the company that owns and maintains the property.

Street appeal
Also known as kerb appeal, it is the attractiveness of the exterior of a property as viewed from the kerb or street. (See *Valuation types*).

Subdivision

Subdivision is a complex and strictly regulated process of dividing a parcel of land into separate allotments. Land with subdivision potential is often advertised for sale as 'subject to council approval (STCA)' and interested parties should be aware of the risks and time involved in achieving a successful outcome.

Subject to finance approval

'Subject to finance approval' is a standard clause that may be included in a contract of sale that provides the would-be purchaser time to arrange a loan for the property. If the loan application is refused, then the contract may be terminated and deposit money refunded. (See *deposit and forfeit for details*).

Sublease

Sublease is a separate lease granted by the head lessee to the sublessee. Sublease normally involves a portion of the property.

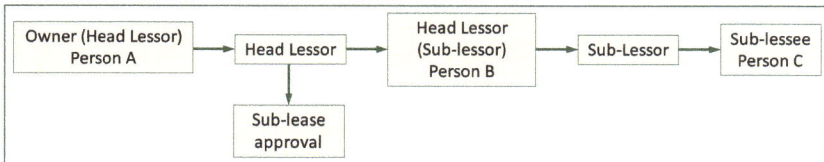

Figure 14: Schematics showing the connections between head lessor, sub-lessor and sub-lessee

Suburbs

A suburb is considered an identified community in a region. The cities of the western worlds are satellite cities or suburbs that started arising in the mid-1900s. The design of the cities was intelligent and timely at that time to provide homes for all and to kick start the building and construction industries during the post WWII era. The suburbs were designed to be self-sufficient in terms of goods and services including employment but not the energy (fuel). Fuel was the key factor for transportation. Mass motoring in the suburbs has pushed the whole civilisation to be dependent on a fuel based economy. There is a connection between our economy and fuel as we rely on foreign oil reserves for supply. Australia is dependent on imported fuel as we do not have much in the way of refinery capacity in Australia as of 2017. Australia's fuel reserve is less than 90 days. (*See imports*)

Surrender

Following negotiations, one party will give up their lawful rights under a lease or other beneficial agreement in return for either compensation or a new agreement that provides additional benefits.

Survey

A map showing the boundaries, improvements, easements and other physical features of a property.

Survey plan

This is a document created by a registered surveyor that designates the specific parameters of a particular lot or lots including size, dimensions, contours, easement, encroachments and rights of way.

T

Tenancy agreement

A document setting out the rights and obligations of both parties (the lessee and the lessor), the rental amount, period of tenancy and any other agreed instructions.

Tenant

A person who has the owner's permission, normally documented through a tenancy agreement, to have possession of real property.

Tenants in common

A form of ownership where, in the event of death, the share in property is not passed to the other tenants in common but according to the person's will or, if no will exists, by the laws of intestacy. This is known as 'no right of survivorship'. If a property is owned as tenants in common, it is possible to own predetermined unequal shares in the property. (See *joint tenancy*)

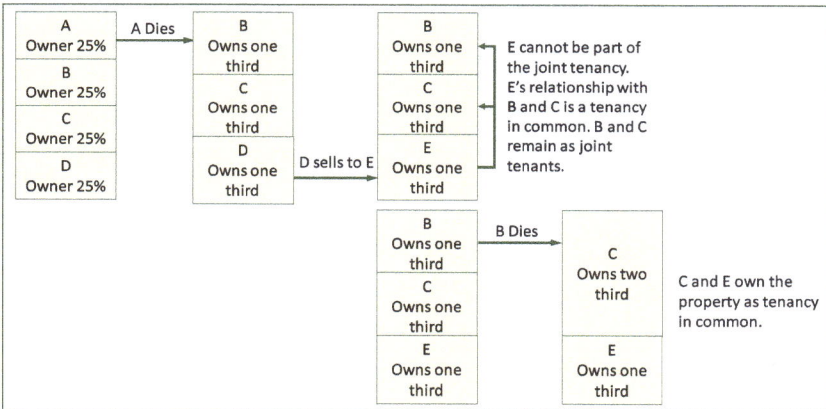

Figure 15: A, B, C and D own a property as joint tenants

Tender Loving Care (TLC)

A term commonly used by a real estate agent in a sales description for a dwelling that suggests it is in need of renovation or repair.

Termination of lease

The process whereby the property owner (landlord) asks the tenant to vacate the property by terminating the lease agreement. The lease termination for a contract usually requires prior notice and this period varies between states and territories. A tenant can also terminate a lease but will likely incur lease break costs. (Refer to *Consumer Affairs* or *Fair Trading* websites for more details).

Title

The document which provides legal evidence of ownership of property.

Title deed

This is a document which evidences the entitlement to land and commonly referred to as 'title'.

Title insurance

Title insurance protects owners and lenders' legal interest against known and unknown title defects on a property. In our current system, the ledgers maintained at the titles office, state revenue office, banks and other parties are different and hence there are chances of errors in title transfer. Possible mistakes could include:

1. A utilities company could have access to install an electrical pole
2. A neighbouring property has a right to use the side driveway on your property
3. Local council could have a right to lay a road through your backyard
4. A covenant exists on the property limiting the types of building materials that can be used

(See *Blockchain* for more details on how the technology would eradicate such errors in the future and possibly avoid the need for such insurances.)

Title search

This is a search of the public records to discover any liens or other impediments to a transfer of an unencumbered title. In other words, a check of title records to make sure the seller is the legal owner of the property and there are no outstanding claims on it.

Townhouse

This is a unit that usually has two or more floors and might be attached to other similar units.

Transfer

In relation to real estate transactions, this is an official document lodged with the Titles Office to transfer ownership of property from one party to another. It is also a process of verifying a change of ownership and noted on the certificate of title.

Transmission

This is a method which allows the executor, beneficiary or trustee of a deceased estate to apply to the Titles Office for a title to property to be passed to them. It is commonly referred to as Transmission by Death.

Tribunal

A tribunal (civil and administrative) exists to provide affordable, timely and quality access to justice for civil matters (concerned with resolving private disputes). The function of a tribunal is to reduce pressure on the courts by hearing small matters that otherwise would create a backlog in the courts. Any person may elect to request a hearing by payment of a small fee.

Triplex and multi-units

As suburbs are rezoned to accommodate more high density housing, some large blocks can accommodate three or more houses called triplex or multi-units. They are normally arranged with the driveway along a side boundary to maximise the full potential of the block. The following example shows the multiplex on a large block of 1189 m^2 comprising six town houses in a neighbourhood residential zone (NRZ) (See Zoning).

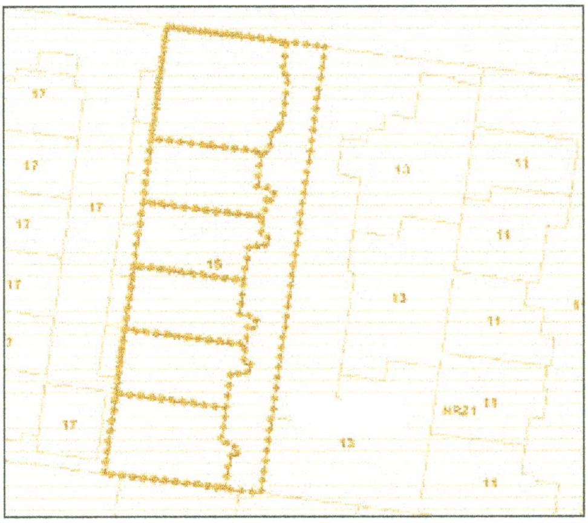

Figure 16: Multiple units in a block of land (six town houses)

Trust

Legal entity where a person or a company (trustee) holds assets (trust property) for another person or group of people (beneficiary or beneficiaries). It can be defined as a fiduciary relationship, and instrument thereof, which places the control and title of property in the hands of the trustee for the benefit of another person.

Trust account

This is a bank account established by auctioneers, real estate agents, solicitors and accountants, approved and monitored by a government agency (Department of Justice or Department of Fair Trading) to handle monies received on behalf of someone else. For example, money paid as a deposit to purchase a property is paid by the purchaser to the real estate agent and the money is banked into the real estate agent's trust account. The money remains in the trust account until the real estate agent receives written instructions from both the purchaser and vendor's solicitors that the funds can be released and paid to the nominated parties.

Trust account is also used in property management to collect rent. Trust Accounts have to be audited by approved auditors and are also subject to spot inspections.

Trustee
A person or company who holds title to assets for the benefit of another.

Trust ledger for rental property
It is the ledger that shows the trust account activity of a rental property. This ledger usually has trust account holder (usually real estate agents company), land lord name and account details, details of payee or payer, amount debited, amount credited and total balance. (See *trust account, balance sheet*).

Tenancy by the entirety
This is reserved for a husband and wife only and both husband and wife have an equal undivided interest in the property. Upon the death of one partner (husband or wife), title to the entire property goes to the surviving spouse. (See *joint tenancy*)

Tenancy agreement
A document that sets out the rights and obligations of both the lessee and the lessor, the rental amount and period of tenancy.

Tenancy at sufferance
A tenant that remains in possession of a property after the lease has expired. A tenant at sufferance has no right to the premises.

Tenancy at will
A tenancy that may be terminated at the will of either the lessor or the lessee.

Tenancy schedule

The following image shows the floor plan of a multi-tenanted property with seven shops with different yields, lease expiry terms, areas and income (The dimensions of the plan are not to scale).

Shop 1	Shop 2	Shop 3	Shop 4	Shop 5	Shop 6	Shop 7
50 m^2	60 m^2	70 m^2	80 m^2	70 m^2	60 m^2	50 m^2
Yield 7%	7.2%	7.5%	7.7%	7.3%	7.2%	7%

Figure 17: **Multi-tenanted commercial property (seven shops)**

A tenancy schedule provides an overview of various factors that might assist in negotiating contract terms during purchase. A typical tenancy schedule may look like this:

Shop number	Floor Area (m²)	Net rent or net income p.a.	Income per square metre	Yield %	Yield in Percentage	Current value ($)
1	50	12500	250.00	7	0.07	178571.40
2	60	14000	233.33	7.2	0.072	194444.40
3	70	15000	214.29	7.5	0.075	200000.00
4	80	25000	312.50	7.7	0.077	324675.30
5	70	16000	228.57	7.3	0.073	219178.10
6	60	14000	233.33	7.2	0.072	194444.40
7	50	12500	250.00	7	0.07	178571.40
Total	440 m²	109000				1,489,885.15

Tenant v. resident

A tenant is any person in possession of a real property with the owner's permission, usually through a tenancy agreement. A tenant is on the lease and is legally bound to all its terms and conditions, including payment of the rental.

A resident is a person who rents a room in a rooming house as their only, or main, residence. A resident does not need to have a tenancy agreement to live in a rooming house.

Terms and conditions

These are the rules that apply to fulfilling a contract and that form an integral part of that contract. A person signing a contract agrees to having read the terms and conditions and that he/she agrees with said terms. Since the wording is often very complex, a signee should seek professional advice before signing. (See *Warranty, Guarantee and Insurance* for more details)

Testator

This is a person who makes a will.

Torrens system

Land registration in Australia is based on the Torrens principle of "title by registration" rather than "registration of title". It is named after Sir Robert Richard Torrens, third premier of South Australia. Each state and territory has unique legislation for property and title. Land ownership is transferred through title registration instead of using deeds, the main aim being to simplify land transactions and to authenticate ownership of the title. It is a government system of recording land ownership and allows property to be leased, sold or disposed of lawfully.

Table 4: **Legislation (property and title) in states and territories in Australia**

Legislation regarding property and title		
State and Territory	Property	Title
New South Wales	Real Property Act 1900	Conveyancing Act 1919
Victoria	Property Law Act 1958	Sale of Land Act 1962
Australian Capital Territory	Civil Law (Property) Act 2006	Civil Law (Sale of Residential Property) Act 2003
Queensland	Property Law Act 1974	Land Titles Act 1994
Northern Territory	Law of Property Act	Land Title Act
South Australia	Law of Property Act 1936	Real Property Act 1886
Tasmania	Conveyancing and Law of Property Act 1884	Land Titles Act 1980
Western Australia	Property Law Act 1969	Transfer of Land Act 1893

Countries following the Torrens system

The Torrens system is widely used in Canada, Ireland, Israel, Malaysia, New Zealand, Singapore, Thailand, and 10 of 48 contiguous states of the United States of America.

U

Under license
In real estate, this is an agreement to take over a property before settlement.

Unregistered mortgage
When borrowing from a bank or other financial institution, they will secure the loan by way of a first mortgage over the property. Some purchasers may have to borrow additional funds to complete a transaction and this loan is normally secured by an unregistered mortgage and caveat. If the purchaser defaults on

their repayments, the lender can register this second mortgage with the Titles Office.

Utilities

These are service facilities such as electricity and water provided as part of land development.

V

Vacancy rate

Vacancy rate in Australia is normally between 2% and 3% with 2.2% for metropolitan properties and 2.4% for regional (May 2017).

Good vacancy rate

A vacancy rate of less than 3% is regarded as a good environment for an investor, with high demand for rental properties.

Bad vacancy rate

If the vacancy rate is above 4% and closer to 7%, then this is considered a bad vacancy rate.

Table 5: **Table showing various vacancy rates**

Vacancy rate (%)	Vacancy rate (decimal)	Vacancy rate (fraction)	Number of days property is unoccupied per year (365 days)	Number of week the property is unoccupied or vacant per year (52 weeks)
1	1/100	0.01	3.65	0.52
2	2/100	0.02	7.3	1.04
3	3/100	0.03	10.95	1.52
4	4/100	0.04	14.6	2.08
5	5/100	0.05	18.25	2.6

Valuation

Valuation refers to the worth of a property. The lending organisation will require a valuation to establish whether the property is in occupiable condition and to assess how much money the lending organisation (banks or financial institutions) can securely lend using that particular property as security. Valuers use a number of methods to arrive at their valuation, the most common for residential property being the comparison method where they compare recent sales of similar properties in the area.

There are three types of valuation of a property:

Type of valuation	Description
Desktop valuation	Usually for properties in capital and metropolitan cities. This uses the median price of the suburb hence no inspection of the property is done.
Kerbside valuation	Inspecting the property from the kerb. Banks usually go for kerbside valuation as there are time and resources are involved in engaging a value for a full valuation.
Full valuation	Banks engage a qualified valuer from an independent valuation company to inspect the property. The valuer writes a full report that include images and other specifications of the property. This is the most common and widely used form of valuation.

Valuation fee

A valuation fee is that paid to a qualified valuer, either by the purchaser or the lending organisations, for a valuation. Residential property valuation fees are sometimes waived by the lending organisations but for commercial property, the valuation fee is normally paid by the purchaser (See *valuation*).

Valuation report

A valuation report serves as a confirmation of the property value for the lender. It will assign separate values for the land and the dwelling built on the land. In the event that the mortgagor defaults on the loan repayments, the mortgagee has the right to repossess the property and will then normally try to sell the property at or above the fair market value stated in the valuation report to recoup the loss. A valuation should be carried out every few years as these reports are useful for insurance purposes. In the event of damage or loss, the valuation report would form the basis of an insurance claim (See *default payment* for more details).

Value buying

This refers to assets that can be bought with existing attractive features such as a high rental yield or a business with a high turnover and profit margin.

Valuer

Some of the major factors that a valuer might use in establishing the value of a property are:

External factors	Internal factors
• climate • educational institutions • employers • hazards and nuisances • industries • legal description • level of business activity • location in block • location of facilities: schools, shopping, recreational, cultural	• air conditioning and other fixtures • architecture style • building to land ratio • construction materials • date of construction • dimensions and floor area • floor plans • heating • interior utility • placement of building
External factors	**Internal factors**
• natural resources • restrictions on a property • political organisation • population density • population trends • public transport • topography • water bodies (ravines, rivers, lakes) and other attractions • zoning	• plumbing • special equipment such as elevators • utilities

Vendee
The person who purchases personal property is called a vendee or buyer.

Vendor
This is a person or persons who offer a property for sale. Also called the seller of an asset or the person disposing of the property.

Vendor terms
Also referred to as instalment contracts whereby, after the purchaser pays an initial amount of money upfront, the vendor provides the balance of the purchase price. This balance, and any interest accrued, is paid by instalments over an agreed period.

Very low density house
This is a single detached dwelling on a large allotment with large setbacks to side boundaries and the street and large areas of private open space. Very low density housing is usually constructed in country towns and on the fringes of metropolitan cities. An acreage house is an example of very low density house.

Villa
The most common interpretation of this term in Australia is a single storey semi-detached dwelling. Overseas it has a far wider meaning.

W

Walk up flats
Walk up flats are a set of residential flats or units that do not have a lift. The units higher than the second storey do not appreciate in value as they are not suited to older or infirm people. Some councils restrict the development of walk up flats to three storeys.

Work Cover insurance

WorkCover is an insurance policy that is compulsory for most employers. If an employee is injured or becomes sick in the course of their work, WorkCover insurance covers any medical expenses, rehabilitation costs and loss of earnings.

Wetlands

These are protected by the Environmental Protection Act. Wetlands are an attractive part of the landscape but also act as a sediment trap, nutrient trap and they filter and retain stormwater. Properties closer to wetlands tend to be in a higher price bracket. Interested buyers are well advised to check flood zoning and flood insurance protection.

Z

Zone

A planning control that allows local government to decide the appropriate use of land. A particular type of zone will dictate whether a planning permit is required for development of the land.

Zoning

The local council or planning authority places an ordinance over land which determines the use of the land and regulates the type and density of improvements that can be built on it. Zoning is aimed at regulating the use of land and buildings to control the rate of growth and the pattern in the area. Each state and territories have their own legal framework for zoning in Australia and they change periodically. Zoning restrictions fall into six basic categories: commercial, industrial, mixed-use, residential, agricultural and public use.

Table 6: Zonings in various states and territories

State	Zones	Authority in the state
Victoria	RGZ – Residential Growth Zone (new) GRZ – General Residential Zone (new) NRZ – Neighbourhood Residential Zone (new) C1Z – Commercial 1 Zone (new – includes some mixed use) C2Z – Commercial 2 Zone (new) LDRZ – Low Density Residential Zone (amended) MUZ – Mixed Use Zone (amended) TZ – Township Zone (amended) RLZ – Rural Living Zone (amended)	Victoria Department of Transport, Planning and Local Infrastructure
Australian Capital Territory	RZ1 – Suburban Zone RZ2 – Suburban Core Zone RZ3 – Urban Residential Zone RZ4 – Medium Density Residential Zone RZ5 – High Density Residential Zone (CZ1 to CZ6 suburb to high density with CZ5 is mixed commercial zone that allows for residential development)	ACT Government Dept of Environment and Planning
Western Australia	Residential design codes (R codes) – no uniform zoning codes	Western Australia Planning Commission
Tasmania	General Residential Zone Inner Residential Zone Low Density Residential Zone Rural Living Zone Environmental Living Zone Urban Mixed Use Zone	Tasmania Planning Commission
South Australia	No uniform zoning codes (zones based on areas, not necessarily residential density)	The Department of Planning, Transport and Infrastructure

State	Zones	Authority in the state
Queensland	Have not yet created a uniformity of zoning codes - need to refer the local government (council or shire)	Queensland Department of State Development, Infrastructure and Planning
New South Wales	R1 – General Residential R2 – Low Density Residential R3 – Medium Density Residential R4 – High Density Residential R5 – Large Lot (Rural) Residential B4 – Mixed Use	Department of Planning and Environment
Northern Territory	SD – Single Dwelling Residential MD – Multiple Dwelling Residential MR – Medium Density Residential HR – High Density Residential RR – Rural Residential RL – Rural Living FD – Future Development CB – Central Business (permits some residential development)	Department of Lands, Planning and the Environment

Chapter 2

Finance and accounting

A

AAA

The highest possible rating assigned by credit rating agencies (to an issuer's bonds, to companies or governments). AAA means the highest degree of creditworthiness.

Abnormal

Abnormal is a term that refers to a sudden change in revenue and expense during a particular accounting period. *See balance sheet.*

Account

An arrangement with a financial institution in which a customer deposit and withdraw money.

The following arrangement works by combining an offset account with your home loans and investment loans. A 55 day interest free period for the credit card means that no interest is charged on a transaction for a maximum of 55 days after the expense is incurred.

Table 7: types of bank accounts in Australia

Account	Description
Savings account	• allows you to save money • interest rate will accrue on the balance but is low compared to other types of accounts • no cheque books • a transactional account for depositing and withdrawing funds
Cheque account	• common but losing popularity • no interest will accrue • holders can write a cheque or use a debit card to withdraw funds • bank can charge a fee if the number of cheques drawn exceeds a fixed amount
Interest-bearing cheque account	• added services • added interest • higher fee to maintain but an unlimited number of cheques)
Offset account	• similar to a redraw facility available within a home loan • funds are offset against a home loan balance for calculation of interest • ATM access, cheque book, online banking • direct credits and direct debits

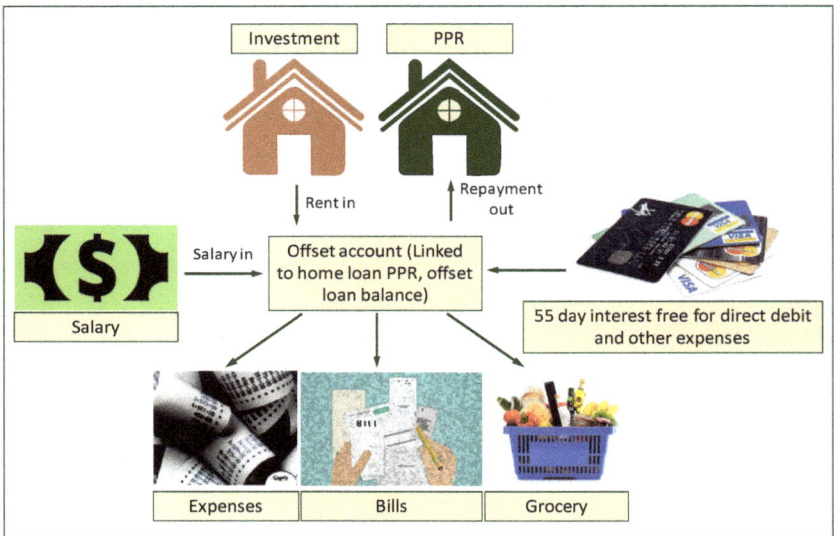

Figure 18: **Image showing the ways to fully utilise an offset account**

Accountant

A member of your A Team, an accountant is a qualified person who is trained in bookkeeping and in preparation, auditing and analysis of accounts. Accountants prepare annual reports and financial statements for planning and decision making, and advise on tax laws and investment opportunities. Ideally your accountant should have experience in property investment and development having their own rental portfolio. Your accountant will be able to advise on the best structure to use in purchasing property, ways to minimise tax, and prepare your tax returns and Business Activity Statement.

Accrual Accounting

Under this accounting system, transactions are recorded at the time they occur regardless of whether the payment is made now or in the future.

Active income
Income received in exchange for work whereby a degree of exertion is required. Active income is in the form of salaries, wages, commission and bonuses.

Amortisation
Amortisation is a process of reducing a loan back to zero from its original principal value by a series of repayments over a specified time. It is also the process whereby intangible assets such as goodwill and intellectual property are expensed over a period of time.

Annual depreciation
This is a measure of how much the value of an asset falls annually mainly due to wear and tear or continuous use of the plant or equipment or machine or vehicle.

$$Annual\ depreciation = \frac{(purchase\ value - scrap\ value)}{(useful\ economic\ value\ (years))}$$

A business purchases a lawn mower for $5000 in 2018. Over time the lawn mower has to be replaced, say 2025. The business can record the reduction in value of the lawn mower in its accounts as depreciation.

$$Annual\ depreciation = \frac{(\$5000 - \$1500)}{7} = \frac{\$3500}{7} = \$500\ per\ year$$

Annual depreciation of the lawn mower is $500

Annual depreciation value is applicable for purchased assets. If the business leases an asset (e.g. computers), the business cannot record the asset's depreciation in value over time and there is no depreciation charge to be used to reduce the taxable profit of the business.

Annual percentage rate
The amount you pay in interest calculated on an annual basis

Annual report
The annual report of a company can give a recent snapshot of how a company is trading in terms of revenue. This is a yearly record of a company's financial condition including a description of the firm's operations, its profit and loss accounts, statement of cash flow and balance sheet.

Annuity
An insurance product that offers the policy holder a fixed monthly or annual income for life.

Asset
Anything of monetary value owned by a person, company or trust including cash, house, car, caravan, etc. Assets are real or personal property in which a person, company or trust has an unencumbered ownership or equity and which has value like real estate, bonds, shares, dividends and other capital goods.

Audit
An audit is an official examination and verification of financial accounts and records. (*See document management system*).

B

Bad debt
A bad debt is money owed to a company or organisation by a customer for goods and services on credit that will likely remain uncollectable, or will be written off.

Balance sheet
This lists a company's assets, liabilities and shareholders' equity at a specific point in time. It is a snapshot of a company's financial position on a particular day. It is now called Statement of Financial

Position. It is a useful 'snapshot' tool for a potential buyer of commercial properties. A typical balance sheet may look like this.

Another way of summarising this is:

Equity = Assets – Liabilities

Table 8: Example of a balance sheet

Assets $		Liabilities and equity $	
Cash	50,000	Debts	50,000
Vehicles	75,000	Mortgage payments	100,000
Plant and equipment	100,000	Maintenance for plants, equipment	10,000
Property (land and building)	1,500,000	Equity	1,590,000
Furnishings	25,000		
Total assets	1,750,000	Total liabilities plus equity	1,750,000

John and Jo currently live in their principal place of residence (PPR). They are keen to purchase an investment property. Following are some details provided to you. Calculate equity in their principal place of residence.

Table 9: Various figures involved in equity calculation

Original loan (A)	$1,000,000
Amount repaid to date (B)	$600,000
Amount owing (C) = A-B	$400,000
Current valuation of this property (D)	$1,250,000
Less amount still owing (E)	$400,000
Total equity (F) = D - C	$850,000
How much can you borrow from the bank with your current equity (Loan value ratio 80 and 20)	Bank could lend upto 80% of the current value of the property.

Balloon payment

This is a large payment to clear the debt at the end of the loan period. For example, if you purchase an item using 'interest-only' finance for a fixed term, then you would pay out the loan at the end of the term using a balloon payment. This deal may work in situations where you have a cash flow restriction but would like to acquire the asset for your immediate needs that may give both short and long term returns on an investment.

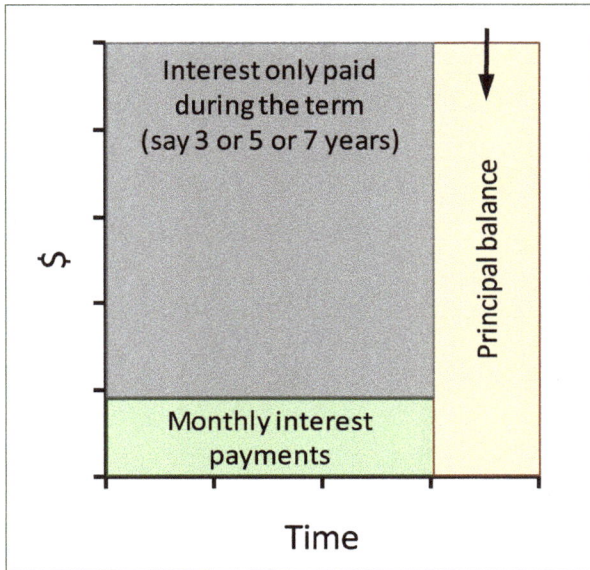

Figure 19: Conceptual diagram to illustrate the balloon payment in a loan

Bank guarantee

A bank guarantee is a means of providing a deposit or bond directly to the vendor. It is an unconditional undertaking given by the bank to pay the recipient of the guarantee the amount of the guarantee on written demand. Bank guarantees require security in the form of cash held on deposit with the bank, or real estate of a type and value acceptable to the bank.

Bankruptcy

A situation in a business where cash levels drop so low that will make the business become insolvent. Insolvency or bankruptcy is a situation when the business has no cash to pay its bills.

Bare trust

The simplest form of trust whereby the beneficiary has the absolute right to the assets within the trust including the income generated from these assets. The trustee has no control over these assets.

Bare trust (also called security trust) is a piece of paper that holds the property (personal and corporate bare trust).

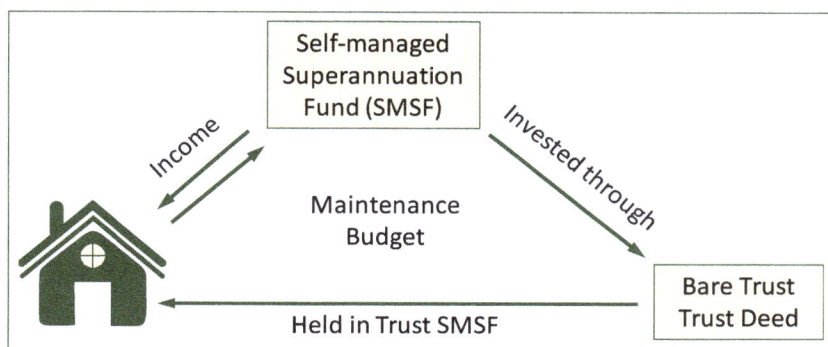

Figure 20: **Schematics of a bare trust**

Basic home loan

This is a simple 'no frills' home loan without any of the extras that may come with other home loan products such as an offset facility.

Beneficiary

A person or associated entity designated to receive income from a trust or estate.

Betterment statement

A betterment statement would be submitted on your behalf by your accountant if the Australian Taxation Office was not satisfied with your income tax return.

Betterment tax

The amount of tax assessed by the Australian Taxation Office as a result of the preparation of a betterment statement.

Blanket mortgage
A single mortgage that covers more than a parcel of property.

'Big four' banks
There are over 30,000 banks in the world. Australia's top four banks, the Commonwealth Bank of Australia, the Australia New Zealand Bank, Westpac and the National Australia Bank, are in the top 100 banks of the world in terms of assets. Three of the four banks were about to collapse in early 1990s: Read our book entitled "*It's My Time: Setting Financial and Personal Goals*" for more details.

Binding offer
A binding offer is an offer, on the terms set out in the particulars of appointment that is obtained in compliance with the appointment. It is sometimes known as a Letter of Intent.

Bitcoin
Bitcoin is an example of cryptocurrency. It exists in the form of virtual coins and each coin created by a miner is listed on blockchain. Bitcoin users set up a virtual wallet to store their bitcoins. (Read our book entitled "*It's My Time: Setting Financial and Personal Goals*" for more information on Bitcoins. (Also see *Blockchain, Cryptocurrency and Fiat currency*)

Bond (government)
This is a loan to a government or corporation at a fixed term and interest rate. Government bonds tend to have a lower interest rate but are more secure. The opposite applies to corporate bonds.

If interest rates drop, a bond with a higher fixed rate is in demand and can be traded on the stock exchange for a capital gain

Bonds
Financial instruments or securities for long term debt. There are different types of bonds: savings bonds, company bonds, government bonds (gilts). Bonds are not always held until the end of their terms.

Bookkeeping
This is the system of recording a company's, or individual's, financial activity such as GST, payments to employees, superannuation, fringe benefits tax, fuel tax credits and business payments. Such records may be used to analyse business activities, seek finance, lodge and pay tax and other reporting requirements.

Book value
The net value of an asset on the balance sheet.

BOOT
Acronym of *Build Own Operate Transfer* and is a means of financing a project (*See public private partnership*)

Borrowing costs
Borrowing costs are the costs related to the application and setting up of a loan, application fees, mortgage insurance, valuation fees (if required by the bank), stamp duty on the mortgage, registration of mortgage and any solicitors fees required by the mortgagee (financial institution).

Borrower qualification and loan underwriting
The process of assessing the level of risk associated with a loan according to the financial position of the borrower.

Break-even point
This is when the amount of money a business generates equals all outgoings of the business (salary, rent, insurance and all on-costs).

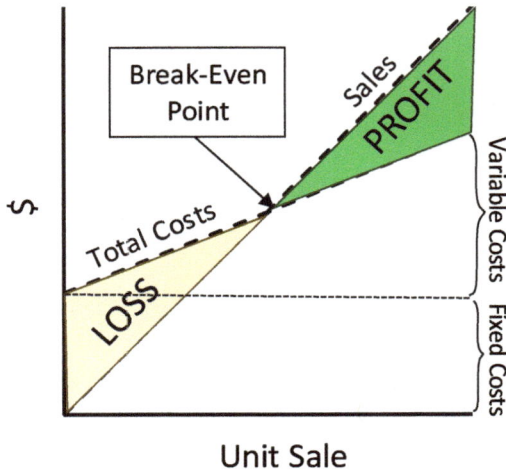

Unit Sale

Figure 21: Break-even point (with variable and fixed costs)

Bretton Wood system

In 1944, the United Nations Monetary and Financial Council adopted the Bretton Woods system. This tore apart the gold standards and created a new system: the US dollar was linked to gold and the rest of the world linked their currencies to the US dollar. After 1944, the US Federal Reserve Bank became the banker of the world in principle. (Read our book entitled *"It's My Time: Setting Financial and Personal Goals"* for more details on current reserve currency and special drawing rights)

Bridging loan

This is mortgage financing between the closure of one loan and the start of another loan. Example: a couple want to build a new home but don't want to sell their current home until they can move straight in. The bridging loan will pay for the new house until they sell their home, pay off the bridging loan and apply for a new mortgage. Normally a bridging loan attracts a higher interest rate.

This is a short term loan providing the purchaser with sufficient finance to effect settlement on a property prior to the general financing becoming available. For example, a bridging loan may be required to settle the purchase of another house before the sale of the existing house settles.

Brokerage

A fee paid to a broker. For example, when obtaining a loan, a fee is paid to a finance broker.

Budget

A budget is an estimation of income and expenses over a specified future period of time, normally a year. It should be compiled and re-evaluated on a periodic basis and seen as a valuable tool to identify potential financial problems. Income - expenses = Funds available for savings

Table 10: Template for a budget (single or family)

Your income (after tax) – Single or Family	
Mortgage / Rent	
Council rates	
Utilities (gas/water/electricity/phone)	
Internet	
Groceries	
Insurance (personal, travel, car, home, landlord)	
Maintenance budget (households)	
Medical	
Entertainment	
Registration/licensing of vehicles	
Vehicle running costs	
Restaurants	
Travel (overseas / domestic)	
Clothing	
Personal goods	
Investments	
Total	

Budget deficit

When a government is spending more in the economy than they are earning in revenue via taxes.

Budget surplus

When a government is making more revenue (rates and taxes) from the economy than they are spending.

Building contents insurance

Building contents insurance covers the contents of a building including (but not limited to) household goods, carpets, blinds, curtains, furniture, furnishings, jewellery, watches, clothing, personal items, and cash. Certain limits are applied to high risk items but the insured person may increase these limits by paying an extra premium.

Business Activity Statement (BAS)

Depending upon the size of a business, there is a requirement to complete the BAS monthly or quarterly. It forms the basis of the payment of business taxes and other obligations to the Australian Taxation Office (ATO) including:

- goods and services tax (GST)
- pay as you go withholding (PAYGW)
- pay as you go (PAYG) instalments
- wine equalisation tax
- fuel tax credits
- luxury car tax.

A BAS is not required if a person owns residential property but no other business interest or if a person owns commercial property with a turnover of less than $75,000 and no other business interest.

If a commercial property has a turnover of more than $75,000 (or if GST is charged but the property is under the threshold of $75,000) then the GST paid on purchases, such as repairs and maintenance, is offset against the GST collected and the difference remitted to the ATO after completion of the BAS.

C

Cap
The maximum interest rate on a loan

Capital
Money used to create income or wealth of a person or company, or the net worth of a business.

Capital cost
This is a substantial one off purchase of physical item such as plant, equipment, building or land.

Capital cost deduction
As of July 2017, this rule applies in terms of capital cost deduction for investment properties. The allowance is a deduction of 2.5 % each year for 40 years (2.5 x 40 = 100 %)

Example:

Suppose an investment (in 2017) is worth $1,000,000. The capital cost deduction of 2.5 % each year equates to a tax deduction of approximately $25,000 per year for 40 years (2057).

Capital expenditure
This is the cost of improvements made to a property to increase its value. These are expenses that (unlike operating expenses such as rates) cannot be deducted as tax expenses in that financial year. Instead they are recorded and taken into consideration to offset capital gains tax when the property is sold.

Capital Gain
This refers to the monetary gain obtained from the sale of an asset when the selling price is greater than the original purchase price. If the purchase was made as a sole trader or partnership, the capital gain or loss is added to the taxpayer's taxable income and the taxpayer is then taxed at that marginal rate.

Capital Gains Tax (CGT)

This is a commonwealth tax on the capital gain received from the sale of an asset which commenced on, or after, 20 September 1985. Assets purchased prior to this date are generally exempt from any capital gain tax liability as is a person's principal place of residence and 5 acres of land around the main house on a farm. Properties acquired before 20th Sep 1985 are referred as pre-CGT assets. CGT is paid when an asset has been sold at a profit or at loss (although it is called Capital Gains Tax regardless) where income tax is paid for services performed or from trading profits. CGT assets include units, land, buildings, good will, leases, foreign currency, land, rights and options.

Capitalised interest

This occurs when interest payments are added to the principal amount of the loan. It is used a lot in the construction industry and also fairly common with bridging finance.

Capitalisation rate

This rate is calculated by comparing the relationship of the net operating income to the sales price of similar properties that were sold in the current market.

Capitalisation rate is a component of return on investment and depreciation. If the cap rate is 10 %, this could be 8 % return on investment and 2 % for depreciation.

$$Value = \frac{Annual\ income}{Capitalisation\ rate}$$

Example: the estimated annual income (net) of a shop in a commercial property is $10,000 per year. The cap rate is 10 %. The value is

$$Value = \frac{\$10,000}{10\ \%} = \frac{\$10,000}{0.1} = \$100,000$$

Capitalisation rate is an indicator of the value of the property that produces income

$$Capitilisation\ Rate = \frac{Net\ operating\ income}{Purchase\ price}$$

Suppose the property discussed in, the purchase price is 1.4 million dollars, then

$$Capitilisation\ Rate = \frac{77,000}{1,400,000} = 0.055 \times 100 = 5.5\%$$

Capital works deduction
A capital works deduction applies to new buildings and extensions, alterations, improvements and structural improvements.

Cash accounting
Under this accounting system, transactions are recorded at the time money is actually received or paid.

Cash flow
This is simply the money moving into (income such as rent) and out (expenses such as rates) of a business or investment. It represents the operating activities of a company and affects its liquidity. It is important that cash flow is monitored as it is a prime factor in business failings. Funds must be available to meet debts as they fall due as well as unexpected expenses such as an increase in interest rates. (See *positive cash flow* and *negative cash flow properties*).

Cash-on-cash return
Cash-on-cash return is a rate of return often used in real estate transactions that calculates the cash income earned on the cash invested in a property. Cash-on-cash return measures the annual return the investor made on the property in relation to the amount of cash invested.

Example 1: on a $1 million dollar property the net income (after all expenses and debt service) is $100,000 in the first year. The cash-on-cash return in this example; $\frac{\$100,000}{\$1,000,000} \times 100 = 10\%$.

Some properties yield less (sometimes less than 5 %) and hence have a low cash-on-cash return but may still represent a good investment if there are encouraging signs such as harbour views, infrastructure improvements, change of zoning, proposed marina, etc.

Charge cards vs credit cards
Charge cards carry no pre-set spending limits. The balance must be paid at the end of every month and, if the account is paid late, the customer faces a flat fee (Diners Club, American Express).

Credit cards have pre-set spending limits. It is considered good practice to pay the balance monthly otherwise a high interest rate (around 20%) is charged on the amount outstanding. If the balance is not paid in full, it rolls over to the next month and interest accrues. A minimum amount must be paid monthly or the customer will be refused further credit (Visa, MasterCard).

Chart of accounts
This is an index of the accounts a company will use to classify transactions. Each account represents a type of transaction such as asset, liability, owner's equity, income and expense. Accounting packages such as MYOB have standard chart of accounts that can be used.

Cheque
A cheque is issued by a bank on its account (cheque or checking account) and is used by the customer for paying bills or withdrawing funds. (See also *accounts*).

CHESS
CHESS is an acronym for Clearing House Electronic Sub register System. CHESS is an electronic transfer and settlement system used by the Australian Securities Exchange.

Clawback clause

If a mortgage broker (or financial advisor) is engaged to seek or to purchase a product (a loan or insurance), the insurance provider or lending institution pays the broker a commission based on the loan or insurance product chosen. If the product is no longer required, the insurance or lending organisation can pull back (clawback) the commission paid to the broker. A clawback provision is a special contractual clause typically included in contracts by financial firms, by which money already paid must be paid back under certain conditions.

Commercial mortgage loan

A loan secured by a commercial property that generates business or rental income.

Compounding

Compounding is the process through which a small amount of money earning interest can steadily grow into a large amount through accrual of interest on interest.

Compound interest

Interest paid both on the sum of the original principal and on the interest accrued from the time it fell due.

Construction cost deductions

Post 15th September 1987 any capital expenditure used to construct income producing property may be allowable as a 2.5% tax deduction for 40 years (40 × 2.5 = 100%). Note the construction cost deduction is only allowed for the time the property is being used as an investment property (either rented or available for rent). (Read our book entitled *"It's My Time: Successful Residential Investing"* for more details on the current changes and updates as of 1st July 2017).

Construction loan

A short term loan taken over the time of construction.

Constructive receipt
A method that prevents taxpayers from intentionally delaying the receiving of rental income to delay paying tax on it. Example: paying rent to a third party

Contingent liability
Also referred to as loss contingency. It is the potential liability that may occur based on the outcome of an uncertain future event. Contingent liability is recorded as an expense, or a loss, on the income statement, or a liability on the balance sheet.

Costs of discharge
The costs incurred for administration when a loan is repaid.

Crowd funding
This is a recent strategy where individuals and groups of individuals raise funds over the internet bypassing banks and government organisations. The funds are managed by an intermediary that takes a percentage fee. There are some pros and cons of crowd funding in the real estate business. Some of the pros are: products are more accessible for investors with little cash or savings and a higher rate of return. Some of the cons are: due diligence limitations and government regulations. (Our book entitled "It's My Time: Successful Residential Investing" has an example of a large residential project completed via a crowd funding model).

Credit card fraud
This is a crime that involves a credit card as a fraudulent source for transaction of funds. A person involved in these fraudulent activities normally acquires an individual's credit/debit card details used over phone, or on the internet, and makes purchases in the cardholder's name. (See second step verification and Blockchain).

Credit history
A record of a person's ability to service present and past debts.

Credit limit
The maximum amount of funds an individual can borrow at any one time.

Creditors
Those to whom a payment is to be made or debt is due.

Credit rating
Standard and Poor's credit rating, *Moody's* credit rating and *Fitch's* credit rating are the three major credit rating agencies that rank countries to gauge their credit worthiness. The ranking is from AAA (highest) to D (lowest). Australia has maintained a higher credit rating since 15th January 1962. *Standard and Poor's* rating for Australia was BBB on 27th Feb 1957. There is another rating called the *Trade Economics* (TE) credit rating. The TE rating scores the credit worthiness of a country between 100 (riskless) and 0 (likely to default). The following are the values as of May 2017.

	S&P		Moody's		Fitch		TERating
Australia	AAA	Negative	Aaa	Stable	AAA	Stable	97

Figure 22: Credit rating of Australia as of May 2017 (AAA and 97 (TE Rating))

Credit reporting
In Australia, we have three main credit reporting agencies that compare credit-worthiness related data on more than 11 million individuals in Australia and New Zealand. It accesses the data from a range of industries: banking, finance, telecommunications, retail, utilities, trade credit, government, credit unions and mortgage lenders. This credit report is used by lending organisation to rate the creditworthiness of a prospective borrower.

- Veda Advantage (previously named Baycorp Advantage)
- Dunn and Bradstreet
- Tasmanian Collection Service

Cryptocurrency

This is a form of encrypted digital currency that is created, regulated and secured by a computer network. Cryptocurrency is a non-conventional currency and is not backed by a government. It is created by a system that generates mathematical codes to provide high level security. (See *Fiat currency*)

Current ratio

Working capital is a measure that compares current assets to current liabilities.

$$Current\ ratio = \frac{Current\ assets}{Current\ liabilities}$$

If a business has current assets worth 6 million dollars and current liabilities worth 3 million dollars, the current ratio of this business is 2. A ratio over 1 is favourable as liabilities coming due can be adequately met by assets.

D

Debts

The amount of money that is owed to someone or a financial institution. Debt should be paid off as quickly as possible unless there are benefits in spreading repayments. There are two types of debt: good debt and bad debt. A mortgage against a positive cash flow investment property is a good debt whereas a credit card debt, or a personal loan at a high interest rate, is considered a bad debt. Bad debts can lead to taking out more loans simply to pay off the interest and downward spiral results. Read our book entitled "*It's My Time: Setting Financial and Personal Goals*" for the following: set financial goals, increase savings from income, manage debt, use investment pay-outs and gain financial independence.

Debt/Equity Ratio (DER)

This is the ratio of mortgage or outstanding balance on a property over equity on the property. A higher debt equity ratio means that the loan value ratio is likely to be lower.

If the mortgage on an investor's properties equates to 1.6 million and the equity from all these properties is 1.2 million dollars, the debt/equity ratio is

$$\frac{1.6 \; million}{1.2 \; million} = 1.33$$

As of July 2017, tighter lending restrictions by APRA to lenders has ameliorated the situation of investors borrowing at a low debt equity ratio.

Debt Servicing Ratio (DSR)

This relates to the amount of income a lender requires a loan applicant to have available to service payments. It is the annual loan repayment as a proportion of net income. Most lenders prefer this to less than 0.35 and will not lend if the ratio is greater than 0.5.

Default

This is when a borrower breaks the terms of the mortgage contract with the lender. Default could occur due to missing repayments or failing to keep the mortgaged property insured. (See *Lenders Mortgage Insurance* for details).

Delinquency

The situation that arises when a borrower does not meet a scheduled payment.

Digital currency

This is a virtual currency that can be traded on exchanges directly between individuals using the internet.

Diminishing Value Method

The diminishing value method calculates depreciation of chattels using a depreciation rate. The depreciation allowed by the ATO each year is calculated and deducted from the written down value from the previous year's depreciation. Unlike the prime cost method, the depreciation allowance is not equal throughout the period but higher in the first year and reducing annually. Investors would therefore choose the diminishing value method to secure greater tax rebates in the earlier years of an investment. (See *prime cost method* and *depreciation schedule*).

Disbursement

A cash payment to settle a debt. The process of paying out money to a number of recipients. Typically, this would be carried out by a conveyancer on the day of settlement. (See *statement of adjustments*)

Disbursement fees

Disbursement fees are essentially any costs incurred by the lender's solicitors for researching the property and lodging the mortgage documents and normally include title search fee, registration of title fee and settlement fee.

Discharge of mortgage fee

A discharge of mortgage fee is paid to the lending institution for attending the settlement and discharging the security on the loan when you are selling a property. It includes preparation of the discharge of mortgage document along with the government fee to register the discharge of mortgage on the certificate of title.

Discounting

Similar to compounding in terms of calculating the value of an investment over time. Discounting is a method which determines what an investment will cost now if it is to be worth a certain amount of money in the future. This will answer the question "For an investment to be worth $1,000,000 at the end of 14 years, at an interest rate of 5 %, how much money is needed to invest now? (This presumes that the interest rate will remain fixed over that period. The effect of inflation would also need to be considered) (See *eighteen year cycle*).

Discretionary Income

The amount of income available for spending or investing after tax and necessities.

Disposable Income

The amount of income available for spending or investing after tax.

Distress sale

If the mortgagor defaults on the obligation to the mortgagee (that is monthly payment of interest, interest and principal), the lender may be able to take possession of the property in order to sell it and use the proceeds to repay the loan, interest outstanding and costs. A distress sale may also happen when an owner needs to raise cash to prevent bankruptcy. (Also known as a fire sale).

Dividend

This is the amount given to the shareholders of the company's earnings usually quarterly. This amount is taxable payment declared by a company's board of directors. (See *franked dividend*).

Dividend cover

This is a ratio showing the number of times a company's dividend is covered by its net profit. Dividend is calculated by dividing net profit by dividend paid.

Double taxation

This is where tax is paid twice on the same source of earned income. It can occur by taxation at corporate and personal levels and also by taxation in two different countries (international trade).

Dovish
A careful monetary policy that encourages lower interest rates.

E

EBITDA
EBITDA is earnings before interest, income tax, depreciation accounting, amortisation of deferred charges and extraordinary items. It means taking net income as a start point. (See *Net income*).

Economic Life
The time remaining during which a property can be profitably and feasibly used.

Eighteen year cycle
It is a term used for property price variations in a market. Statistics shows that Western economies show this trend over an 18 year real estate cycle. This theory may not necessarily apply to Australia as Australia's property market did not crash both in 1990s and in 2008. Read our books entitled "*It's My Time: Setting Financial and Personal Goals*" and "*It's My Time: Successful Residential Investing*" for more details on the Australian property market, our housing market's reliance on overseas and the effect of migration in the property market. (See *One Belt One Road, Relationship between capital growth and rental return*)

Equity
This term refers to the value of a property less any outstanding loans.

Equity loans
A loan secured against the equity in a property for the purpose of renovating or securing a second property. (See *cross collateralising*).

Establishment fees

Fees charged by a lending institution to set up a loan.

Exchange rate

This is the rate at which one currency can be traded for another. The exchange rate of a currency is based on economic conditions which, in turn, are based on four factors: Gross domestic product, inflation, employment and interest rates.

Table 11: **Comparison of factors affected by stronger and weaker currency**

Weak currency	Strong currency
Low interest rates, high inflation, falling Gross Domestic Product, high unemployment and low confidence in investors	High interest rates, stable inflation, rising GDP, low unemployment, high confidence

The Australian dollar was floated in 1984 which meant that its value was no longer fixed but could vary according to supply and demand compared with other currencies.

Exit Fee

A fee charged by a financial institution when a customer withdraws from a loan or investment.

Exit strategy

This ensures business or real-estate deals are prepared for the termination of contracts, project deals or business relationships.

F

Facility

This is a pre-determined arrangement offered by a financial institution to a business such as a short term loan or an overdraft facility.

Fiat currency
This is currency minted by a government and its value is determined by supply and demand. The currency is not created by the free market, nor backed by any asset like gold, silver or property. It is the traditional currency unique to a country (USD, AUD) or a region (Euro). (See *Bretton Wood system, Cryptocurrency*).

Fidelity cover
An insurance taken out by professionals against losing money held on someone else's behalf.

Fidelity guarantee
A fidelity guarantee is another type of indemnity insurance against fraudulent embezzlement or fraudulent misappropriation of funds set aside for management of a body corporate, including the sinking fund.

Fiduciary
A person or organisation responsible for managing someone else's assets.

Finance application
The finance application form varies a little between financial institutions but generally requires the names and addresses of the applicants, assets and liabilities of each applicant, employer details, salary and wage income, and contract of sale and estimate of rental income if purchasing a rental property. If seeking funds for a development then the financial institution will also want to see a feasibility study, marketing plan, construction estimates, council approved plans, risk analysis, project overview and developer and builder's history.

Financial feasibility study
This is where an assessment of a potential project is undertaken, in terms of income and expenses, to ascertain if there is profit potential. It is sometimes referred to as 'number crunching'.

Financial goal
A financial goal or financial target is an objective which is expressed in, or based upon, money. The financial goals are short term (less than 12 months), medium term (1 to 5 years) and long term (5 years or more). A template for financial goals can be found later in this book.

Financial institution
This is an entity that accepts money as savings or investments and in turn provides funds to borrowers at an interest rate set by the Reserve Bank of Australia. The financial institutions in Australia are regulated by APRA. (See earlier definition).

Financial planning
Financial planning is about setting financial goals and the development of strategies to meet them.

Finder's or spotter's fee
This is money paid when a person finds a property that doesn't meet their requirements but meets the requirements of another investor. It is an incidental and likely once off happening to the person finding their own property. All state governments require real estate transactions to be handled by licensed real estate professionals and there are penalties imposed if people are found to be operating outside of licencing requirements.

Fixed interest loans
With this type of loan, the interest rate is fixed for a specified period of the loan, generally between one to five years, although some

banks offer fixed interest loans up to ten years. At the end of the fixed term, the loan generally converts to the current variable interest rate or may rollover to a further fixed term. Fixed interest loans provide certainty for that period with regard to repayments but the drawback is that, generally, you can't make additional repayments. There are also substantial penalties, known as break fees, if you want to pay the loan out early, or refinance.

Fixed vs variable interest rates

When choosing between fixed and variable rates, an investor must consider many factors but the most significant is somewhat out of everybody's control – what will the Reserve Bank decide to do with the cash rate in the coming months/years and how will the banks respond with their setting of interest rates? Another important factor is changes to lending policy dictated by the Australian Prudential Regulation Authority. For example, in 2017 APRA advised lending institutions to restrict interest-only loans favoured by investors and this resulted in a substantial rise in IO loan rates.

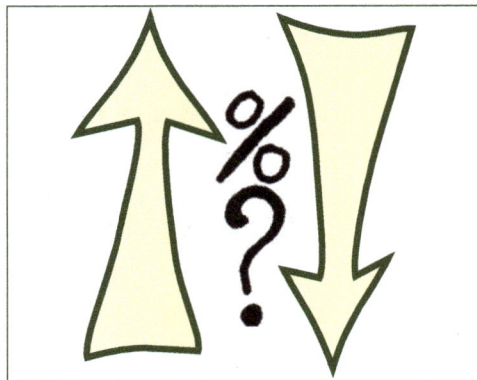

In the current economy, with interest rates at an all-time low most investors are opting for loans at variable interest rates. However there are advantages in both types of loans:

Table 12: Features of fixed and variable interest loans

Fixed interest	Variable interest
Interest rate will not vary during the term of the loan (remains unchanged even though the official cash rate might rise or fall)	Interest rate is free to rise or fall based on the official cash rate set by the RBA
Interest rate is set for a fixed period (commonly 1, 2, 3, or 5 years)	Interest rate varies over the full term of the loan
Penalties may apply for early repayment of the loan	Not applicable
Advantageous when rates increase	Undesirable when rates increase
Undesirable when rates drop	Advantageous when rates drop
In times of interest rate volatility, investors are wise to fix a shorter fixed period which can be changed on the expiration.	Since all lenders respond to the market differently, investors can improve their situation by 'shopping around' to other lenders for a better rate.
Offset facility not available	Loan interest can be offset by funds in a savings account
Limited redraw available	Redraw largely unlimited
Less flexible	More flexible

Floating rate
An interest rate which changes over the term of a loan.

Foreclosure
Foreclosure is the process whereby the lending organisation institutes legal action to repossess a property when the mortgagor defaults on monthly loan repayments.

Foreign registered trusts
These are trusts that are based overseas that you can buy in Australia.

Fortnightly or bi-weekly mortgage
This refers to the frequency of loan repayments.

Freehold

Freehold is the highest form of ownership. No time limit is imposed on the ownership hence the right exists in perpetuity. Ownership of the property is fee simple which means that it is a legal interest in property or real estate capable of being inherited without limitation.

Fully amortized mortgage

This is the sum of two loan components – principal and interest. The total repayment remains the same each month but the earlier payments in the loan term comprise mostly interest. The amount of repayment applied to interest decreases each month while the amount applied to the principal increases each month.

G

Gazumping

Particularly relevant in New South Wales, this occurs when a vendor has agreed to sell the property to a certain buyer but then receives a better offer from another buyer before the sale has been settled and then sells to the highest offer.

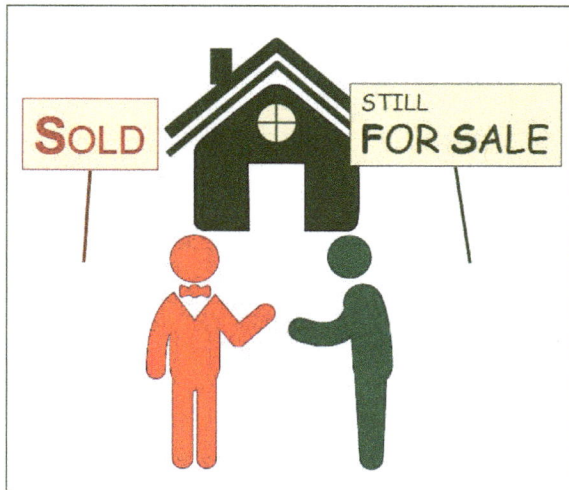

Figure 23: Image showing the Gazumping process (buyer(red), vendor(green))

Genuine savings

As a first home buyer or an investor applying for a loan, lenders expect to see a record of savings. The savings could be generated over a period of time or an amount of money held over a period of time would be acceptable. The rental income from a property or a lease in place on a property would also be seen as periodic income.

Goods and Services Tax (GST)

Goods and services tax (GST) was introduced on 1st July 2000 and is charged at 10% on all taxable supplies from GST registered entities. Residential rent and mortgages are input taxed and cannot include GST. When purchasing a house for living or rental, the transaction is not subject to GST. However, the first buyer of a newly built house has to pay GST. The federal government collects GST from consumers across the country but returns the GST collected to the states.

Table 13: Taxable supplies, GST free and input taxed supplies

GST transactions	Description
Taxable supplies	Goods or services from a business that has an annual turnover of over $75,000
GST free supplies	Fresh food (but not snacks or ice cream), education and child care, health and medical services, exports, purchase of an established business
Input taxed supplies	Residential premises for rent, financial supplies, sales of residential premises, fund raising activities

Goods and services tax (GST) on short term and long term accommodation

An owner of 'bed and breakfast' accommodation or 'AirBNB' style housing, is required to charge GST on the supply of accommodation, meals and any other services provided to guests. Input tax credits may still be claimed for any GST included in the prices of goods and services purchased for the business.

Gross

In terms of finance, gross is a total amount before deductions. A person's gross wage is what their employer pays them before deducting income tax or any other amounts. In the following example, gross salary is $80,230 before tax and other deductions.

Period of payment	Day/Month/Year 01 / 07 / 2016	to	Day/Month/Year 30 / 06 / 2017			
			TOTAL TAX WITHHELD $			19,286
				Type	Lump sum payments	Type
Gross payments	$		80,230	S A $	0	
CDEP payments	$		0	B $	0	

Figure 24: Screen shot of a payslip showing total tax withheld and gross payments

Gross building area

The gross building area is determined by measuring the area of each floor plan to the outside of exterior walls. It is used for site coverage calculations and in development applications.

Guarantor

A person or company that provides a guarantee. If the borrower defaults on the loan, the guarantor will pay all or some of the loan.

H

Hawkish

An aggressive monetary policy that is likely to lead to higher interest rates

Home equity loan

A loan for any purpose secured by a mortgage over a property.

Home improvement loan

A loan using an applicant's house as collateral for improvements.

I

Illiquid
A term referring to an asset which cannot be readily converted into cash.

Immovable assets
These are assets that are not movable and cannot be moved without destroying or altering it (properties, land, property rights, plants, large piece of equipment).

Income
Gross income is the total income from a property before all expenses are deducted. Net income is gross income minus all expenses.

Income tax
This is a tax levied by the tax office on assessable income (income that is to be included in an income tax return). According to the ATO, there are many types of income:

1. Employment income
2. Super pensions, annuities and government payments
3. Investment income (interest, dividends, rent)
4. Foreign income
5. Crowd funding
6. Other income (insurance payments, compensation, prizes, awards)

Indenture
This is a written agreement between the issuer of a bond and the bondholders, usually specifying the interest rate and maturity date.

Input tax
An indirect tax or valued added tax that is levied on raw materials and capital goods that a business uses for its daily operations.

Input taxed supply

This is a supply for which the vendor cannot charge GST and also cannot claim GST incurred in relation to that supply. There are input taxed sales and input taxed purchases. Residential rent is input taxed which means that landlord pays out GST on most of the goods and services for the rental property but cannot claim it back and must not charge GST to the tenant on the rent. This is designed such that property investors do not gain an unfair advantage over home owners.

Instalment Activity Statement (IAS)

This is a form for reporting PAYG instalments or PAYG withholding by certain investors or businesses that are not registered for GST.

Interest

Money paid by a borrower in return for the use of money lent by another, or money paid for not requiring a debt or loan to be repaid. Banks and all lending organisation make profit based on the interest accrued or amortised at regular intervals.

Simple interest

The total amount of interest over a period of time is calculated by multiplying the principal, term or period, and the rate of interest.

$$Simple\ Interest = \frac{pnr}{100}$$

Where p is principal, n is the period or term in years, r is the rate of interest.

Simple interest is not commonly used. Some car loans are some amortised using simple interest and some consumer loans are calculated on this basis but, in almost all financial transaction in property development, compound interest is used.

Compound interest

This is calculated by adding simple interest to the capital and recalculating interest on the sum. It is a bonus for anybody wanting to accrue savings but a burden when making repayments on a loan.

$$Compound\ Interest = P[(1 + i)^n - 1]$$

P = Principal, I = Interest Rate, n = number of compounding terms

Example: A personal loan of $25,000 is taken out to purchase a car at an interest rate of 10 % for a period of 7 years. (Note: It is not considered good financial strategy to take out a personal loan to purchase an item that depreciates in time and where there is no return on the investment).

$$Compound\ Interest = \$25,000[(1 + 0.1)^7 - 1]$$

$$= \$25,000[1.9487 - 1]$$

$$= \$25,000[0.9487]$$

$$= \$23,717.93\ Total\ interest\ over\ the\ 7\ year\ period$$

The following table shows how the interest 'compounds' (builds) over the 7 year period:

Year	Principal	Interest only 10%	Total balance (principal and interest)
1	25000	2500	27500
2	27500	2750	30250
3	30250	3025	33275
4	33275	3327.5	33602.5
5	36602.5	3660.25	40262.75
6	40262.75	4026.28	44289.03
7	44289.03	4428.90	48717.93
Total interest		$23,717.93	

Interest cover ratio

This is a measure of a company's ability to meet its interest payments.

Interest only (IO) loans

This is a type of loan whereby the interest only is paid and the principal remains the same for the entire term. This means lower repayments but the borrower is left with a larger lump sum at the end of the term (the value of the lump sum is diminished by the effects of the inflation).

Example: An investment property worth 1 million dollars is purchased with 20 % deposit and an interest only loan at 5% on a 30 year term. The monthly repayments would be $3333.33 (800,000 x 0.05/12) assuming the interest rate is constant at 5% for 30 years.

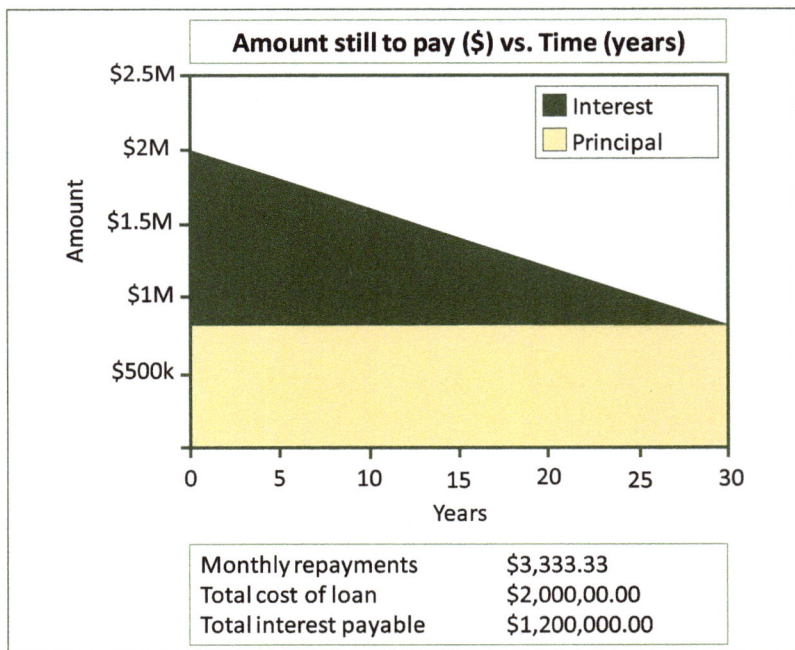

Amount still to pay ($) vs. Time (years)

Monthly repayments	$3,333.33
Total cost of loan	$2,000,00.00
Total interest payable	$1,200,000.00

Figure 25: Graph and numerical representation of interest only loan on a million dollar property

In the example illustrated below, the lender gives a better rate of 4.5% but this time for principal and interest payments. The repayments increase from $3,333.33 to $4,053.48 but, at the end of the term, the loan has been completely repaid.

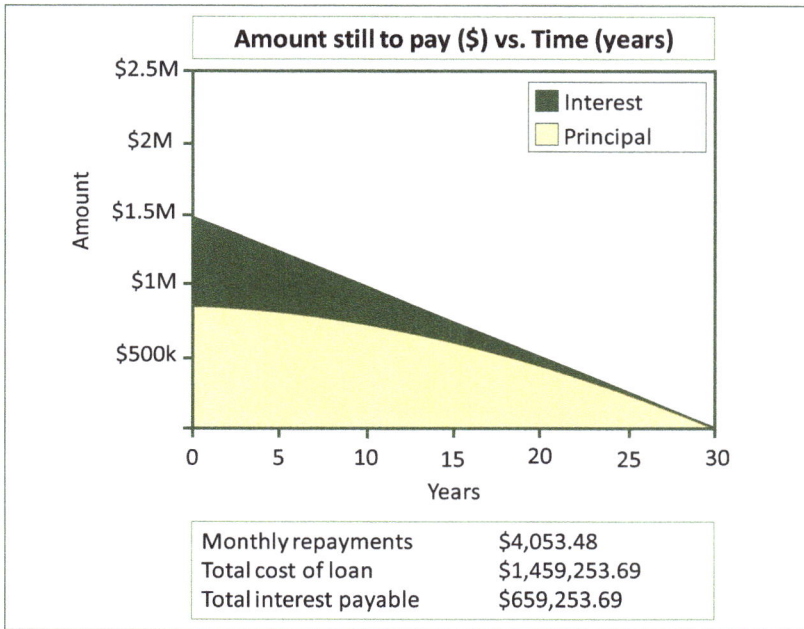

Amount still to pay ($) vs. Time (years)	
Monthly repayments	$4,053.48
Total cost of loan	$1,459,253.69
Total interest payable	$659,253.69

Figure 26: **Graph and numerical representation of principal and interest loan on a million dollar property**

Repayment frequency

Monthly repayments are the most common but, if principal and interest loans are repaid fortnightly or weekly, there are savings to be made. The following examples illustrate this:

Scenario 1: $500,000 at 5% interest only loan (30 years loan term)		
	Repayment	Total annually
Weekly repayment	480.77	25,000
Fortnightly repayment	961.54	25,000
Monthly repayment	2083.33	25,000

Scenario 2: 500,000 at 5 % principal and interest loan		
	Repayment	Total annually
Weekly repayment	618.98	32,186.96
Fortnightly repayment	1238.22	32,193.72
Monthly repayment	2684.11	32,209.32

Interest Cover Ratio (ICR)

Interest cover ratio is a measure of a company's ability to meet its interest payments. It is equal to earnings before interest and taxes (EBIT) for a period, often one year, divided by interest expenses for the same time period.

Example: Bill has applied for a $1,000,000 loan at an interest rate of 5 %. If the lender assessed Bill's application using a buffer rate of 7 % then the lender would need to see $70,000 in net rent income for Bill to qualify for a lease doc loan. If the property was actually generating $140,000 in rent, then Bill would have an ICR of 2.

Interest rate change

Lending institutions will almost certainly increase their interest rates if the RBA increases the official cash rate. Branch managers usually get notified on a Friday afternoon before the banks make the official announcement on the weekend.

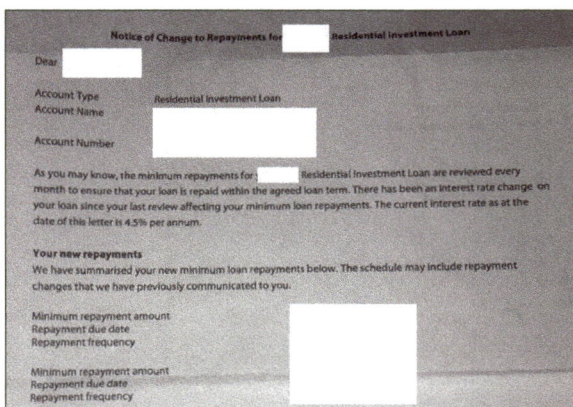

Figure 27: **Letter from a bank advising of a change in repayments on an investment loan**

Internal Rate of Return (IRR)

Annualised return on investment (value of cash returns with cash invested) Internal rate of return calculation is an extension of the net present value (see *net present value*)

$$Cash\ Flow = (Investment\ acount) \times (1 + i)^t$$

$$i = rate\ of\ return, \qquad t = term$$

If the rate of return is 20% and the investment amount = $100,000 then cash flow after 3 years would be:

$$Cash\ Flow = (100,000) \times (1 + 0.20)^3 = \$172,800$$

Introductory loan

A reduced rate loan for new borrowers before going to current market interest rates. This loan is also called a Honeymoon loan.

Inventory

A list of items included in a purchase that are not attached to the property, nor fitted. Examples of this are beds, chairs, tables, rugs, movable furniture.

J

Joint tenants

A form of ownership of property, often by married couples, where, in the event of death, the deceased share is passed to the surviving party (See *tenancy in common*).

L

Lease document lending

A lease document loan for commercial or investment property does not require full evidence of an applicant's income but instead relies on the strength of the rent income from the property used to secure the loan.

Legal fees

Legal fees will normally be for time involved on the buyer's behalf by legal practitioners in the conveyancing (transfer) of the property and any disbursements costs. (See disbursement costs).

Lender's Mortgage Insurance (LMI)

This is insurance paid by the loan applicant (borrower) to protect the lender against payment default. It is normally applied in residential loans if borrowings are above a loan to value ratio (LVR) of 80%. This means an applicant needs to have at least 20% of the total value of the property and stamp duty costs as a deposit to avoid paying LMI.

It is worth noting that payment of the LMI does not absolve the borrower from responsibility for the debt.

If the LVR is above 80%, an applicant may still be able to secure a loan if a third party (normally a relative) is willing to guarantee the loan. In the case of default, this passes the onus of debt onto the guarantor. LMI is not applicable if the loan is guaranteed.

LMI can either be paid upfront or capitalised into the loan, which means payments are made over the life of the loan.

Liabilities

The debts owed by an individual or a company.

Line of credit

This is a facility whereby a specific amount of credit is lent to the borrower and the principal is not required to be repaid until the end of the life of the facility. It has similar principles to a credit card facility.

Line of credit account

A loan account which a customer can use for deposits and withdrawals up to a pre-arranged credit limit.

Liquid asset
An asset that can easily be converted to cash.

Loan application fee
A fee charged by a lender for processing a loan. Also called an establishment fee, it is to compensate the lender for the time spent assessing the loan application. The loan application fee may be waived at the discretion of the lender, whether or not the loan is approved. A waiver, or a reduced fee, is often applied for returning customers.

Loan processing
The steps involved in creating a loan from application through to closing.

Loan service fee
This is a monthly fee applied to the loan on the monthly repayment date

Loan to Value Ratio (LVR)
This is the amount of your loan shown as a percentage of the market value of the property or asset to be purchased. Using this ratio, the lender works out whether the loan amount can be recovered in the event of defaulting on the loan. It is also used to determine whether lenders mortgage insurance may be required.

This may vary between banks and the property being purchased. The LVR can also be influenced by economic factors, legislation and by controlling bodies such as APRA. Generally, the LVR for residential property is 80%, for commercial property 65 – 70%, for vacant land around 65% and, for other properties that banks view as less favourable, it maybe 40 – 50%. Purchasing a residential property valued at $500,000 would require a deposit of $100,000 for an 80% LVR.

Low doc loans

This type of loan requires the borrower to provide minimal financial disclosure to the financial institution to secure the loan. They are useful for self-employed people. The interest rates are normally higher and some lenders may charge mortgage insurance on properties with an LVR of 60 – 80%.

Low start loans

A loan that starts out with low repayments that gradually increase.

Lump sum repayments

These are additional ad hoc repayments, made over and above the minimum repayment requirement.

M

Marginal rate of tax

This is the rate of tax paid on salary that falls above a certain income threshold.

Minimum repayment

This is the amount that a borrower (or mortgagor) is contractually obliged to repay each month, in order to repay a loan within the agreed term.

Minimum repayment on credit card

The lowest amount the account holder must repay each month, or at each billing cycle date, to avoid a penalty. Note that if a credit card holder pays only the minimum payment by the due date, the remaining unpaid balance will accrue interest and the amount the cardholder owes will increase (See *Compound interest, Credit card*).

Money supply

The amount of money circulating in an economy. When the money circulation increases, the value of spending also increases.

Governments increase the money supply to stimulate the demand and to increase its spending. Government increases spending via defence, building houses, schools, hospitals, transport infrastructure, health care, education, security and so on. Read our books entitled "*It's My Time: Setting Financial and Personal Goals*" and "*It's My Time: Strategies in Action*" for more details on the relation between investment and spending, stimulating demand, production increase, business expenditure, wages, goods and investments.

Mortgage
A mortgage is given as security for a loan and sets out the terms and conditions of the loan, including the rights of the financial institution in the event that the borrower defaults on the loan. The mortgage is registered on the title to the property. In other words, it is a charge over property given by the owner (borrower or mortgagor) to a lender (mortgagee) to secure repayment of a loan or to ensure satisfaction of a debt. (See *gage, live gage* for details).

Mortgage broker
A mortgage broker is a professional who has knowledge of the mortgage market and will be able to find the best mortgagee best suited to a customer's needs. The broker acts for the borrower, not for the lender. However the mortgage broker is paid a commission by the lender based on the size of the loan amount.

Mortgage discharge fee
A fee some lenders charge for discharging a loan.

Mortgage duty
It is a duty charged on the amount secured by a mortgage.

Mortgage offset
An account in which the funds are offset against a home loan to reduce the amount of interest to be paid.

Mortgage protection

Mortgage protection is a simplified form of life insurance available to those with a mortgage. This is often confused with Lenders Mortgage Insurance which is quite different (See earlier definition).

Mortgage trust

A unit trust which invests in mortgages.

Mortgagee

The mortgagee is usually a lending organisation, often a bank, which lends money to purchase a property and uses said property as security for the loan.

Mortgagee sale

Where a property is sold due to the owner's inability to meet the mortgage payments on a loan. Often known as a fire sale.

Mortgagor

This is the borrower named in a mortgage agreement covering a mortgage loan where the property is offered in support of the loan (mortgaged) (See *encumbrance*).

Movable assets

These are tangible assets that are movable (paintings, computers, jewellery, vehicles, etc.).

N

Net profit

The profit after tax, interest and extraordinary items.

Net present value

It is the difference between cash inflow (present value) and cash outflow (present value). The net income in year one divided by 1+r where r is the cost of funds (interest rate) for year one and then added to the same calculation for years 2, 3 and so on. The value of r in each year could be changed to CPI and this would give a NPV in today's dollars. Net present value for a period of two years is

$$\left\{ \frac{(income - expense)^1}{(1+r)^1} + \frac{(income - expense)^2}{(1+r)^2} \right.$$
$$\left. - purchase\ price\ an\ asset \right\}$$

The formula can be extended for as many years as the asset is owned. In essence the formula is the net income in year one divided by 1+r where r is the cost of funds (interest rate) for year one and then added to the same calculation for years 2, 3 and so on.

Net worth or net wealth
The difference between total assets and total liabilities.

Non-conforming mortgage
A product developed for people who have difficulty conforming to the eligibility criteria applied by most financial institutions for mortgage loans. The interest rates are usually higher than those of most mortgage loan products and there may be higher exit fees and many other special conditions. In the wake of the sub-mortgage crisis in the United States, lending institutions are very wary of such products. (For further details read more from our book entitled "*It's My Time: Setting Financial and Personal Goals*").

O

Official Cash Rate (OCR)
Used in Australia and New Zealand, this term refers to the interest rate charged on overnight loans to commercial banks. This is the basis on which all other interest rates in Australia operate.

Offset account

This account is generally linked to a mortgage account such that the funds held within are deducted from the loan amount for the purpose of calculating loan interest

Description	Amount
Offset account contains	$100,000
Interest is paid on	$900,000 instead of $1 M

Ongoing fee

A fee charged over the life of a loan.

Ordinary income

Income according to ordinary receipt. Ordinary income is usually defined as income other than long term capital gain. Examples are wages, salaries, tips, commissions and bonus.

Outstanding balance

The outstanding balance is the present value of the balance remaining on a loan at any point in time. (See *pro-rata and early termination fee*).

Overheads

These are fixed costs associated with operating a business such as rent, utilities and administrative costs.

P

Peer-to-peer lending

It is a non-conventional lending process in which a borrower and a lender are matched by an online agency. There are a few regulations but the borrowers are screened for risk.

Personal loan

This is a type of loan given to a borrower for any worthwhile purpose. The interest rates for personal loans are usually higher than for home loans.

Positive cashflow
Properties generate a cash flow profit when the income exceeds the outgoings.

Pre-qualification
Before commencing a formal loan application, this is an indication from a lender as to whether the application is likely to be successful.

Prime loans
These are those made to well qualified borrowers (See *subprime loan*).

Prime and subprime market
The market for mortgage loans is categorised by the creditworthiness of the borrowers that draw the loan. The highest-rated borrowers are rated A (called prime market) with lower ratings for those with questionable ability to meet their obligations (subprime).

Prime rate
The interest rate banks charge their preferred customers.

Principal
The original amount borrowed on a loan or the remainder of the original borrowed amount that is still owing (excluding the interest portion of the amount).

Interest only loans	you pay interest only every month
Principal and interest	you pay both interest and principal every month

Private treaty sale
The sale of a property through a real estate agent.

Profit and loss statement
A financial statement that summarises revenue, costs and expenses

incurred resulting in a company's net profit or loss over a specific period such as quarterly or yearly. It is now called an Income Statement. (Our book entitled "*It's My Time: Introducing Commercial Investing*" will look at the significance of various details on a balance sheet and profit and loss statement and how it will help to make an informed decision before purchasing a commercial property).

Profit margin

If a business is generating a revenue of $100,000 and the net income (profit) is $50,000, then

$$Profit\ margin = \frac{Net\ income}{Revenue}$$

$$Profit\ margin = \frac{50,000}{100,000} = 0.5\ or\ 50\ \%$$

Proforma

This is a description of financial statements that have one or more assumptions or hypothetical conditions built into the data.

Progress payment (residential)

This is a periodical payment made to a builder at defined stages of construction (see earlier). The owner, or representative, must testify that construction has reached that stage before the release of funds. The percentage of payment, and the different stages, are mostly uniform across Australia but each state has minor variations. For recipients of a First Home Owner Grant, this is normally credited at the first progress payment. (See *accounts*).

Promissory Note

A written promise to pay a stated sum of money to someone on a certain date or on demand.

R

Real return
A return adjusted for inflation.

Record keeping
This is the process of keeping or recording information that explains business transactions. Under Australian Taxation law, it is a requirement to keep records.

Redraw facility
The bank holds any amounts you have paid on your loan over and above the minimum required in this facility and allows you to access these 'surplus' funds in the future if required.

This is an added feature of a variable loan account whereby a customer is permitted use of personal savings to make repayments in excess of the agreed monthly amount. These deposits will reduce the debt, and hence the interest payable, until such time as the customer wishes to redraw the funds. The lender will impose restrictions in terms of the number of such transactions and the maximum amount deposited. For example, if a customer's agreed monthly payment is $1,200 but he deposits $1,500 each month for six months, then, an amount of $1,800 (6 x $300) is available for redraw after that period. This may be withdrawn as one lump sum or in smaller amounts over a period of time until the $1,800 has been fully redrawn.

Refinance
This is to increase one's debt to make additional funds available 'for any worthwhile purpose' by taking out a new loan using the same property as security. It is also when a new loan is taken out to pay off an existing one or to extend the original loan over a longer period of time, reduce fees or interest rates, switch banks, or move from a fixed to variable loan.

Reserve Bank of Australia (RBA)

The Reserve Bank of Australia is the central bank of the Commonwealth of Australia responsible for controlling inflation through its monetary policy and setting of the cash rates (currently at a record low of 1.5%). It also aims to aid the stability of the Australian dollar and targets full employment and economic prosperity and to insure the safety and soundness of the financial system. The Reserve Bank has an autonomous power to create or reduce or destroy the money and to lower or raise interest rates.

Table 14: Connection between interest rate and economic activity

Interest rates	Economic Activity	Mechanism behind this
Raise	Slow activity (inflation)	• Takes money out of the system (through tax and othindustreiser modes) • Increase in interest rate • We spend less and borrow less (more on savings)
Lower	Stimulate activity	• Creates more money in the system • Interest rates fall • We are more likely to borrow and spend

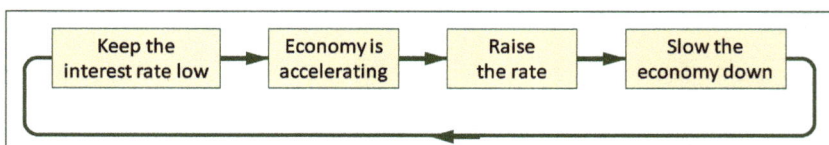

Figure 28: Connection between interest rate and economy

One of the main functions of the Reserve Bank is to establish the cash rate (the building block for the interest rate used by financial institutions) and the availability of money to service the national economy. The Reserve Bank controls money by adjusting supplies and can loan money to the government. It is a three step process.

1. The government creates an informal document acknowledging debt called an IOU (I owe you). When the government

needs more money than they receive from taxes that we pay to ATO, the government asks the treasury department for the money.

2. Treasury then receives an IOU or a bond from the Australian government. Treasury, through the bank, gives the IOU to the reserve bank. The Reserve Bank writes a cheque for this amount mentioned on the IOU and hands it to the financial institutions.

3. Money is created and it can be used to pay government bills.

Reserve currency

This is foreign currency held by the Federal Reserve Bank and other financial institutions used to make trade payments. The US dollar is the currency most commonly held in reserves globally. Read our books entitled "It's My Time: Setting Financial and Personal Goals" on special drawing rights.

Reserve requirement

A percentage of total deposits that a bank must keep in reserve as currency (see Vault cash). There are no reserve requirements on banks in Australia. APRA can force the banks to increase the reserve requirement as a buffer if a financial crisis prevails or looms.

Retention of title

A type of clause that can be included in contracts where a buyer may physically receive property, but doesn't take legal ownership from the seller until the full purchase price is paid for example if early access is granted to allow work to be undertaken.

Return On Investment (ROI)

This is a calculation that works out how efficient a business is at generating profit from the original equity provided by the owners/ shareholders. It is a way of thinking about the benefit (return) of the money invested into the business. To calculate ROI, divide the gain (net profit) of the investment by the cost of the investment: the ROI is expressed as a percentage or a ratio.

$$Return\ on\ investment = \frac{Net\ profit}{Cost}X100$$

If an investor buys a property for $1,000,000 and sells the property a year later for $1,500,000 then the net profit is $500,000.

$$Return\ on\ investment\ (ROI) = \frac{500,000}{1,000,000}X100 = 0.5\ X100 = 50\ \%$$

The ROI on the property purchase is 50%.

Revolving credit
Revolving credit is also called equity overdraft. The advantage of equity overdraft is that the funds are accessible anytime without pre-approval. Interest is only paid on funds withdrawn (See *redraw facility*). A credit card is a type of revolving credit. The borrower can withdraw, repay and redraw funds any number of times within a set limit or within a credit limit. (See *credit cards*).

S

Salary sacrifice
This is a voluntary deduction from a person's salary and paid into their superannuation savings. This has the effect of lowering a person's taxable income into a lower tax bracket. It is particularly tax effective for those paying a high rate of tax because, at the time of writing, the tax rate applicable is 15%

Second mortgage
A mortgage which is taken out on a property which already carries a mortgage. It is paid off only after a first mortgage is paid.

Secured
A loan guaranteed by security over specific assets.

Security
A general term for stocks, shares and investments or an asset used as collateral on a loan. It is an instrument that memorialises the transfer of funds.

Self- Managed Superannuation Fund (SMSF)
The self-managed superannuation fund is a superannuation trust structure providing a pension to members in retirement. It differs from other funds in that members are also trustees and each fund is limited to four members.

Shadowing
Shadowing is the process of creating values for variables that do not rely purely on the market value. It allows an analyst to evaluate their value in any number of projected conditions.

Shortfall of funds
Shortfall of funds is the unavailability of funds at a particular point of time, to meet your financial obligation or objective. Shortfall may occur at any instance of development: renovation, subdivision, or construction.

Sinking fund
A fund formed by periodically setting aside money for the gradual repayment of a debt or replacement of a wasting asset. A body corporate's sinking fund is effectively a deposit which exists to allow a body corporate to pay for repairs and maintenance of a building.

The money in a sinking fund can be spent on several different things. Firstly, it can be spent on anticipated capital expenditure, or non-recurrent items. In a large strata scheme, this often includes large or one-off items, such as painting the building or major structural repairs to common property. The sinking fund can also be used to replace major capital items in a scheme. This might include items such as common property fences, or carpets in a lobby. Sinking funds can then also be spent on any other reasonable expenses which should be reasonably met from capital, such as pool furniture.

The sinking fund is raised through three main avenues:

- Owners' contributions to the sinking fund
- Interest received from the fund's investments
- Money from insurance pay-outs (for major or capital items which have been destroyed or damaged)
- The sinking fund levy (owner's contribution), is often kept and administered by a community management company such as SSKB, on behalf of a body corporate.

Body corporates are also required to raise an administration fund. This is used for regular maintenance of common property, such as gardens, as well as insurance charges and administrative expenses – including secretarial fees and postage. Money cannot be transferred between the sinking fund and the administrative fund, and vice versa.

A proposed sinking fund budget must accompany the Annual General Meeting notice when it is distributed to lot owners every year. After the sinking fund budget has been prepared, a committee is able to determine what amount will be levied to lot owners for the sinking fund levy.

Payments from the sinking fund for repairs or major expenditure can only be made if there is either a written request for payment in the form of a tax invoice, or written evidence of payment, including a receipt. All payments from the sinking fund must be made from the financial institution account.

Split-rate mortgage
This type of loan allows a borrower to split a mortgage loan into fixed rate and variable rate segments and take advantage of the benefits of both (See *fixed rate mortgage* and *variable rate mortgage*).

Spotter's fee

This is also called a finder's fee. This is money paid when a person finds a property that doesn't meet their requirements but meets the requirements of another investor. It is an incidental and likely once off happening to the person finding their own property. All state governments require real estate transactions to be handled by licensed real estate professionals and there are penalties imposed if people are found to be operating outside of licencing requirements.

Superannuation

Refers to money accumulated for a person's retirement during their working life. Superannuation is tax effective because it is not subject to the full rate of normal tax and is secure because it cannot be accessed until a certain age. Superannuation is not an investment asset in itself but a special fund where a manager invests in a range of assets. Note that a separate administration fee is payable to every fund managers if multiple accounts are held. (This is commonplace as workers leave a company which is tied to a particular fund and start work for another company which is tied to a different fund. Workers rarely think of consolidating their savings).

Superannuation guarantee

This is a government backed guarantee that every employer in Australia must pay into a superannuation fund on their employee's behalf. This was set to steadily increase from 9% to 12% over a seven-year period from 1st July 2013.

T

Taxation in Australia

Tax is a fundamental part of social and economic infrastructure that will allow government to provide services to its people. In Australia, there are at least 125 separate taxes of which 99 taxes are levied by federal government, 25 by the state government and 1 by the local government (council rates). It should be noted that the individual number of taxes varies based on the perspective of individuals or organisations operating across more than one state or jurisdiction that affect its rates, thresholds and exemptions. According to government statistics, Australia has the greatest reliance on tax revenue from capital, labour and land. The International Monetary Fund defines tax as "compulsory unrequited payments, in cash or in kind, made by institutional units to government units". The following are some of the top 10 taxes that make up 90 % of tax collected in Australia:

- personal tax
- company tax
- Goods and Services Tax
- fuel excise
- payroll tax
- conveyance stamp duties
- land tax
- superannuation funds

Tax breaks
A tax break is a tax concession or advantage allowed by the Australian Taxation Office. Salary sacrifice, and absence of capital gains tax on your primary residence, are two favourable tax breaks in Australia.

Tax deductible
A type of expense that can be used to reduce taxable income.

Tax deduction
This is the deduction of expenses incurred in earning an income from a person's salary. Some expenses can be deducted fully in one year and others are deducted over time. The list of items that can be deducted varies every few years as regulations and legislation changes. A typical example is that "from 1 July 2017 all travel deductions relating to inspecting, maintaining, or collecting rent for a rental property will be disallowed." We

have discussed a few case studies on recent legislations changes related to tax deduction in our books entitled *"It's My Time: Successful Residential Investing"* and *"It's My Time: Introducing Commercial Investing"*.

Tax file number (TFN)

Tax file number is a unique number to identify each taxpayer in Australia. This number is issued by the Australian Taxation office to lodge a tax return at the end of financial year (financial year: 1st July to 30th June). The TFN is normally shared by the individual with various government bodies, for example Centrelink. This is not compulsory but it will most likely adversely affect benefits that are being applied for. TFN is a unique number and should be protected to prevent fraud. There is no age limit for a TFN, however if the individual is:

- 12 years old or under – a parent or guardian must sign on behalf of the individual
- 13 to 15 years age – the individual or a parent or guardian can sign
- 16 years or older – the individual must sign

Taxable income

Taxable income = assessable income - deductions

Assessable income is all the income that is earned during the tax year (1st July to 30th June) (see *ordinary income*).

Tax invoice

This is an invoice required for the supply of goods or services over a certain price. A valid tax invoice is required when claiming GST credits.

Tax return

A document used to record individual or company income for the financial year from 1st July to 30th June. (See *Australian Taxation Office* for details).

Term of loan

This is the length of time required to pay off a loan plus interest. The loan term usually varies between 1 and 30 years. The loan is 'amortised' for this period which means that the periodic payments are all made equal even though more interest accrues in the earlier part of the term.

Trust deed

This is an instrument that serves as security for a note. The borrower is the trustor and the lender is the beneficiary. A trust deed is also a document that contains the rules for the operation of a Discretionary, Unit or Hybrid trust.

Trustee

Manages assets held in a trust and is a nominee of the beneficiaries A trustee is like a straw man or a puppet controlled by the beneficiaries.

U

Underwriting

The process of analysing risk and determining an appropriate charge for taking on the risk. It involves a review of a borrower's credit, value of security and certain legal documents.

Unsecured creditor

This is a person or entity who has lent money without taking security over the asset.

Unsecured loan

This a loan that is not backed up by collateral.

Unsecured notes

The deposits that are not secured against a specific asset and that rank alongside unsecured creditors if a company is wound up.

V

Variable interest rate
This is when the interest rate of a loan changes with market conditions for the duration of the loan.

Vault cash
Currency in reserve inside a vault of any bank. It is usually recommended or preferred that the banks expect customers to give a prior note if they would like to withdraw a large amount of cash on a business day. In particular banks in regional parts of the country may have limited vault cash. (See *Reserve requirement*)

Vendor finance
Vendor finance is finance offered by a seller (vendor) to finance the sale of goods, services or real estate to a buyer (purchaser). Vendor finance agreements vary considerably in terms of the amount of money lent, the period of the loan and amount of interest, if any. Vendor finance is not common, however in regional parts of the country vendor finance may work better for both sides (vendor and purchaser). Properties in regional parts of Australia could be on the market for a long period and this could encourage the vendor to offer vendor finance. In some cases, the vendor and the purchaser agree to a higher price for the property in return for the vendor finance. Sometimes, the vendor may finance 20% – 40% of the purchase price allowing the purchaser to obtain bank finance for the balance. The advantage to the vendors is that it increases the market available and the prospects of a sale. The vendor may secure the loan with an unregistered second mortgage and/or a caveat. The three major types of vendor finance model practised in Australia are:

1. Deposit finance
2. Lease options
3. Instalment sales

Venture capital
This is the start-up capital for a new business or project.

W

Wealth
The value of savings and assets owned by a person or a trust that has a list of beneficiaries. Wealth could be created through savings, investments or inheritance. Wealth is not usually spent in day-to-day living unless the income stream ceases.

Wear and tear
Often referred to as fair wear and tear, it is the depreciation of an asset due to general usage. For example, over a period of time, carpet will wear more in areas where people walk (traffic paths) than in other areas.

Working capital
This is the money that a business has readily available to meet day to day expenses.

Write down
This refers to reducing the book value of an asset when it is no longer sellable at the higher price. It should not be confused with write-off (to decommission or dismantle).

Written down value
Also called *book value* or *net book value*.

original cost a depreciating asset
— total depreciation claimed against it

Write-off
In finance terms, this is when a bad debt or worthless asset is cancelled from an account.

Chapter 3

Investment

A

Accumulation phase
A period during which the investor builds up or accumulates property or funds. It has particular relevance to superannuation during which time funds are being deposited.

Activity levels
The number, or volume, of sales in the market.

Act of God
This is a term used in insurance policies. Act of God is an event that occurs without human intervention and is due to a natural calamity such as bushfire, flood, cyclone or earthquake (see *insurance*)

Actual cash value
The price which property will realise on the open market after all reasonable efforts have been made to secure a purchaser who will pay the highest price.

Adding value
Adding value to a property is important to increase the potential for capital gain. It may allow the property to be refinanced sooner due to the added value, it may improve the rental return, and it may make the property easier to rent.

Adding value is achieved primarily through renovations. These could be as simple as tidying up the garden and cosmetic renovations, including painting and new floor coverings, to structural renovations such as adding a deck or carport.

Affordability

This is what a person can afford to spend on buying a home after taking into account assets, liabilities, income and expenses.

Allocated pension

An allocated pension is the process of investing a set amount of money with a financial institution that in turn pays you an income. Please note that the return from an allocated pension is not guaranteed in advance and this income may increase or decrease depending on the economy and market conditions. (*See annuity*)

Angel investors

People that provide finance and invest in the future of a start-up business. These investors dilute the ownership by receiving shares in return. Angel investors normally hold sufficient shares in the business.

Annuity

After investing a set amount of money with a financial institution, an annuity pays a guaranteed income for a set period or a lifetime. It provides peace of mind in that the recipient knows how much he/she will get and how long it will last. (*See allocated pension*)

Appreciation

This is an increase in a property's value due, primarily, to increased inflationary trends. Appreciation is the opposite of depreciation. Most of the time land appreciates in value and the building on the land depreciates in value. The value will go up due to various factors such as inflation, Consumer Price Index, modernisation, shortage of land, etc. If a block of land is purchased for $500,000 and, after 5 years, the value of the land has increased to $600,000, the appreciation is $100,000. Note that any profit generated from an investment property is subject to Capital Gains Tax (CGT). (*See depreciation*).

Arbitrage

This is a practice of buying an asset (tradeable) in one market and simultaneously selling it at a higher price in a different market. It is also a practice of selling an asset in one market and buying it for a cheaper price in a different market. This is mostly practised in stock and bond markets. Arbitrage is doable now where huge transactions of stocks and bonds would occur in a few milliseconds via computers.

Asbestos liability insurance

This is critical to personnel in a trade that deal with asbestos either directly or indirectly. Public liability insurance policies and professional indemnity insurance does not necessarily cover asbestos-related incidents. (Refer *Certificate of insurance*).

Asset allocation

The splitting of a portfolio between different asset classes such as cash, shares, managed funds, property is called asset allocation.

Asset Class

A group of similar assets including shares, property, fixed interest or cash.

Asset inflation

Asset price inflation is a phenomenon showing a rise in the price of assets, as opposed to ordinary goods and services. It might make a person who has numerous properties appear wealthy but it is just an illusion. This type of increase in wealth is simply the redistribution to those who owned wealth (illusion of wealth) away from those who do not. In real terms, we cannot say how wealthy we are if the housing price doubles or stock market prices double. (See *sub-prime mortgage*)

Asset mix

The spread of investments between cash, fixed interest, shares and property.

ASX

Sometimes referred to as Sydney Stock Exchange, is an Australian public company that operates Australia's primary securities exchange. ASX is a market operator, clearing house and payments system facilitator. About 40 % of the total value of all companies listed on the ASX is taken up by ten companies. The companies break up into two main groups – Industrials and Resources.

Industrials – S and P (Standard and Poors) / ASX industrials – Telstra, Woolworths, Fosters, Qantas

Resources – BHP Billiton, Rio Tinto, Woodside Petroleum

Authorised capital

Authorised capital is the maximum number of shares that a company is permitted to issue.

Average unimproved value

Land tax is assessed on the total unimproved value of your assessable land holdings, including investment properties, on a quarterly basis as at 1st July, 1st October, 1st January and 1st April. The principal place of residence is exempt from land tax.

$$Land\ tax = \frac{(Average\ unimproved\ value)\ \times\ (Rate\ of\ the\ number\ of\ days\ in\ a\ quarter)}{Number\ of\ days\ in\ the\ year}$$

B

Bank deposits

Money deposited in banks for a fixed term.

Base rent

This is the minimum periodic rent specified in a commercial lease. In addition to the base rent, the tenant's rent could include the tenant's share of common area maintenance and lighting, a share of building operating expenses and (in large shopping centres) a percentage rent based on gross retail or food sales.

Bear market

This is a market condition when prices decline sharply against a self-sustaining background of widespread pessimism.

Benchmark

The benchmark interest rate is the official interest rate for short term cash investments set by major banks.

Blue chip

Blue chip companies are those with a reputation as a good investment in both good and bad economic climates. (Blue chip comes from a poker game where the highest value is blue in colour). (See bear and bull markets, low, medium and high risk).

Figure 29: **Blue chip used in Poker game (highest valued chip of all coloured chips)**

Bond

A certificate that serves as an evidence of a debt and the terms under which it is undertaken. There are different types of bonds: savings bonds, company bonds, government bonds (gilts). Bonds are not always held until the end of their terms.

Boom phase

The stage of the cycle before a downsizing. It is characterised by positive market sentiment and a previous period of strongly rising property prices.

Bricks and mortar
A term that can apply literally to the actual building materials but more commonly refers to an investment in property (as opposed to an investment in the stock market).

Bull market
Bull market is a period of buoyant and optimistic market when there is rise in share prices and other prospects of further price rises.

Bull run
This means a continuous increase in share prices.

C

Call option
The right but not the obligation to buy an asset at a set price or day. A call option gives you the right but not the obligation.

Capital flight
A drop in investor confidence that leads to transfer of investment funds from one country to another. Read our book entitled *"It's My Time: Setting Financial and Personal Goals"* on One Belt One Road and how it impacts the Australian real estate market. (See *foreign investor tax*)

Capital growth and return
If a sale advertisement states that a property has 10 % capital growth and 5 % rental return it means that, if you invest $500,000 in the property, there is a likelihood of a $50,000 price increase every year on the property and the property generates $25,000 per year in rent. It is quite common that property in urban areas has higher capital growth and lower rental returns with the opposite applying to rural areas.

Relationship between capital growth and rental return

Example: A house in Page St Albert Park, VIC 3206, was sold on 21st Jan 2014 for $2,310,000, and re-sold to another owner for $4,735,000 on 25th Feb 2017:an increase in value of $2,425,000 in just 3 years. Let us assume an 80% loan with a 5% interest rate was taken out:

Table 15: Relationship beween capital growth and rental return on a property

Purchase price	$4,735,000
80 % loan	$3,788,000
5 % interest rate (investment property) per annum	$189,400
Weekly mortgage payment	$3,642
Weekly rental	$2,500
Loss per week	$1,142
Loss per year	$59,384
Loss for five years	Approximately $300,000
Capital growth on the property for five years	$2,425,000

It is clear to see that, although the rental was insufficient to meet the cost of interest, the capital growth far exceeded any loss.

Principal amount (property value on day 1)	Rate of increase in the value of property (per annum compounded)	Rate	Number of years	$(1+i)^n$	Value of $(1+i)^n$	$P(1+i)^n$ ~ 200,000 (dollars)
$100,000	1 %	0.01	70	$(1+0.01)^{70}$	2.0067	$200,676
$100,000	5 %	0.05	14	$(1+0.05)^{14}$	1.9799	$197,993
$100,000	10 %	0.1	7	$(1+0.1)^7$	1.9487	$194,879
$100,000	15 %	0.1	5	$(1+0.15)^5$	2.0113	$201,139
$100,000	20 %	0.1	4	$(1+0.2)^4$	2.0736	$207,369

Capital losses

There are occasions when a property is sold for a slightly higher price than when purchased but, after taking account of the expenses incurred in the sale, there is a capital loss. Record of such loss will be made and offset against a future capital gain

Cash flow (Positive and negative cash flow properties)

Positive cash flow: Income – outgoings = a surplus

Example: A property in a mining town is worth $750,000 with a rental yield of 12% p.a.(See appendix V for questions to ask a real estate agent in a mining town)

Table 16: **Positive cash flow property**

	Value in dollars	Calculation
A. Purchase price	$750,000	
B. Annual rental return (12% yield)	$90,000	750,000 × 12%
C. 80% of total value	600,000	750,000 × 80%
D. Interest only payment (5%)	$30,000	60,000 × 5%
E. Principal and interest payment (4.5%)	$36,481	Calculators are available at many websites such as: https://www.moneysmart. gov.au/
F. Banks calculate 80% of the rental towards the debt service ratio	$72,000	(90,000 × 80%)
G. Cash flow towards service of the debt	$35,519 (a surplus)	(72,000 – 36,481)

Negative cash flow: Income – outgoings = a deficit

Example: A property in a mining town is worth $750,000 with a rental yield of 5 % p.a.

Table 17: Negative cash flow property

		Value in dollars	Calculation
H.	Purchase price	$750,000	
I.	Annual rental return (5% yield)	$37,500	(750,000 * 5%)
J.	80% of total value	600,000	(750,000 * 80%)
K.	Interest only payment (5%)	$30,000	(60,000 *5%)
L.	Principal and interest payment (4.5%)	$36,481	www.moneysmart.gov.au/
M.	Banks calculate 80% of the rental towards the debt service ratio	$30,000	(90,000*80%)
N.	Cash flow towards service of the debt	-$6,481 (a deficit)	(30,000 – 36,481)

The following are some of the terminologies with examples that will illustrate the metrics of properties finance.

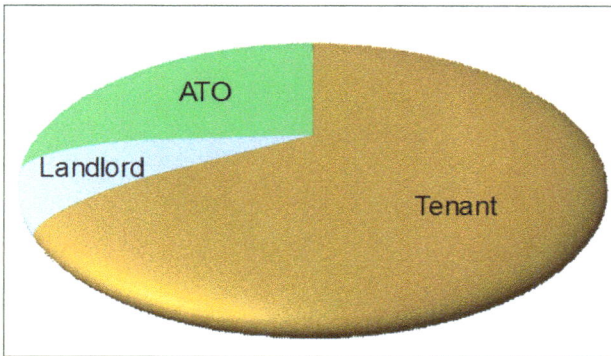

Figure 30: **Relationship between rent from tenant, landlord (outgoings) and tax that determines positive, neutral or negative cash flow properties**

Accelerated amortisation – Accelerated amortization is reducing the principal amount in excess of the minimum requirement so that the loan is paid off in a shorter period of time.

Suppose you borrow $500,000 at 6% for 30 years for your PPR.

Home loan - $500,000

Interest rate – 6%

Home loan term – 30 years

Repayment frequency – fortnight

Principal and interest repayment (monthly) - $1382.92

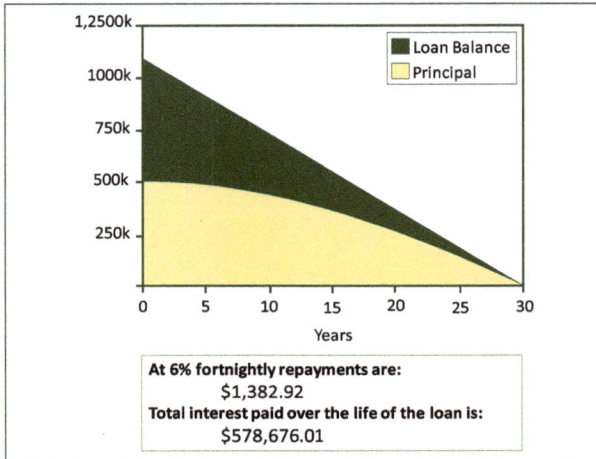

Figure 31: **Graph showing principal and interest paid on $500,000 loan**

The following shows the effect of a reduced interest rate of 5.5%. The mortgage payment will reduce by 70 dollars.

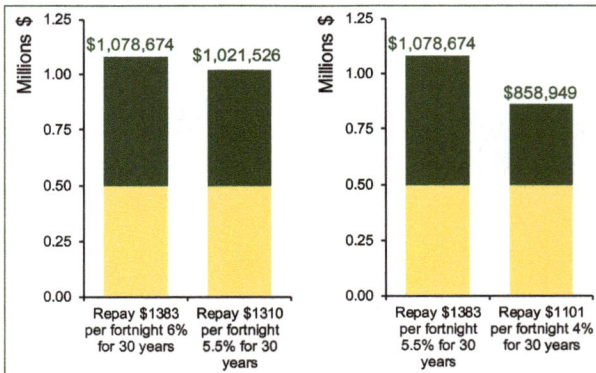

Figure 32: **Bar chart showing the difference between regular payment and additional payments (accelerated amortisation)**

The following shows the effect of increasing repayments by $117 per fortnight. The 30 years loan will be paid off in 24 years and 6 months.

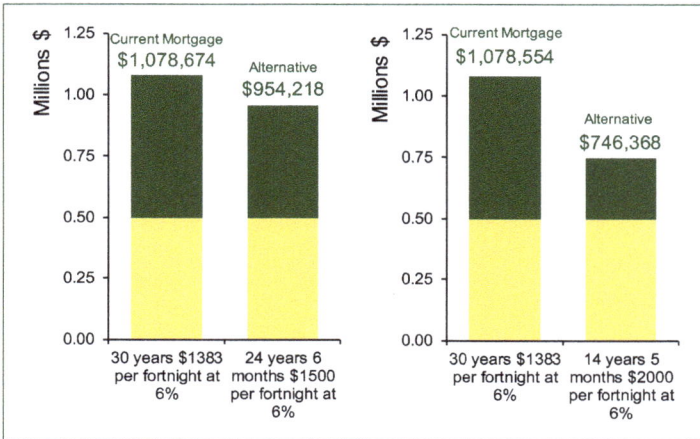

Figure 33: **Bar chart showing the difference between regular payment and additional payments (accelerated amortisation)**

Certificates of deposit

These are fixed-term savings certificates issued with a set interest rate by banks. The interest rate depends on the length of maturity. This is issued by a bank to a customer who deposits funds for a specified length of time at a specified interest rate.

Churning

Churning means excessive trading by a broker in a client's account largely to generate commissions. It can happen in industries such as franchise, insurance and mortgage. Churning is an illegal and unethical practice that violates Australian Securities and Investment Commission rules. (See appendix 1 for consumer protection and fair trading practices).

Clear title

A title free of lien or questions over ownership.

Commercial broker
One who lists and sells commercial property that includes offices, shopping malls, medical suites, retail and wholesale businesses, hotels and serviced apartments

Commercial property rent
A residential property investor (landlord) does not charge GST to the tenant on rent but GST is added to commercial property rent. Commercial property investors must register for GST and an ABN and such registration allows for the claiming back of any input credits (GST charged on goods and services).

Commodity
A commodity is a product that trades on a commodity exchange, including foreign currencies, metals, minerals, agricultural and food products, financial instruments and indices.

Currency pair
Two currencies that are being traded, for example the Australian dollar and US dollar, US dollar and Euro. Trading an AUD/USD currency pair is also called trading the "Aussie"

D

Day trader
This is an investor who trades shares every day or an investor who buys shares and sells them in the same day.

Debenture
This is the debt backed only by the integrity of the borrower, not by collateral. This is documented by an agreement called an indenture. Debenture is a bond and indenture is the agreement for this bond. (See *indenture*)

Deferred maintenance
A practice of deferring non-essential maintenance on a property for tax or budget purposes. Example: a broken door handle, a missing roof tile or rising damp.

Depreciation

This is the loss in value of property or goods below the replacement cost. In respect to property, an allowance can be claimed on a tax return for the decline in the value of certain assets such as fixtures and fittings.

In real estate, a building depreciates in time whereas land appreciates in time. (See *capital cost deduction for details*). However, the land value can depreciate if the land is contaminated and there is a liability to carry out the remediation work. Although it is possible to recover previously unusable land through the cleaning up of contamination, this has relatively little impact on the reduced value.

Table 18: Percentage of depreciation on various assets

Asset	p.a. Depreciation
Vehicles and automobiles	20 to 30% of original value
Furniture	20 to 30%
Apparels and clothing	30 to 50%

Depreciation allowance

This allowance is a proportion of the costs (also known as the book value) of an asset which can legitimately be claimed annually as an expense.

Depreciation factor

$$Depreciation\ factor = \frac{Estimated\ future\ life\ of\ the\ building}{Total\ life\ of\ the\ building\ (from\ day\ one)}$$

Depreciation method

A method used to measure loss in value, either accrued or future, of an asset through depreciation.

Depreciation schedule

This is a list of depreciable assets which enables the maximisation of cash return from a property. The two main elements are:

1. Capital works deduction – the structural elements which are irremovable
2. Plant and equipment – removable assets which have a limited effective life

Deregulation
This is the process of scrapping of rules that stop foreign investors or companies from competing in Australia on an equal footing.

Diversification
Diversification is an investment risk management technique. It means having funds invested over a range of products or asset classes in a portfolio, for example shares, property, cash and fixed interest. For property, further diversification can be achieved across different types of property and regions.

Divestment
The selling of an asset.

Dividends
Profits paid to the shareholders of a company

E

Earnings per share
This is an indicator of a company's profitability. It is the net income divided by the number of shares in an issue.

Exclusive use
This gives the occupier(s) of a lot in a body corporate the right to the exclusive use (or other special rights) to a part of the common property or a body corporate asset.

F

Face value
The original price at which the bond was issued initially. Also called par value.

Forex
Foreign exchange and trading refers to buying and selling of currencies. The trading of currencies is among banks, financial institutions, individuals and governments.

Forex market
Where currencies are bought and sold purely to make profit via speculation. It is open 24 hours, 5 days of a week. Small fluctuations in currency price when trading large volume can provide profits or losses. The market provides service to banks, financial institutions, individuals, business, and governments that need to buy or sell currencies other than that used in the country. The education sector is one of the largest export businesses where Australia attracts over 600,000 students per year. (Read our book entitled *"It's My Time: Setting Financial and Personal Goals"* on how international education improves the currency value of our dollar and the Australian economy).

Franked dividends
A franked dividend is the dividend paid by a company out of profits on which the company has already paid tax.

Fund managers
They normally respond to economic news, guestimate movements in local and global stock markets and analyse the market as to when to buy, sell or hold.

G

Gearing
Gearing means borrowing money to purchase an income producing investment. An investment is 'geared' if the purchaser borrows money to finance its acquisition. Gearing enables an investor to purchase more property than they may otherwise have been able and therefore benefit from the increased exposure.

Positive gearing is a leveraged investment whereby the income generated from the property exceeds the total costs involved in purchasing and maintenance, hence allowing for a positive cash flow.

Good covenant

Property tenanted to a good covenant is a better investment than similar property rented to a generic tenant. A good covenant is a tenant that is regarded as a low risk and never fails to pay rent on time or breach an agreement. A state or federal government based organisation, or a company with a good reputation, are examples of good covenants. (See *Anchor tenant*).

Government bonds

Known as *gilts* these are the least risk type of bond as the risk of government default is so slim. However, the dividend is low.

Growth assets

Assets such as property where the return is made up of capital growth and income above the rate of inflation.

H

Hedge fund

An investment team of wealthy investors and a fund manager that make money by using investment techniques to hedge against losses whether the market rises or declines.

Hedge fund (international)

These are offshore investment funds which are speculative and use borrowed capital.

Hedging

This is a strategic method to maintain a market-neutral position where investors purchase shares they think are likely to increase in price while also selling shares they think will decrease in price.

I

Improvements
Capital expenditure on a property that adds value to the original purchase price by improving its appeal. It is distinguished from general repairs or maintenance in that the original character of the property is improved and the value is increased.

Inflation risk
This is the risk that inflation will cause a decline in the purchasing power of the future dollars to be received from an investment.

Initial Public Offering (IPO)
An initial public offering is when a company is offering shares to the public for the first time.

Investments
These are defined as purchase of goods or a monetary asset that are not consumed today but are used in the future to create wealth, or sold at a higher price for a profit. Key investments in Australia are fixed interest bonds, shares, managed funds and property. (Read our book entitled "*It's My Time: Setting Financial and Personal Goals*")

Investment company
Buys and sells different businesses, financial assets, equities and bonds using the pool investor's funds, potentially giving its clients access to markets they could not afford to enter alone. (Our book entitled "*It's My Time: Setting Financial and Personal Goals*" contains more details on the top 10 strategies: property market, commodities, and bonds, shares, gold, wine and so forth.

J

Junk bonds
Bonds of very high risk companies

L

Landlord insurance

This is the most common type of insurance amongst property investors. The general components of landlord insurance are:

1. Building and / or contents
2. Malicious damage by tenants
3. Workers compensation
4. Loss of rent
5. Accidental damage caused by natural disasters including fire, flood and other calamities

```
              LANDLORDS RESIDENTIAL INSURANCE

                                              SUM INSURED
                                              -----------
BUILDINGS                                      $300,000
   (including Replacement Benefit)
CONTENTS                                        $10,000
SPECIAL CONTENTS                              Not Insured
TOTAL SUM INSURED FOR ALL CONTENTS              $10,000
LOSS OF RENT                                    $16,800
RENT DEFAULT AND THEFT BY A TENANT              Insured

Excess applicable to all above $500
   Additional excesses apply for claims for
   earthquake, tsunami, vandalism or malicious
   acts by tenants, deliberate or intentional
   acts by tenants, rent default and theft by a
   tenant.  These are shown in the policy
   wording.

LIABILITY                                    $20,000,000
WORKERS' COMPENSATION                         Not Insured
```

Figure 34: Screen shot of a landlord residential insurance policy

Leverage in Forex

The option for individuals to trade higher values of currency than the cash in their Forex account would cover.

Leverage in loan

Using an asset as security for borrowing. It can also mean gearing.

Limited liability

When the liability of shareholders is limited to the unpaid value of their shares. Limited liability is a type of investment in which a partner or investor cannot lose more than the amount invested.

Line fee

An additional interest payment levied on the full amount of a construction loan and is payable from the time the loan is approved until it is fully repaid. It is usually in the range 1% to 2% and the cost is capitalised on the loan.

Liquidity

Liquidity is a measure of the ability to sell an investment quickly (the inability to do so is known as illiquidity). Cash is the most liquid asset and property is the most illiquid asset. It is also a measure of the extent to which a person or company or organisation has cash to meet its immediate and short-term obligations.

Liquidity risk

The risk that an asset may not be easily and rapidly be sold for cash at its current value.

Listed company

This is a company that has agreed to abide by the Australian Securities Exchange (ASX) listing rules so that its shares can be bought and sold on the Australian Stock Exchange.

Loss of rent insurance

This insurance cover will insure the landlord against lost rent in situations that make the property unable to be occupied. The tenant has the right to move out or will have the right to ask for the rent to be reduced if the property is damaged. This policy does not apply for periods of vacancy.

M

Maintenance and repairs

The lease should include a clause that stipulates the tenant (lessee) or landlord (lessor) should at all times maintain, repair, amend, replace or renew if there was a need for maintenance and repair. The landlord usually takes care of maintenance in residential properties whereas the tenants takes care of maintenance in commercial properties.

Managed fund

A unit trust that pools the investment money of a number of individual investors. The fund is managed by a professional on behalf of the investors. (See *joint venture* and *partnership* for details).

Management/expense ratio

This is a great tool to compare the ongoing costs of various funds.

Manufacturing equity

Manufacturing equity is a strategy to increase the equity in a property. Renovating or extending is by far the easiest method but, subject to council approval, adding another dwelling is also a consideration.

Margin call

A request from a foreign exchange (Forex) broker for an investor to increase their deposit when the investment value has dropped below a certain point.

Margin loan

A margin loan allows an investor to borrow funds to invest and uses managed funds or shares for security. These loan arrangements are for investors who manage their funds and who invest in projects that have both higher returns and higher risks.

Margin trade
A method of buying shares in which a day trader borrows a part of the sum needed from the broker that is executing the transaction.

Market capitalisation
This is the total value of a company's shares at current prices, as quoted on the exchange and is a way of telling the overall worth placed on a company by the investing public.

Market value
The price at which the bond is traded

Master trust
This is an investment platform which allows administration under a single trustee and offers access to a wider range of investments and direct shares than other public offer funds, with ownership held by a pool of investors.

Medium cap
These are companies that have market capitalisation of more than $100 million but are not regarded as blue-chip companies.

Merger
This is the combination of two or more companies into one, through an acquisition or a pooling of interests.

Mezzanine finance
Unsecured debt finance for companies which may not have access to equity capital or traditional bank finance. In property finance, developers often use mezzanine loans to secure supplementary financing for development projects typically in cases where the primary mortgage or construction loan equity requirements are larger than 10 % of the project cost.

Millennium bug

Millennium bug or the Y2K bug was the "problem faced by computer programmers when dealing with dates beyond December 31, 1999 because twentieth century software represented the four digit year with only the final two digits" (year 1900 and year 2000 would look same as the year was represented by DD – MM – YY). There is a direct connection between the millennium bug and the global financial crisis that crippled the US real estate market in 2008. Our book entitled *It's My Time: Setting Financial and Personal Goals*" contains more information on this connection.

N

Negative gearing

Where the income from the asset does not cover the holding costs (loan interest, rates, utilities) of the asset. Negative gearing is a leveraged investment whereby the costs are planned to exceed the income generated for taxation purposes. Negative gearing lowers the overall taxable income of the investor such that less tax is paid.

A property which generates positive cash flow (income exceeds holding costs) is said to be positively geared. (Our book titled *"It's My Time: Setting Financial and Personal Goals*" and "*It's My Time: Successful Residential Investing*" provide more details on strategies to purchase negatively geared, positively geared and neutral properties).

Net income

This is the real profit the project or company is making. In terms of property development, financial feasibility on a project is very important as the feasibility will indicate the real profit that the project will make rather than the revenues it will generate. (Read the book entitled *"Real Estate Investor or Gambler*" by John Bone for more details).

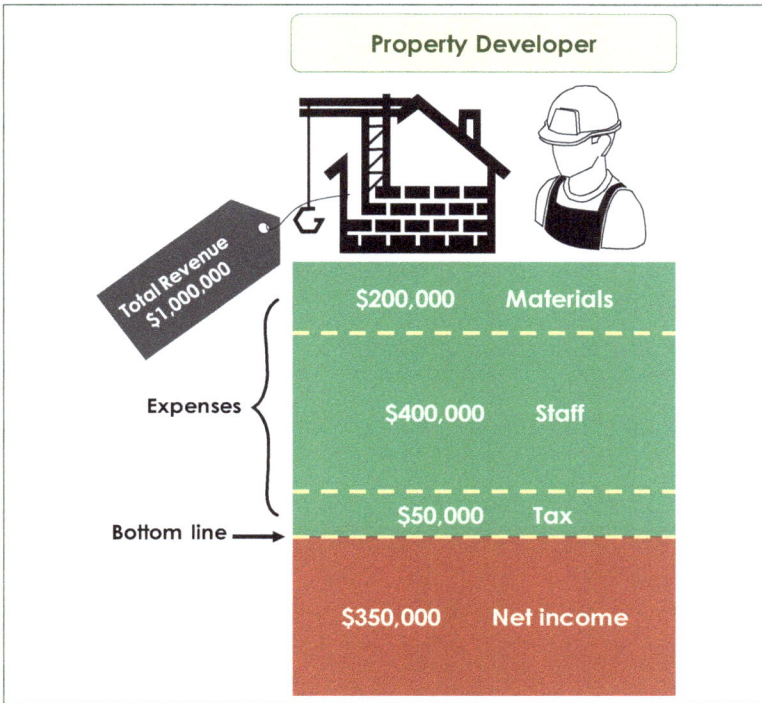

Figure 35: **Image showing the difference between total revenue and net income**

Net Operating Income (NOI)

Net operating income is a property's yearly gross income minus vacancy and operating expenses. If the property's net income is $100,000 per year, with a 3% vacancy rate, and $20,000 operating expenses, NOI is calculated as follows:

Property income (A)	$100,000
3% vacancy rate	0.03
Vacancy rate (B)	$3000
Operating expenses (C)	$20,000
Net operating income (A-B-C)	100,000-3,000-20,000
Net operating income (A-B-C)	$77,000

Net rent

Net rent is the rental return after deduction of all outgoings: rates, insurance, repairs, maintenance, management, body corporate fees and land tax. If the net rent is a positive amount then the property is positively geared.

Example:
A property is purchased at $500,000 with the intention of achieving a 10% net rent.
10% x $500,000 = $50,000 per annum
$50,000 / 52 = $961.54
The weekly rent after all outgoings must be $961.55.

Novated lease

An agreement among an organisation (employer), a financier and an employee where an employer leases a car for the employee. This lease agreement allows the employee (user of the vehicle) to use pre-tax income for the vehicle repayments. A novated lease also reduces the overall taxable income and will increase cash flow. The eligibility to apply for a novated lease varies with employers.

O

Operating expenses

These expenses, unlike capital expenses, are immediately tax deductible in the financial year in which they accrued.

Outgoings

These are all operating expenses associated with owning and running an investment property such as council rates, water rates, insurance and strata levies for apartment buildings. The landlord normally pays the outgoings for residential property but, in commercial property, some or all of these outgoings may be paid by the tenant depending upon the terms of the lease. (See *residential vs commercial* for more details).

Overcapitalise

To spend more money on property improvements than the amount of value added to the market price of the property.

Overheads

These normally include the rental cost of a property, utility bill, office supplies, stationery and indirect labour (salaries and wages of employees not directly involved in creation of goods and provision of services).

P

Passive income

Income received that is not directly related to the hours worked. Income received in exchange for some ongoing effort but where comparatively less time is spent than on money earned as active income. Passive income is in the form of rent from property, dividends from stocks and shares and interest from bonds.

Penny stocks

Commonly called penny dreadfuls. These are cheap stocks that offer the prospect of big gains.

Placement

When a company makes a private issue of new shares to raise funds.

Ponzi (or pyramid) scheme

This is a fraudulent practice whereby returns are paid to existing investors out of funds received from new investors. This might work when economic conditions are conducive but ceases when investors stop spending. (Read our book entitled "It's My Time: Setting Financial and Personal Goals" for examples of other scams that occurred in Australia and how those scams helped us in terms of new social and economic reforms).

Pooled investment

This is an investment in which a number of individuals give money to a professional manager, who manages the assets as a pool. Examples are superannuation funds, unit trusts, cash management trusts and managed funds.

Portfolio

This is a range of investments (property, shares, bonds and cash) held either by an individual or by a group of people or by an organisation.

Positive gearing

This is when a property generates a profit immediately through having the rental income exceed all expenses including the mortgage repayments on a loan.

Preference shares

This is the capital stock that provides a specific dividend that is paid before any dividends are paid to common shareholders, and that takes precedence over common stock in the event of a liquidation.

Private certifier

An authorised agent who assesses a development application against building rules and has the same power as a local government (see *Development approvals*). The private certifier must possess building surveying qualifications and must be registered. (See *Insurance*).

Product Disclosure Statement (PDS)

A full financial description of a product being offered for a public investment as required by ASIC.

Property trusts

Unit trusts which enable individuals to invest in a pool of commercial properties.

Prospectus

A legal document, requesting funds from the public, which provides full details about the offering.

Pump and dump

This is a manipulative trade technique often practised by a rogue trader that encourages investors to buy shares, pushing the price up so that the trader can then sell their own shares at a higher price.

R

Rates

Council rates are paid to local councils and shires to fund the installation and maintenance of infrastructure and the provision of services such as waste collection.

WARD	ISSUE DATE	LEVEL OF VALUATION	DATE DECLARED	SITE VALUE	CAPITAL IMPROVED VALUE	NETT ANNUAL VALUE
	15/08/2014	01/01/2014	07/07/2014	212,000	298,000	14,900
Waste Management Charge			Waste Charge $259.00		1	$259.00
Developed Land					298,000	$958.05
Municipal Charge			Municipal Chg $52.75		1	$52.75
Payments & Adjustments						-$8.17
State Government Charges						
Fire Service Levy Residential Fixed			$102			$102.00
Fire Service Levy Residential Variable			(.000109 x val)		298,000	$32.48
					TOTAL AMOUNT	$1,396.11

Figure 36: **Council rates**

Real estate investment trust

This is a managed fund that specialises in investment property.

Renovation

Renovation is a method of adding value to a property. It may be a low-cost cosmetic renovation or a more extensive project which requires council approval.

Table 19: **Various renovation strategies**

Renovation type	Strategy	More information on tax implications and reducing assessable tax
Basic renovation	Buy, renovate and sell	Read from our book "*It's My Time: Setting Financial and Personal Goals*"
Cosmetic renovation	Buy, renovate and sell	Read from our book entitled "*It's My Time: Successful Residential Investing*"
Value renovation	Buy, renovate, rent or sell	Read from our book entitled "*It's My Time: Successful Residential Investing*"
Preference renovation	Buy, renovate, rent or sell	Read from our book entitled "*It's My Time: Successful Residential Investing*"

Rental guarantee

This is the promised rate of return on an investment offered by a property developer. A rental guarantee is not a reliable way to invest as the development company could become insolvent rendering the rental guarantee worthless. (See *insurance*).

Rent reviews

This is an appraisal, normally facilitated by the property manager, to ascertain if a rental is in line with market standards for the local area. Rent reviews normally occur annually. Residential rent reviews are normally based on market comparisons, but commercial rentals may be tied to the Consumer Price Index (CPI), or an agreed percentage rate adjustment applied. Commercial rental might be calculated using the formula:

$$Revised\ rent = Old\ rent \times \frac{CPI_1}{CPI_2}$$

CPI_1 = consumer price index for the quarter ending immediately

prior to the commencement date

Rental yield

This is the annual rate of rental return on an investment property against its purchase price or current value.

Repairs and maintenance
Expense on a property that restores something to a working or an acceptable condition but does not add to the original value of the property. This refers to any expense incurred for general maintenance or repair to a rental property. Such expenses are usually allowed as a tax deduction. Care needs to be exercised to differentiate between a repair and a capital improvement. For example, replacing a broken window pane is a repair but replacing a timber framed window with an aluminium window is an improvement. (See *Improvements*)

Responsible entity
The person responsible for managing the unit trust or a property syndicate.

Return
The amount of money received from an investment.

Return on assets
This is a measure of company's profitability.

Return on equity
This is a measure of how well a company used reinvested earnings to generate additional earnings. It is a percentage of income versus the value of an asset less any debts against it.

Return on investment
This is the income that an investment provides each year or a financial benefit flowing from an investment (usually expressed as a percentage)

If $100,000 is invested in a project and it returns $1000 per month. What is the annual rate of return?

(Annual return/investment) x 100

= (1,000 x 12/100,000) × 100 = 12%

Risk in investments

Risk includes the possibility of losing some or all of an original investment or that an investment's actual return will differ from the expected return. Read our book entitled *"It's My Time: Setting Financial and Personal Goals"* for further details.

- Low risk investments – bank savings account, government bonds, prime property on long term leases.
- Medium risk investments – blue chip stocks, residential and commercial properties.
- High risk investments – mining stocks, technology stocks, options and warrants, hedge funds, speculative property developments.

Risk management

Managing various risk factors in an investment or company.

Risk profile

A description of the type of investor a person is, based on the level of risk or volatility that is acceptable.

Risk/reward ratio

Australia is one of the top five countries in the world with a better risk reward ratio for investment. Risks in an investment market are potential threats to an investor's plans that could happen due to inflation, interest rate changes, timing in the market or regulation changes (tax deductions). In general, the higher the risk, the higher the potential reward.

Rogue trader

One who makes high risk speculative unauthorised financial trades.

Royalty

This is money paid to a property owner or business owner, either in a percentage or in a constant amount, for extraction of some valuable resource from the land or constant amount for each sale.

Royalty from mining or land

Gina Rinehart's original Hamersley royalty (which she inherited from Lang Hancock) was worth millions of dollars in the form of:

1. The Hamersley royalty paid by Rio Tinto (which was secured by Lang Hancock);
2. Royalties from Hancock Prospecting's 50% stake in the Hope Downs mine, which is run by Rio
3. The Roy Hill mine

Rule of 72

The 'Rule of 72' is a simplified way of determining how long an investment will take to double, given a fixed annual rate of interest. By dividing 72 by the annual rate of return, investors can get a rough estimate of how many years it will take for the initial investment to double.

If $100 is invested at 10% return, it would take 7.2 years (72/10) to turn into $200

If $1000 is invested at 6 % return, it would take 12 years (72/6) to turn into $2000

$$Number\ of\ years\ to\ double = \frac{72}{intrest\ rate}$$

Rule of 80 / 20 (Pareto principle)

This rule was originally proposed by Vilfredo Pareto in the early 1900s. It states that roughly 80% of the effects are derived from 20% of the causes. For example, 80% of a country's wealth is owned by 20% of the population.

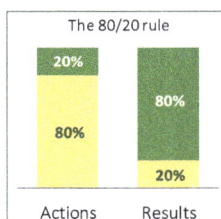

The 80/20 rule

Actions	Results
20%	80%
80%	20%

Figure 37: **Pareto Principle (80 20 rule)**

S

Savings bonds
Cash deposits on which a regular interest rate is paid

Scalping
A strategy where a trader holds his / her position (share or financial asset) for just a few minutes or even seconds.

Shares
Shares are also known as stocks. It is a slice of ownership in a company that publicly trades on the stock market. Australia has one of the highest rates of share ownership in the world.

Small cap
These are stocks that have relatively small market capitalisation and the value is less than $100 million.

Smart investor
A smart investor is one who buys property at a low point of the economic cycle and sells at the highest point. These types of investors mostly use properties for trading rather than holding. (See *pump and dump and rogue trader*).

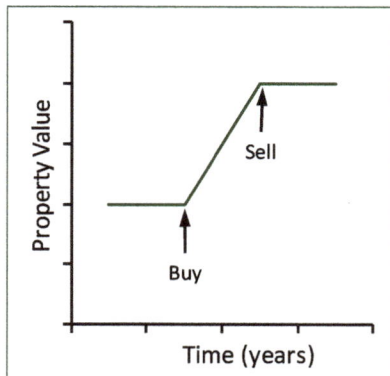

Figure 38: Graphical representation of a smart investors' purchase technique

Speculator

This is a person who buys any commodity such as property with the intention to selling, usually in the short term, in a higher market. Such speculators would typically purchase an off-the-plan property with a 10% deposit and sell the property when it is near completion (usually 18 to 24 months) to another buyer for a profit. Note that CGT penalties apply if the property is owned for less than 12 months.

Standard and Poor (S &P)

S & P classifies all companies on the ASX in accordance with the Global Industry Classification Standard (GICS).

Standard and Poor ratings

This is a tool that investors use when purchasing bonds and other fixed income investments. For example, when a government or company borrows money, through issuing bonds, that debt is then assigned a value based partly on the credit rating. There many types of ratings for different market sectors and many classifications within each group. The reader is encouraged to visit the S & P website for a more thorough treatment.

Stock broker

An intermediary that charges a flat fee and / or commission on the trades they execute and also making money from the bid offer spread.

Stocks

These describe ownership of shares in general whereas *shares* refers to ownership of shares in a particular company.

Structure

The way the ownership of an asset is managed. That is, the legal entity that owns a property, for example: individual or joint names, company, trust, self-managed superannuation fund.

Sunset clause

This is a statement in the Contract of Sale that refers to the maximum time during which the developer has to complete the project. Lang Hancock and his daughter Gina Reinhart signed a contract with a mining agent in the late 1970s that did not have a sunset clause (meaning there is no due date on the contract). This meant that the mining company must share their profits as long they as they mine the property that Gina owns.

Sweat equity

This is the equity accrued in a property by the mortgagor who increases the value through his/her own labour, or 'sweat'.

Purchase price of a rundown house in January 2017	$500,000
Mortgage on this property (60/40 LVR) in January 2017	$300,000
Stamp duty	$30,000
Renovation costs including your time to improve the equity (3 months)	$50,000
Value the property in July 2017	$750,000
Equity in January 2017	$580,000 – $300,000 = $280,000
Equity in July 2018	$750,000 – $300,000 = $450,000
Sweat equity (you have created in 6 months)	$170,000

T

Treasury bills

These are short-term government securities that mature in a short term (within 3 to 12 months of issue). Also known as T bills, they are risk free

U

Underwriting

A strategy to cover a potential risk in return for a fee.

Unit trust
This is a form of pooled investment where many smaller investors buy units in a trust that is promoted and managed by professional investment managers. This is governed by a trust deed and has trustees and a managed company.

Utilities bill
A utilities bill covers utilities including water, electricity, gas, telephone and internet. It comes under overheads.

V

Volatility
This is the extent of fluctuation in share prices, exchange rates and interest rates.

W

Wall Street
Wall Street is a street in Manhattan, USA. In financial terms, Wall Street refers to the stock market companies that dominate the US and global economy. Wall Street is represented by three stock exchanges: the National Association of Securities Dealers Quotations (NASDAQ), the New York Stock Exchange (NYSE), and the NYSE Amex Equities (formerly known as the American Stock Exchange) (See *Main Street*).

Weighted Average Lease Expiry (WALE)
The yield or cap rate may not apply for a commercial property where there are multiple tenants since the lease end date will vary. The WALE may be more useful:

$$\text{WALE} = \frac{Net\ income\ of\ a\ property \times \text{lease expiry (in years)}}{Total\ net\ income\ of\ all\ properties\ in\ the\ commercial\ property}$$

$$\text{Lease expiry in years} = \frac{Lease\ term\ in\ months}{12}$$

Figure 39: Commercial property with multiple tenants (seven in total)

Example for calculating lease expiry in years:

Table 20: Initial steps involved in calculating lease expiry

Shop number	Lease from	Lease to	Number of months	Total number of months in a year (D)	Lease expiry in years
1	1st July 2017	31st Dec 2017	6	12	0.5
2	1st July 2017	31st Mar2018	9	12	0.75
3	1st July 2017	30th June 2018	12	12	1
4	1st July 2017	30th June 2018	12	12	1
5	1st July 2017	31st Dec 2018	18	12	1.5
6	1st July 2017	30th June 2019	24	12	2
7	1st July 2017	30th June 2019	24	12	2

Weighted average lease expiry (used to multiple tenanted properties)

$$\text{WALE} = \frac{Net\ income\ of\ a\ property \times \text{lease expiry (in years)}}{Total\ net\ income\ of\ all\ properties\ in\ the\ commercial\ property}$$

Table 21: Calculation of weighted average lease expiry (from the previous table)

Shop number	Lease expiry (years) A	Net income ($)	Net income / total net income (B)	WALE = A×B
1	0.5	12500	0.115	0.06
2	0.75	14000	0.128	0.10
3	1	15000	0.137	0.14
4	1	25000	0.229	0.23
5	1.5	16000	0.147	0.22
6	2	14000	0.128	0.26
7	2	12500	0.115	0.23
Total		109000		1.24

WALE for this property that comprises seven shops is 1.24

Y

Yield

This is the net income or profit derived from any investment and expressed as a percentage of the purchase price. Yield is only used in commercial and resi-mercial properties

$$Yield = \frac{Net\ income\ (ex\ GST)}{value} \times 100$$

If a property is on sale for $1,000,000 and net income is $100,000 per year:

$$Yield = \frac{100000}{1000000} \times 100$$

$$Yield = 0.1 \times 100 = 10\ \%$$

The above equation can also be written as

$$Value = \frac{Net\ income\ (ex\ GST)}{Yield}$$

If a property has a yield of 7% and the net income is $70,000 per year:

$$Value = \frac{70000}{0.07} = 1,000,000$$

Note that if net income increases, or yield decreases, then value increases. For commercial properties, the rent increases every year (based on the contract terms) for the first few years based on the CPI and thereafter by market review.

High yield property

This is a property with a high return on investment. However, such properties tend to be associated with a higher risk.

Yield increase

There are several ways to increase the yield obtained from a property: reducing the price paid for the property or increasing the rental returns by renovating, furnishing, higher usage, option to purchase, vendor finance, etc. (Read our book entitled *"It's My Time: Setting Financial and Personal Goals"* and *"It's My Time: Successful Residential Investing"* on methods of increasing the yield).

Chapter 4

Building / Renovation

A

Acid etch

A process using a fairly strong water and hydrochloric acid solution (approximately five parts of water to one part acid) used to etch a concrete surface which has a smooth, steel-float finish. It is applied when the concrete needs to have a 'key' for bonding.

Acoustic board

A material used in the construction of walls and ceilings to reduce noise.

Addition

Any construction or change in a building which increases the overall area of the structure.

Aggregate

Grammatically this means the 'sum of the parts' but, in building terms, it is crushed stone and one of the constituents of concrete. Aggregate is usually blue metal, granite or basalt rock.

Air space

A cavity or space in walls or between various structural members. It is an essential element of a system of insulation. It also refers to the space above particular commercial buildings that may be rented out for mobile phone transmission or advertising.

Anchor bracket connector

A device securing one part of a structure to another for stability.

Angle iron

An iron or steel bar with an L-shaped cross-section.

Architect

A person who is qualified to design buildings, prepare the working drawings and specifications of the building and, in many cases, also supervises the construction.

Architecture ('design concept sketch')

When a client meets with an architect, she or he will produce a concept sketch, similar to that shown below, based upon the client's preferences. The architect will issue a design brief that will show site details and a schedule of accommodation. A final design is then sent to a draftsperson to produce working drawings (usually 1:200 or 1:500 scale) for builders and others involved in the construction process.

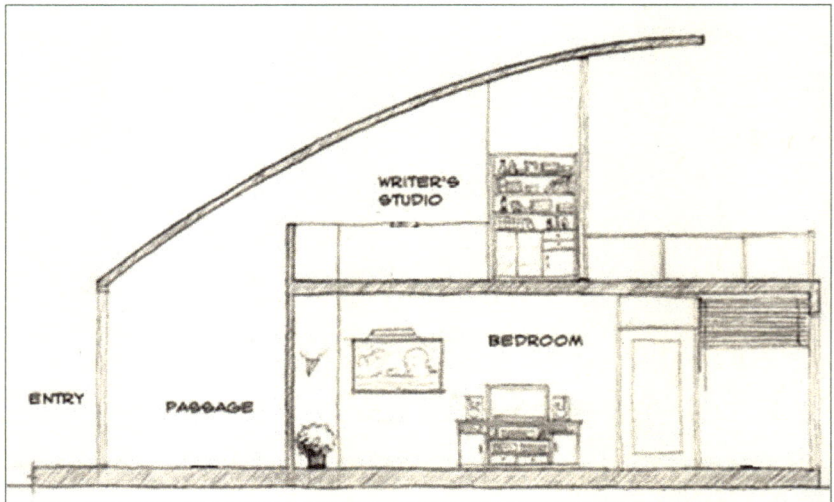

Figure 40: Design concept sketch

Asbestos

An inorganic material used in older buildings as boiler insulation, floor tile, ceiling coatings, and pipe wrap. Asbestos is a risk to health if fibres are released into the air. There has been a total ban on the manufacture, use, reuse, import, transport, storage or sale of all forms of asbestos since December 2003. The presence of asbestos in a property is likely to be associated with a drop in the value of the property. Local authorities and licensed asbestos removalists can assist with both managing and removing the asbestos from the site. (See *Asbestos liability insurance*).

Asphalt

Sometimes known as bitumen, this is a black, petroleum-based product used to surface roads

Architrave

The timber moulding around a window or door. It can be plain or decorative.

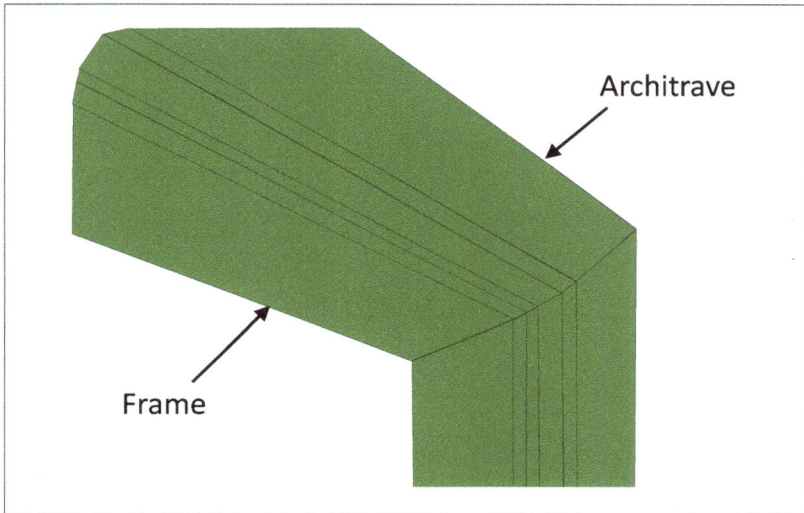

Figure 41: **Image showing frame and architrave**

Australian Height Datum (AHD)

This was adopted by the National Mapping Council as the datum to which all vertical control for mapping is referred. The acronym (AHD) is shown on all elevations using this datum.

Awning window

This window is hinged at the top and is opened with the bottom moving out on a spiral screw.

B

Backfill

Replacement of excavated earth into a hole or against a structure.

Bagging

This is a method of coating brickwork with a thin mortar slurry applied using a bag or sponge. This process is normally carried out by the bricklayer and is not smooth like render. (See *Rendering*).

Balcony

This is normally an extension of an upper floor which is surrounded by a balustrade. The exception is a Juliet balcony which does not protrude from the building but does have the balustrading.

Balustrade

A railing or wall to prevent people from falling over the edge of stairs or a balcony.

Barge board

Also called a *verge board, it* is a board that is attached to the projecting gables of a roof. A bargeboard gives stability and weather protection to projecting gables and conceals the ends of horizontal timber or purlins of the roof they are attached to. (See *roof types*).

BASIX

The New South Wales Government introduced this legislation to ensure any new buildings are designed to meet environmental outcomes of 40 % less water consumption and 25 % less energy usage.

BASIX Certificate
A document certifying that a building complies with the government's Building Sustainability Index.

Bat
A cut piece of brick usually more than half the length (eg half-bat, three-quarter bat)

Batten
Sawn timber that is mounted horizontally across the rafters to hold the roof cladding. (See also *counter battens*)

Batter boards
Support boards attached to pegs which hold layout lines showing the outline of the foundation.

Bay window
A window that projects from the wall and has glazing all around.

Beam
This is a principal load-bearing member of a building constructed of timber, steel or concrete.

Bearers
These carry the loads from the floor joists and usually run along the direction of the longest wall. Joists and bearers are laid perpendicular to each other. (See *Joists*).

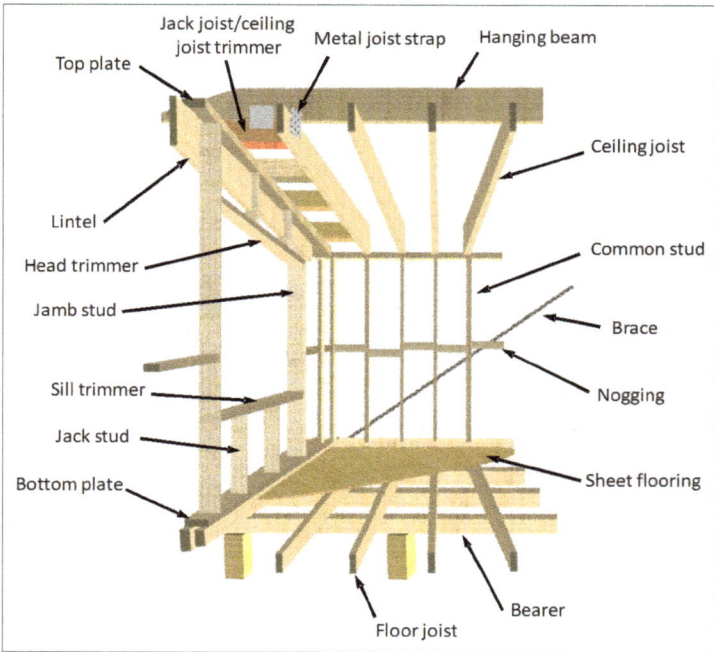

Figure 42: **Photo showing joists and bearers.**

Bearing wall

A wall which supports a part of a building, usually with a floor or roof above it. Also referred to as a load-bearing wall.

Bedrock

A solid rock underlying soils and other superficial formations. It represents an ideal foundation material.

Benchmark

A level datum point used by a surveyor when surveying land.

Benzene, toluene, ethylbenzene and xylene (BTEX)

BTEX are naturally occurring organic compounds in crude oil. The primary sources of BTEX are motor vehicle emissions, aircraft exhaust and cigarette smoke. They are toxic chemicals and often comprise some of the chemicals involved in leaking underground petroleum storage tanks. (See *contaminated sites*).

Bevel
A sloping surface cut at an angle other than 90 degrees.

Blue board
A thick cement sheet that is painted with a blue primer. Blue board is used as an external wall material and is coated with render.

Bifold door
An internal door that slides open while its panels fold up and stack neatly against the wall. It creates an illusion of extra space and ingress of natural light. (Read our book entitled "*It's My Time: Successful Residential Investing*" for staging, styling, and interior design for better appeal to occupants and tenants).

Bill of Quantities (BoQ)
A schedule detailing the quantities of materials and labour needed for construction. A Priced Bill of Quantities also includes the prices of these items.

Birdsmouth notch
A cut in a rafter that fits over a wall plate or beam.

Bleeding
Also known as *leaching*, this is when the tannins in timber bleed through to the surface and present as a yellow or brown stain.

Block splitter
A mechanical device, usually hydraulically powered, used to split logs.

Bolster
A short-handled chisel with a wide blade used for cutting bricks.

Bond (brick pattern)
This is the way bricks are laid in a wall, or paving, so that they interlock. The simplest pattern is called a *stretcher* bond. This is

laid by placing each successive course, or layer, so that each joint is staggered by one half-brick length.

Bottom plate
This is the timber at the bottom of a wall frame.

Box gutter
This is a gutter which is not on the external edge of the roof. It was popular in the 1960s and 1970s with flat roof design for residential houses but could cause problems if gutters become blocked.

Brace
This is normally a diagonal member used to resist lateral forces and or movements of a framed structure. Also referred to as bracing.

Bracket
A prefabricated metal connector used to connect two structural members.

Bricks
Generally a standard size building component made of clay and fired in a kiln. There is a wide variety of types, colour and textures available and these vary across regions. Bricks are laid in courses using mortar to hold the bricks apart.

Bricks are manufactured by using different clays and mixing with additives (such as oxides) and by varying both the burning temperature and the amount of kiln time. The darker colours are harder, stronger and chemically resistant. As well as being used in building construction, bricks are ideal for paving.

Brick construction (solid brick)
A building that is built with brick on both internal and external walls.

Brick paving
There are many different patterns used in brick paving: running, stack bond, herringbone, basket weave, diagonal herringbone, double basket weave, and capped herringbone.

Brick ties

These are galvanised wire ties used at regular intervals to join the internal and external walls of a cavity brick wall or to tie the external brick veneer to a timber frame.

Brick veneer construction

A building that is built with brick on external walls only. Internal walls are usually constructed of timber with a plasterboard lining. The brickwork is not load bearing and is considered a 'veneer' covering to the internal timber frame.

Builders' sand

A clean beach sand that has been washed to remove all salt and organic matter. Available as bulk or bagged. Also called plasterers' sand.

Building agreement or contract

This is an agreement between the customer (owner) and the builder setting out what work is to be carried out, by when, and how much it will cost. Both parties sign the agreement.

Building Application (BA)

This is the documentation, including detailed drawings, of the proposed construction submitted by a town planner, architect or builder to the local council for approval. This application is submitted after Development Approval (DA) has been received and the drawings are more comprehensive with engineering specifications and detailed schematic drawings of the proposed construction.

Building (floor) area ratio is the ratio between the building area and the land area.

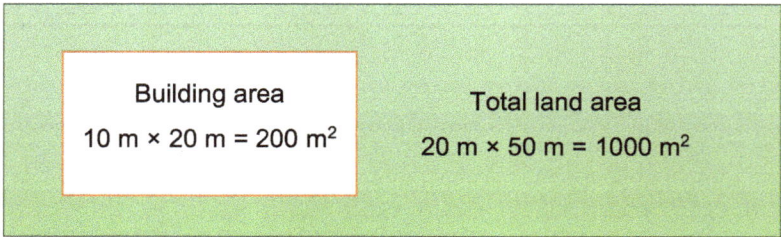

Figure 43: **Sample calculation illustrating the building floor area ratio**

$$Building\ area\ ratio = \frac{building\ area}{land\ area} = \frac{200}{1000} = 1:5$$

Building certificate

This certifies that a building plan adheres to the Building Code of Australia (BCA) and local building codes.

Building Code of Australia

This is a national set of regulations for use in the design, construction, alteration or demolition of buildings and sets out procedures, acceptable methods and materials as well as minimum and maximum values.

Building and construction is regulated in Australia through the building code of Australia (BCA). It contributes to the safety of the building and protects the health, safety and general welfare of occupants and public in new and existing buildings and structures. Insurance companies expect that a building is built to an appropriate standard and insurance becomes void if the building does not conform to BCA standards.

The National Construction Code (NCC) sets out the minimum technical requirements for new buildings (and new building work in existing buildings) in Australia. In doing so, it groups buildings by their function and use. These groups are assigned a classification which is then how buildings are referred to throughout the NCC. There are different classes of buildings in the BCA. All classes of buildings in Australia (Class 1A to Class 10C) are discussed in our book entitled "It's My Time: Successful Residential Investing".

Building compliance report

This report will state whether the constructed work complies with relevant building codes (*See Building Code of Australia*)

Building inspection report

This report provides an intending purchaser of a building an assessment of any existing defects. Normally it does not address pest infestation and a separate report for this is highly recommended.

Building line

This refers to a line, parallel to the property boundary, beyond which a building cannot be located.

Building permit

Formal approval of building plans by the designated local council as meeting the requirements of prescribed codes. It is an authorization to proceed with the construction or reconfiguration of a specific structure at a particular site, in accordance with the approved drawings and specifications.

Details of relevant planning permit (if applicable)

The issuer or provider of the required insurance policy is: Owner builder

Details of relevant planning permit (if applicable)

Planning permit no:		Planning permit date:	
Nature of building work:	Construction of dwelling and garage	Total new floor area m^2:	
Stage of building work:	All	Cost of building works:	
Part of building:	All parts	BCA classification:	1A and 10A

Inspection requirements: The mandatory notification stages are:

inspection of footings (shed)
inspection of pre-slab
inspection of framework
inspection of occupancy permit

Occupation or use of building: An occupancy permit is required prior to use of occupation

Commencement:	Building work must be commenced by:	15/05/2007
Completion:	And must be completed by:	15/05/2008

Figure 44: **Sample copy of a building permit**

Building Surveyor

Building surveyors are responsible for ensuring buildings are safe, accessible and energy efficient and therefore have an impact on the design, planning and functionality of buildings.

A building surveyor remains involved for the duration of the building project. They carry out inspections – or have a building inspector carry out inspections on their behalf – to sign off each mandatory notification stage of construction. You can only appoint one building surveyor to a building project.

Once building work is complete, the building surveyor is responsible for issuing the occupancy permit or certificate of final inspection.

A registered building surveyor is authorised to:

1. Assess building permit applications for compliance with the relevant Building Act and Regulations and National Construction Code.
2. Issue building, occupancy permits and certificates of final inspection
3. Conduct building inspections at the mandatory notification stages
4. Serve Direction to Fix notices for non-compliant building work
5. Serve building notices and orders under the relevant Building Act

Bulkhead

This is a lowered portion of the ceiling usually to hide a beam, drainage pipe or air conditioning ducting but can also be used as decorative feature.

Bullnose

A paver or brick having one edge rounded off. It is often used around swimming pools and in steps

Butt hinges

The wings of the hinge are of equal size with one screwed to the edge of the door and the other to the frame so that only the knuckle of the hinge projects.

C

Cantilever
A projecting beam or girder supported at only one end. A diving board (springboard) and a balcony support are examples of a cantilever.

Carpet underlay
A thin layer of cushioning material laid under the carpet to provide comfort underfoot. It also provides insulation against sound, moisture and heat and reduces wear and tear on the carpet. It is commonly made of foam sponge rubber.

Cathedral ceiling
Also referred to as a raked ceiling, it is where the ceiling line follows the line of the roof timbers.

Caulk
It is used to fill a joint to make it watertight or airtight

Ceiling
This is the upper surface of a room or building and can be constructed of a variety of materials such as plasterboard, timber and (in older houses) cement sheet.

Ceiling joist
This is a structural member spanning the room and supports the ceiling. It also ties together the top wall plates on opposite sides of the room.

Cement rendering
Applying cement mortar (sand and cement) to a brick, stone or blue board surface.

Certificate of Occupancy
A local government permit, usually provided by a building surveyor, allowing a dwelling to be occupied. It is issued after the Certificate of Final Inspection.

Chair
A component designed to support the reinforcing steel and hold it in the desired position during the pouring of concrete. Chairs sit on pressed metal pans to prevent the plastic underlay from being damaged. Also known as a bar chair

Chamfer
A small bevel or slope on the edge of a board or timber. The word also refers to the process of removing the edges of lengths of timber.

Charged storm water system
This is a system consisting of sealed PVC storm water piping, including the downpipe that provides for the discharge of rain water from the roof to a termination point at the kerb. A section of the pipe always remains full which can cause problems.

Chuck
The part of a drill or other tool which holds a removable cutting implement. Chucks are operated with a chuck key.

Cleat
A small piece of wood fastened onto something to give support.

Clout
A nail with a large flat, circular head. It is usually galvanised.

Coach bolt
It is also known as a carriage bolt, or cuphead bolt, it has a round head and a square neck which embeds in the timber to prevent turning when the nut is tightened.

Coach screw

A screw with a square or hexagonal head which can be turned with a spanner.

Collar beam

A beam (usually made of timber) that connects the mid-points of opposing rafters to prevent them from spreading. It is sometimes referred to as a collar tie but the latter is normally made from steel.

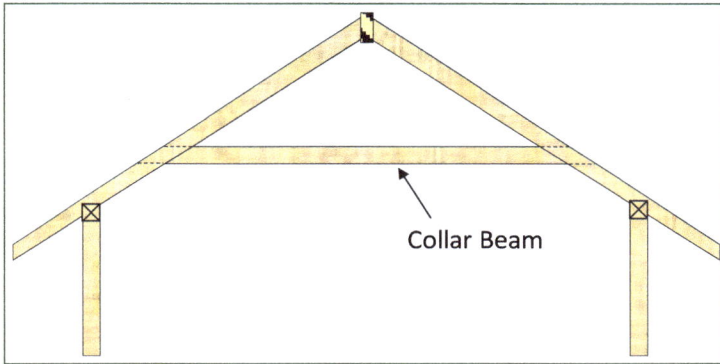

Collar Beam

Figure 45: **Image showing a collarbeam**

Compo

A slang term for mortar.

Compo mortar

A bricklaying mortar which consists one part hydrated lime, one part Portland cement and six parts brickies' sand. A weaker mortar than 3:1 cement mortar but more economical and more workable.

Concrete

A composition of cement, water, fine and coarse aggregate, sometimes with special admixtures.

Construction sequence

The process of construction of a building or infrastructure.

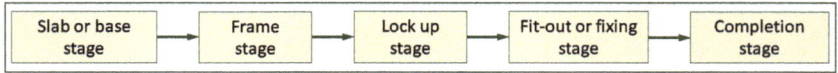

Figure 46: Image showing construction sequence

Construction stages

(Further details are included in our book entitled *"It's My Time: Successful Residential Investing"*).

Table 22: Stages of construction

Name	Activities
Clearing the site	Soil testing, site levelling, fencing, power supply, portable toilet, silt barrier, peg out
Base or slab stage	Setting out, under slab drainage, pouring the footings, moisture barrier, termite protection
Frame stage	Timber or steel frame, gutters, insulation, plumbing, electrical
Lockup stage	Installation of windows, doors and remaining walls
Fit out or fixing stage	Plumbing and electrical fit-off, cornices, tiling, cabinets, shelving, reveals and architraves
Completion stage	Painting, detailing, complete electrical, clean up, pre-completion inspection, install appliances, utility connections

Contour map

A contour map shows the variation in level over a tract of land. Contour lines are imaginary lines joining all points of the same level and are usually assigned a value corresponding to the height of that line above a fixed datum. Land with closely spaced contour lines is steeply sloping and widely spaced lines suggests flatter terrain. Circular lines indicate a depression or a peak. A contour survey is usually carried out by a surveyor on a proposed development site to assist architects, draftspersons, and other professionals to locate buildings, retaining walls and infrastructure.

$$Gradient = \frac{Vertical\ rise\ or\ fall}{Horizontal\ distance}$$

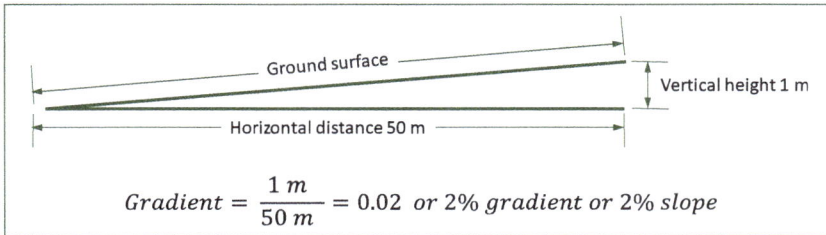

$$Gradient = \frac{1\ m}{50\ m} = 0.02\ or\ 2\%\ gradient\ or\ 2\%\ slope$$

Figure 47: **Slope calculation**

A typical contour plan would look like this:

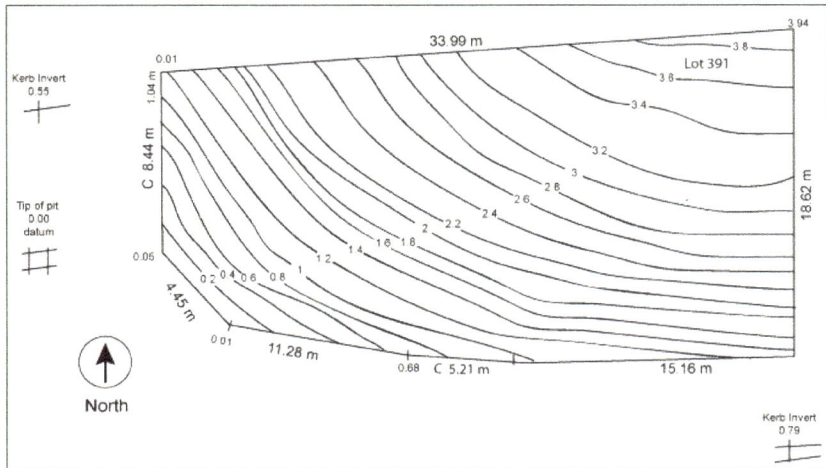

Figure 48: **Contour map showing contour lines**

Along the north boundary on the contour plan the difference in level is 3.93 m (3.94 – 0.01).

Distance is 33.99 m

$$Slope = \frac{3.93}{33.99} = 0.116\ or\ 11.6\%$$

Contour survey

A survey of the building site that identifies the amount of rise and fall over the lot. The datum (starting) point is normally a front corner of the property.

Cornice

A preformed moulding that covers the intersection of wall and ceiling.

Cost per m²

A commercial property has a net internal floor area of 500 m². It was sold this week for $500,000.

$$Floor\ price = \frac{Sale\ price}{Floor\ area} = \frac{500,000}{500} = \frac{\$1000}{m^2}$$

This parameter can be helpful when comparing properties if the floor area is known. If a property has an area of 1000m² then the price should be approximately (1000 × 1000) = $1M

Cost plus

A contract that pays the builder's actual costs plus a management fee which may be expressed as a percentage of the costs or a fixed amount.

Counter battens

Sawn timbers mounted vertically along the line of the rafters to which conventional battens are attached. They are used to assist with ventilation and control of moisture by providing a separating layer. (See *battens*)

Counterboring

A boring technique which conceals the heads of bolts and nuts after insertion.

Countersunk

A special drill bit is used to enlarge the top of a screw hole so that the screw head will sit below or flush with the surface.

Course step-down

This is the stepped-down edge of a concrete slab on which the outer brick wall sits.

Crawl space

A narrow opening between the ground and the underside of the floor of a building. This space is just sufficient for access to install or repair any utilities.

Cut and fill

This method is used on sloping ground to provide a level area by cutting away higher ground and using that to fill the portion of the slope immediately below it.

D

Damp Proof Course(DPC)

This is a continuous layer of an impervious (not allowing liquid to pass through) material between a floor and a wall to prevent the upward or downward movement of moisture. Common materials are bitumen coated aluminium, PVC, copper or lead. For brick walls, it can also be created by the use of an admixture added to the brick mortar.

Darby float

It is a large wooden float or trowel about one metre long used mainly for plastering and rendering.

Deco rock (Decomposed granite)

A type of reddish brown aggregate that is formed by natural decomposition of granite rock and is used, sometimes with cement, to create a stabilised and durable material. It is commonly used in driveways and pathways where a firm surface is required.

Deck

A deck is a raised timber structure normally constructed adjacent to the rear of a dwelling, normally outside the main access door. It is often constructed in combination with a pergola.

Defects liability period

A set period after a construction is completed during which time the builder or contractor may return to the site to rectify the defects. This period varies from 12 to 24 months.

Defective works

Building work that does not comply with the Building Code of Australia.

Demolition

Disassembly and removal of an existing structure from a site and preparing the site for new construction.

Demolition permit

Investors that purchase properties with the intention of demolition need to know that demolition is to be carried out in accordance with legislative and planning requirements. If a property has a heritage overlay then the process of obtaining a permit is far more complex and demolition may not be permitted at all.

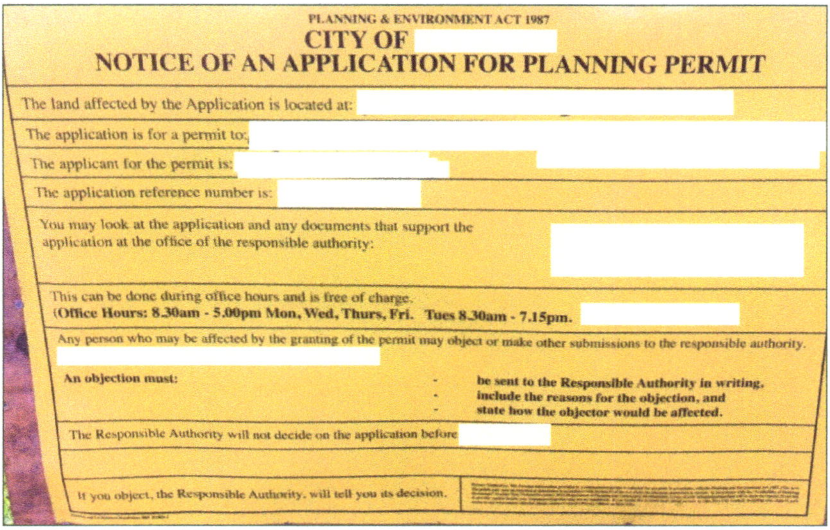

Figure 49: Example of notice of an application for a planning permit (displayed in front of a project, usually on a fence door)

Demolition permit procedure

A permit is normally applied for by a building surveyor on behalf of the owner.

Although many councils have different procedures, the following documents will always be required:

1. Copy of the title
2. Plan of subdivision (title plan)
3. Plan of the existing building.

Depending on the circumstances, the following may also be required:

1. Planning permit
2. Hoarding consent (if close to street frontage)
3. Service of protection works notices (if adjacent to adjoining buildings)
4. Tree removal permits
5. Asset protection permit

Prior to demolition, the owner must also apply for abolishment of services to the property.

Deposited plan

As the name suggests, it is a copy of the plan held by (deposited with) the Land Titles office. The plan shows the exact bearings and dimensions of the block of land and any easements.

Derelict

This refers to the intentional abandonment or renunciation of property. Also used to describe the condition of a building.

Detention pit

This is designed to slow down the flow of storm water from private property into public drainage systems. Pits may be required for each individual lot or in the case of a land subdivision, one large pit to service the whole subdivision. Councils have different policies with regard to the use of these detention pits.

Developer

Developers buy property to redevelop into (mostly) higher density housing either for sale or rental.

Development approval (DA)

The planning permission required from local council to proceed with a development.

Development capital

Investments made in smaller companies looking to expand in their particular field.

Dial Before You Dig (DBYD)

A free referral service designed to assist in preventing damage and disruption to infrastructure networks (utilities). This service provides information on the location of underground utilities anywhere in Australia.

Dilapidation report

This is a report on the condition of a property at a given point in time and will record the condition of existing defects. It records any existing damage, and the state of any aspects of the property that are likely to be affected by construction work, excavation or demolition.

Domestic building insurance

This insurance protects homeowners should the builder default, become insolvent or die before completion (See *construction sequence and construction stages*).

Door furniture

This covers all fittings on a door except the hinges.

Door jambs

The vertical side of a door frame. A door jamb set refers to the two sides and the top which together form the door surround.

Double hung window

A window where both panes are vertically sliding and balanced by cords and weights, springs or balances.

Downpipes

The drainage pipes from a guttering to either rain water tanks or an underground drainage system.

Draftsperson

This is the person who transfers design details into a plan. In the building industry, a draftsperson will work closely with an architect or structural engineer. In smaller companies, a building designer (as opposed to a qualified architect) will also be the draftsperson.

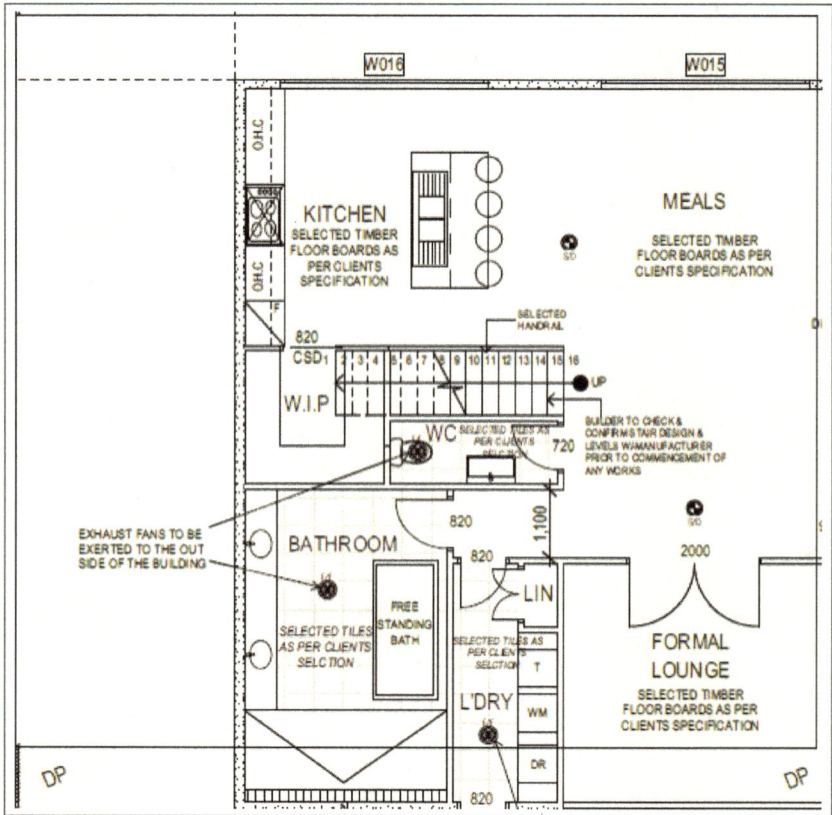

Figure 50: Schematics of a drawing showing various features of a home

Drainage control measure

This aims to prevent or minimise soil erosion by controlling water flow through a building site such that flow concentrations are minimised.

Draw down

This is associated with the construction phase of a development where the developer will access funds from the financial institution to pay the builder at specific milestones. The developer may employ a quantity surveyor to confirm that the value of work performed up to that specific milestone is no more than the amount the builder is claiming. These milestones are described under construction stages).

Drawdown schedule
A schedule of trigger points for release of loan funds: for example dates, progress stages or percentage of works completed.

Dressed All Round (DAR)
This is timber that has been planned on all sides.

Dual occupancy
A block of land zoned to allow for two dwellings to be built on a single title.

Dual water
This is where a block is serviced by town water and grey water services. The grey water is connected for toilet flushing and garden watering. It is ideal for new home construction when new piping can be installed easily.

Duplex
This is a building containing two homes with one central wall. They are often designed as mirror images for design/building efficiencies. In South Australia they are commonly referred to as maisonettes.

Figure 51: An artist's impression of a duplex property

E

Earth leakage safety switch

This is a safety device designed to prevent electrocution and fires. The switch is installed in the meter box and measures loss of current flow. It switches off the power instantaneously if a significant loss is detected.

Easement

This is a restriction on the land title which requires part of the land to be left free of any building for some purpose. (See *facade easement, avigation easements*).

Eaves

The lower or outer edge of a roof which projects over the side walls of a structure.

Edifice

A large structure or building: for example a cathedral or an abbey.

Efflorescence

This is a white powdery substance that sometimes appears on brick walls when salt and other materials come to the surface. (See *rising damp*)

Egress

This can refer to the act of exiting an enclosed space or it can refer to the physical exit itself

Electricity supply meter box

This is where the smart meters, safety switches and residual-current devices are located.

Elevation

A drawing of one of the external faces of a building. It also refers to the height of land above a datum. (See *Contour map*)

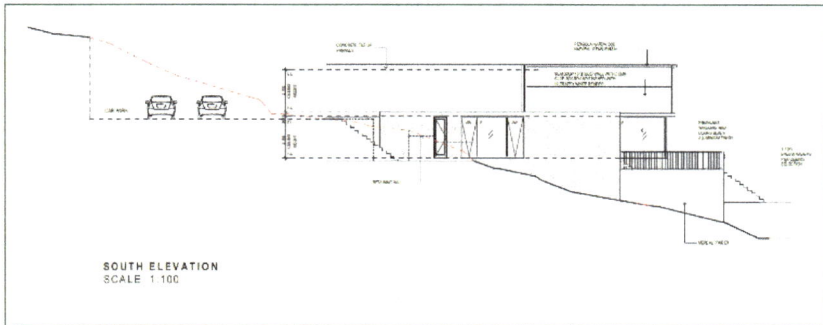

Figure 52: **South elevation map of a proposed building on a very slope land**

Encroachment

When part of a building illegally intrudes into another property.

Engineer

Generally speaking, an engineer is a qualified professional, normally registered with an allied association, involved in the field of design, construction, management or research. Following are some of those who might be involved in building:

Civil – designs and maintains roads, bridges, dams and similar structures.

Hydraulic – designs water distribution networks, sewerage, stormwater drainage and water storage systems.

Structural – designs the structural components of a building to withstand applied loads, wind loads and the weight of the structure itself.

Electrical – designs the electrical distribution systems. In recent times, electrical engineers have become involved in storage using battery systems.

Geotechnical – designs footings for the building based upon results of a soil test to investigate the foundation properties. On sloping sites, design of retaining walls might be required.

Escalation clause (contracts)

For building contracts over $1M, it is an addendum to a contract which allows for the effect of rises in labour rates, inflation, etc. For contracts under this amount, its inclusion must be approved by the Director of Consumer Affairs.

Excavation

The removal of virgin soil or rock from the ground usually for the purpose of construction.

Exterior Insulation and Finishing System (EIFS)

This is a cladding system that provides weather protection and sound insulation to buildings. It looks like traditional *stucco*.

F

Facade

The front or face of the house. It is commonly referred to by style names such as Colonial, Federation, Traditional, Tuscany and many more.

Facade easement

This is a conservation easement, mostly applying to heritage property, where there is a restriction in place to keep the original facade of the property

Factoryettes

These are small industrial units that are easy to manage with minimum maintenance.

Fall

This is a plumbing term for the amount of slope of a drainage pipe, run of guttering, or a shower base. It is also used to refer to the slope of an area of land, usually with reference to natural drainage.

Fascia or Fascia board

A long and straight board that runs along the lower edge of the roof, attached to the ends of rafters. It holds the gutters in place and supports one side of the eaves lining.

Fibrous cement sheet ('fibro')

A building material made of compressed fibre cemented into sheets. Prior to the discovery of the dangers associated with asbestos, the latter was used in its manufacture as the fibre. This was known as *asbestos cement sheet* or simply *AC sheet*.

Fibrous plaster

This is gypsum plaster reinforced with sisal or fibre glass.

Finial

This is a decorative finish at the top of a gable.

Fire-rated wall

A fire-rated wall is one that extends from the foundation through to the roof. It provides occupants in an adjoining dwelling with sufficient time to escape safely by ensuring the wall maintains sufficient structural adequacy, integrity and insulation.

Fit out

The completion of the interior shell space of a building.

Fixed cost

A cost that does not change with variation in the amount of goods or services produced or sold.

Fixed-price contract

A common form of domestic building agreement and allows for variations to the building work during the construction process. Once the fixed price agreement is executed, the builder agrees to complete the building project for a fixed sum.

Flashing

Thin pieces of impervious material installed to prevent the passage of water into a structure from a joint. Metal flashings are made of lead, aluminium, copper, stainless steel and zinc alloy.

Flood zone (flood-prone area)

Properties within a flood zone are considered to have a higher risk of flooding. The federal government raised the idea of making flood cover mandatory in insurance policies after the 2011 Queensland floods, prompting many insurers to include flood cover as a standard definition in insurance policies. However, the idea was not legislated. Building insurance usually covers loss or damage due to fire, storm, impact (car, tree etc.) but some budget policies do not cover damage due to flood.

The eastern seaboard of Australia is mostly prone to storm and flood damage

- Is your property located within a flood plain?
- Does the insurance company and the local council have the same definition of a flood plain area?
- Do you have clear understanding of flood mentioned in the policy?

Note: A flood zone is different from a flood plain. The latter refers to land that is immediately adjacent to a water course and will flood during times of high discharge.

Floor Space Ratio, FSR (Floor Area Ratio, FAR)

This is the ratio between the area of a building compared to the area of the land. It is used by councils to control development in built-up areas.

Footings

This is the part of a structure which transfers its weight to the foundation beneath. A footing is designed to transfer loads from a building to the supporting foundation. Pad footings, strip footings, waffle raft slabs, raft slabs, footing slabs, bored piers, driven piles and screw piles are some of the major footings used in Australia.

Formwork
A mould or support structure into which concrete is poured.

Foundation
The underlying soil or rock upon which a footing is founded.

Frameless shower
A shower that has no framing around it in any form. A frameless shower screen is held in place using special chrome or stainless steel clamps or fixings where the panel adjoins the wall and / or floor.

Friable asbestos
Asbestos that is crumbly and brittle in nature and likely to release asbestos fibres and particles into the air. Asbestos fibres are light, remain airborne for a long time and can be carried over long distances. Pleural plaques, asbestosis, lung cancer and mesothelioma are four major asbestos related diseases. A property that has friable asbestos should be assessed carefully through licensed professionals and consultants.

Freestanding building
A structure that is not attached to another structure. This information is relevant to the premium paid for an insurance policy.

Frog
It is a recess pressed into a clay brick before firing which assists bonding.

G

Gable or Gable end
The top part of a building's end wall which forms a triangle to meet the roof.

Galvanising
It is an electrolytic process that coats raw steel with a protective layer of zinc, recommended for all external steel work.

Gauge
It is a measurement used to specify the thickness of sheet metal, and for the diameter of screws and bolts. It can also refer to a measuring tool.

Geotechnical report
This is a report provided by a geotechnical engineer, following a site investigation, into the suitability of the surface soil and the substrates for supporting a building. (See *Engineers*)

Glazing
This is the glass element of windows and doors. It also refers to the surface finish on floor and wall tiles as well as roof tiles.

Going
It is the width of the tread of a step, from one riser to the next.

Green building
A building that minimises the cost of utilities (water, electricity, gas) and also has minimal environmental emissions

Gross Floor Area (GFA)
This is the total combined space that is designated as living space in a dwelling. The GFA often refers to the internal square metered area under the roof line but excludes balcony and garages. Councils will allocate a percentage of the site allowed for GFA and development is restricted to that percentage. For example, on a 600 m² site with a 50% GFA allowance, the council would permit a dwelling of up to 300 m².

Grout
This is the joint filling material used in tiling of walls and floors.

Gutters

A metal or plastic trough fixed below the edge of a roof to remove rainwater collected on the roof (See *Roof types*).

Gyprock

A proprietary plasterboard lining material for internal walls and ceilings.

H

Habitable

Being in a condition suitable for human occupation or habitation

Half bath

A small room in a house, often known as a powder room that contains a toilet and wash basin but no bathing facilities (bathtub or shower stall).

Half-lap joint

It is a timber joint made by cutting recesses into both components to a depth of half the thickness of the timber, and overlapping the timbers.

Header

A wall framing member used over a door or window opening.

Header brick

It is a brick that is laid such that the small end of the brick is exposed.

Header course

It is a course composed of header bricks only.

Heating and air conditioning ducts

Metal fabrications used to distribute heated and cooled air from a central heating or cooling system (usually located in the roof space) throughout a house or a building.

Height Restrictions

Councils generally designate a maximum height for a building measured from the natural ground level. For residential construction, this may be eight metres to the top of the roof line while in flight paths for aircraft, there may be height restrictions for multi-storey developments.

Hip

A sloping ridge formed by the junction of two pitched roofs which join perpendicular to each other.

Hip roof

A sloping end of a roof where the ridge line splits and terminates on the external corner.

Home inspection

An evaluation of the condition of a property.

Home Owners Warranty Insurance

This is an insurance required for builders, in all states except Queensland, before they can commence residential construction projects. It is designed to protect consumers from faulty workmanship and non-completion of a building where the builder dies, disappears or becomes insolvent.

Housing joint

It is a method of jointing two timbers. It is typically used to house a shelf into the upright end of a bookshelf.

I

In-situ concrete

Any concrete poured and left to set where it is intended to remain eg. a slab-on-ground.

Insulation
Material used to reduce the rate of transfer of heat through a building material. Efficiency is rated by means of an R value: the higher the R value, the better insulation properties the material has. Polyurethane foam, fibreglass, cellulose, expanded polystyrene, rockwool, and glass wool are some of the insulating materials used in building and construction.

Intercom
An intercommunication device, talkback or door phone that functions independently of the public telephone network. This is a device that allows a person to communicate with someone who is inside a building or a different part of the building or structure.

J

Jamb
This is the inside of a door frame.

Jig
A device used to hold a component during machining.

Joint strike
A trowel used to finish a mortar joint to a particular style.

Joist
This is a horizontal beam supporting a floor or ceiling. (See *bearers*)

Joist hanger
A metal anchor which is attached to the bearer and supports the end of a joist.

K

Knee brace

It is a short, diagonal bracing member usually applied between a post and a beam. Bracing is essential to prevent swaying.

L

Lagging

This is material wrapped around piping for insulation or protection of pipes and is used to reduce heat loss in hot water pipes.

Laminated timber

Layers of timber glued together, horizontally or vertically, to form a structural member.

Landing

This is an intermediate platform between two flights of stairs.

Larry

A long-handled hoe with a hole in the blade used for mixing mortar in a wheelbarrow.

Lath

A thin, narrow strip of wood used mainly in older style 'lath and plaster' walls.

Lattice

This is a framework of crossed wood or metal strips used as a screen.

Ledger

A horizontal timber fastened to a wall to support floor joists or similar.

Level
A builder's tool for determining correct vertical and horizontal alignment.

Lime
Hydrated builders' lime is a useful additive for bricklaying mortars as an aid to workability.

Lintel
A beam over an opening such as a door or window and supporting loads above the opening.

Load-bearing wall
A wall that supports a roof load or has sufficient dead load to warrant individual footing support.

Lock up stage
The point at which a home's external wall cladding and roof covering is fixed, the flooring is laid and external doors and windows are fixed.

Louvres
These are overlapping blades made of timber, glass or metal built into an adjustable frame or opening and designed for ventilation and control of light penetration.

M

Manhole (more recently known as an access hole)
An opening for access into a ceiling or below the floors of a house.

Masonry bolt
A bolt with a metal or plastic sleeve which expands to grip the masonry around a pre-drilled hole.

Mastic
A plastic waterproofing sealant used to fill joints between two materials.

Medium Density Fibreboard (MDF)
An engineered composite product, stronger than particle board, made by breaking down hardwood and softwood residuals into wood fibres and combining it with wax and resin. MDF is similar to plywood in density and usage but is more often used as kitchen cabinetry.

Merchantable (merch) grade timber
A lower quality of timber used for non-structural applications.

Mezzanine
An intermediate level between the floor and the ceiling.

Moulding
This is a decorative strip generally of wood used to conceal joints.

Mortar
A mix of sand, cement and water (and perhaps lime) used for laying masonry blocks such as bricks and stone.

Mortice and tenon
A mortice is a rectangular hole cut into one piece of timber. A tenon is a tongue-shaped section designed to fit into the mortice to form the joint.

Mulch
A covering placed around plants mainly to prevent growth of weeds and to retain soil moisture. There are many types of mulch but most are chipped wood or organic materials (leaves, grass clippings, cocoa hulls, straw, hay, pine needles, stone, bark and sawdust).

Mullion
This is the vertical member in a window or between two adjoining windows or garage doors.

N

Nationwide House Energy Rating System (NatHERS)
A star rating system that rates the energy efficiency of a home based on the inclusion of many design features to facilitate energy and water conservation. The number is out of 10. 6 stars is the minimum requirement for all new dwellings.

Newell
The bottom or top post of a stair balustrade.

Nogging
A horizontal timber strut fixed between stud walls or joists in framed construction to provide stiffening.

Nosing
The internal sill finish of a window. It also refers to the leading edge of a stair tread.

O

Off the plan
To buy a property after viewing the plans but before construction has commenced. This practice is popular because of the potential savings on stamp duty but inexperienced investors should exercise caution.

P

Panelled door
A door with sunken raised panels on its faces.

Path mesh

A lighter grade of prefabricated steel reinforcement designed for light paving work.

Pediment

The projecting triangular gable over an entrance, door or window or forming the gable end of a roof.

Pergola

A free-standing structure or a structure that is attached to the property, mostly at the rear. The design is heavily controlled by council regulations and a building permit is required.

Perpends

The vertical joints between bricks.

Pier

A column or post supporting a superstructure such as beams or floor bearers.

Pitch

This is the angle of the slope of the roof and usually expressed in degrees for example most tile roofs require a minimum 15 degree pitch.

Plan

There are different types of plans involved in a project: site plan, floor plan, cross sections, footing plan, drainage plan. (Our book entitled "It's My Time: Successful Residential Investing" contains more details on plans).

Planning permit

It is a legal document that gives permission for use or development of a particular piece of land. A planning permit application is to be submitted to the council to obtain a permit.

Office Use Onl

Application No.:   Date Lodged: /   /

Application for a **Planning Permit**

If you need help to complete this form, read MORE INFORMATION at the end of this form.

⚠ Any material submitted with this application, including plans and personal information, will be made available for public viewing, including electronically, and copies may be made for interested parties for the purpose of enabling consideration and review as part of a planning process under the *Planning and Environment Act 1987*. If you have any questions, please contact Council's planning department.

⚠ **Questions marked with an asterisk (*) must be completed.**

⚠ **If the space provided on the form is insufficient, attach a separate sheet**

ℹ Click for further information.

Figure 53: **Sample of a planning permit**

Plaster

A mix of lime or cement, sand and water used to cover walls and ceilings.

Plasterboard

Commonly referred to by a tradename of Gyprock, these are sheets of varying sizes used to line walls and ceilings.

Plate

When applied to timber framing, this term means a horizontal loading member. A bottom plate may be found at the base of a stud wall and a top plate will be on top of the studs, supporting the ceiling joists and rafters.

Plug and waste

This term refers to a circular object capable of retaining water in a hand basin or sink by arresting the flow. Traditionally made of rubber, and tapered to create a 'wedge' fit, there are now numerous versions including the popular 'pop-up' model and a 'push-down' incorporating a strainer for kitchen sinks.

Plumb
This is a term used by tradespeople to signify something is verticial and even 90 degrees to level.

Polished concrete
A type of decorative concrete produced by grinding a rough concrete surface using abrasive pads and applying a liquid coating.

Pointing
A restorative process of filling joints in brickwork or masonry.

Post cap
A cap used to prevent water entering the end grain of a timber post.

Post support
A metal stirrup into which the base of a post fits, with a projection that is embedded in concrete.

Power point
In Australia this is a three pin (10 ampere or amp) flat pin socket outlet. The term General Purpose Outlet is no longer used.

Pressure-treated
A description for timber which has been treated with a CCA solution – copper, cadmium and arsenic. It gives timber a characteristic greenish-grey colour and provides long-term protection from insect attack.

Prime cost
An amount to cover fittings and materials that are part of the building contract but either have not been selected or their price is not known at the time the contract is entered into.

Table 23: Table showing prime cost calculation and tax deduction

Original cost $5000		
Year	Percentage	Tax deduction
1	20 %	$1000
2	20 %	$1000
3	20 %	$1000
4	20 %	$1000
5	20 %	$1000

Prime Cost (PC) items

A prime cost item is an allowance in a contract for the supply of items not yet finalised. Example: electrical fittings, taps, door handles. (See *Provisional Sum* items).

Project specification

A building plan cannot illustrate all the details of construction; it would be unreadable. A project specification document contains the finer details of the project including: preliminary site works and foundations, footings, brickwork, carpentry, windows and doors, thermal insulation, roofing, electrical, internal wall and ceiling linings, fixings, painting, wall and floor tiling, carpets, glazing, stormwater and sewer drainage, and a schedule of fittings.

Provisional Sum items

An allowance in the contract for the cost of foreseeable necessary work including the supply of materials not fully described or decided upon at the time of contract commencement. Examples: site work costs, excavation works. (See *Prime Cost* items).

R

Raked ceiling

Sometimes called a cathedral ceiling, it is where the ceiling line follows the line of the roof timber and sometimes with the roof timber exposed.

Rafter

A rafter is one of a series of sloping structural members that extend from the ridge or hip to the wall plate and supports the roof cladding.

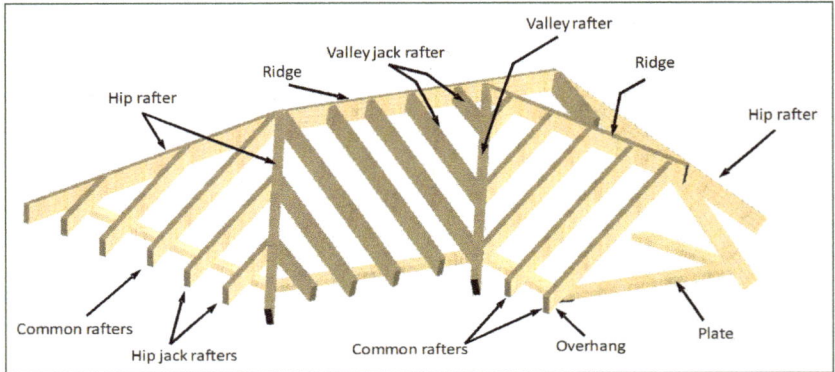

Figure 54: **Image showing ridge, rafter, joist and wall studs**

R value

Measure of the thermal (heat) conductivity of a material used in building and construction.

Reactive soils

Many soils contain clay that is subject to varying degrees of swelling and shrinkage due to changes in moisture content. In the worst case, the soil would be classified as E meaning extremely reactive. (See *soil classification*)

Rebar

Slang for reinforcement bar, this is used to strengthen concrete sections.

Rebate (rabbet)

A recess or step, usually of rectangular section, cut into a surface or along the edge of a piece of timber to receive a mating piece.

Reinforced concrete
In-situ or precast concrete that utilises steel bars or wire mesh for added strength. (Read our book entitled "*It's My Time: Successful Residential Investing*" for all major materials used in the building and construction industries).

Reinforcement steel
A steel bar, or mesh of steel wires, used as reinforcement in concrete. Also called *reinforcing bar* (rebar).

Render
The application of a thin premixed cement-based coating to any surface - normally brick, block, mud or cement sheet.

Restumping
Also called re-blocking. This is the process of removing existing stumps and replacing them with new stumps under a house. This is done by placing jacks in the areas around the weak or worn-out stumps, followed by lowering the bearers back onto the new stumps. This process is prone to cause minor damage to brittle fixings on the floors and walls of the structure. The main reason for restumping is concrete cancer in old concrete stumps or subsidence. Old *fibro* or *weatherboard* homes are often restumped. (Read our book entitled "*It's My Time: Successful Residential Investing*". (See *Bearers, Underpinning*).

Retaining wall
A structure designed to retain soil where there exists a sudden change in ground level. It may be constructed from timber, steel, masonry, rock, compacted earth or any combination of these. Generally retaining walls over one metre high will require engineering design and approval.

Retarder
A chemical added to concrete, usually on hot days, to prevent it setting too quickly.

Retemper

The addition of water to a setting concrete mix. It is not a recommended practice as it results in a weakened mix.

Ridge

The horizontal line at the top of a pitched roof. A duo ridge is where there is a sloping roof on two sides and a mono ridge is where there is only one sloping roof. For example, a gable roof would have a duo ridge and a skillion roof would have a mono ridge.

Rise and Fall clause

A clause in a building contract which allows the price to go up or down according to a specified index.

Riser

The vertical section between the treads of stairs. It also refers to vertically oriented piping used to deliver fluids, gas and electrical power upwards in high rise buildings.

Rising damp

Moisture absorbed from the ground rises up through walls, floors and masonry via capillary action. Common symptoms of rising damp in a building are band of dampness causing paint to flake or to peel. It is often accompanied by a white powder-like substance which is the result of the crystallisation (solidification) of soluble salts brought up from the soil.

River sand

A clean sand, free of salt and organic matter.

Roadbase

Crushed gravel, or aggregate, used beneath the paved layers of a road.

Roofline

The outline of the roof of a building.

Roof materials

The characteristics of the roof cladding are based on the intended purpose of the building that it covers. In some instances, it may affect the premium paid for building insurance.

Figure 55: **Steel sheeting (Colorbond)**

Steel roofing	This is the most common type used in Australia. Zincalume and Colorbond products can resist rust for decades and reflect heat well. Being lightweight, savings can be made on the roof substructure. Access to the roof space is not as easy as with a tiled roof.
Concrete and Terracotta tiles	Concrete and terracotta tiles are another popular choice. They do require more maintenance than steel, mainly due to the formation of lichen and moss, but provide greater sound insulation. They are prone to cracking but individual pieces are easily replaced.
Other materials	Shingles are laid in a similar fashion to tiles but with a greater overlap. They can be made of many materials such as asphalt, slate, fibre cement and plastic. Shakes are a special type of shingle made from wood.

Roof types

There are various architectural styles that Australia has seen in the past few centuries: Victorian style, Workers Cottage, Queenslanders, Post-war triple-fronted brick veneer, and modern homes. In the Modern homes roof design particularly, there are many variations. Our book entitled "It's My Time: Successful Residential Investing" contains more details on the pros and cons of types of roof and the covenants on type of roof selections, including specific angles. It also details how roof type varies with climatic conditions and local weather in different parts of Australia.

Table 24: Different types of roof used in Australia

Roof type	Description
Flat	A low-pitched style of roof with no attic space.
Skillion	Sometimes known as a *shed roof*, it has a greater slope than a flat roof for better drainage.
Gable	This is an inverted 'V' shape and the pitch can be steepened to increase the attic space.
Hip	This can be seen as a gable with the ends sloped back at the same pitch as the sides.
Hip and Valley	A valley is created at the intersection of two perpendicular roof structures. Most modern homes feature a hip and valley.
Dutch gable	This is created when the hip end is dropped to create a triangle at one or both ends of the house.
Clerestory	One side of the roof is extended up and over the other to create a clerestory window.
Dormer	A dormer window is introduced into the side of a gable.
Combination (Verandah)	This style is more popular in warmer parts of Australia as the verandah creates shading to doors and windows for the entire day. The roofing material of the verandah may be straight or curved (Bullnose).

Roof pitch

This is the slope of a roof. The minimum angle for a tiled roof is 15 degrees but corrugated steel roofing can be laid as low as 5 degrees.

Roughing in

This is the preliminary stage of installation for plumbing, electrical wiring, communication wiring done at framing stage.

Router
A cabinet-making tool, which has a vertical spindle and chuck with a high-speed cutter designed to cut different shaped recesses in timber.

Run
The 'going' or width of a step. The total run is the horizontal distance between the top and bottom of a flight of stairs.

S

Sacrificial joint
In concrete paths or driveways, this is a false joint about 25 mm deep. Its purpose is to cause the slab to break along the joint line as expansion and contraction takes place.

Sandblasting
The process of blasting an abrasive granular material onto a surface for the purpose of cleaning. Sandblasting can be used to clean, grind or decorate a surface. Traditionally sand was used but this has now been replaced with safer materials, such as garnet.

Sarking
This is a sheet material placed under the roof covering material to provide reflective insulation and additional waterproofing.

Sash
This is the frame that supports the glass in a window.

Scale
This is the relationship of the size of the drawing to the size of the actual object for example 100:1 is a common scale for building construction but landscape plans maybe 50:1.

Scarf joint
The joining of two lengths of timber by cutting the ends so that they overlap and fit together.

Screed
A layer, usually of mortar or sand, used as a bed for tiles, or a finishing application to rough concrete.

Screed board
A length of board, used in conjunction with screed rails, used to level the screed.

Screeding
The process of levelling concrete or sand to a true and even finish.

Screed rails
Two pieces of timber used on each side of an area to be paved which act as the level for the resultant bed.

Seasoned timber
This is timber that has been dried to a stable moisture content prior to use. Unseasoned timber will shrink over time as the timber dries resulting in movement in the building structure.

Section
A cross-section of a plan.

Security door
A door that prevents unauthorised entry from intruders and provides better protection against inclement weather.

Sediment control measure
This aims to trap and retain sediment caused by erosion on a building site. Normally a barrier is placed on the low side of the land to prevent silt or soil washing from the land into the street drainage system.

Select grade
A grade of timber which is clear of natural characteristics but with sufficient features to retain the look of real timber.

Semi-detached
Two buildings sharing a common wall. Also called a duplex. (See *subdivision for an image*).

Setback
The distance from the front boundary to the front of the house, from the side of the house to the side boundary and from rear of the house to rear boundary. Each council has minimum setbacks.

Shade cloth
Woven fabric, usually made from synthetic fibres, and available in several grades specified by their light transmittance. For pergola and shade house use, grades of 80 to 90 percent are recommended (which will block out 80 to 90 percent of the light).

Shadow diagram
A diagram representation of the shadowing effect by a proposed new dwelling or high rise building or nearby structure on an existing property. It looks at the effect at different times of day and in different seasons.

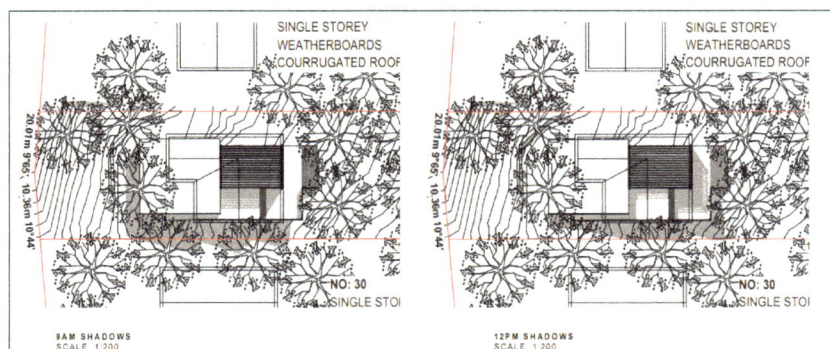

Figure 56: Shadow diagram of a single storey family dwelling at 9 am and 12 pm

Shingles
These are thin pieces of roofing material laid in overlapping rows on a roof.

Shower rod and curtain
Now only seen in older homes and overseas, these are part of a 'shower-over-bathtub' system and prevented shower water from splashing out over the floor.

Shower screen
Glass is the most common material used for shower screens and may be toughened safety glass (frameless or semi-frameless) or laminated (fully framed). Thickness is between 6mm and 10mm.

Shower tray
A shallow, mostly square, base with raised edges used for forming a shower compartment.

Sill
The lower horizontal portion of a window or door.

Sinkhole
A sudden opening or depression in the land.

Site
A site is land that has been worked to make it ready for the construction of a building (residential, commercial or industrial). Land is generally considered as the ground or soil.

Site plan
A site plan is a bird's-eye view showing the footprint of a building on the block of land where it is going to be built.

Skew nail
To fasten with a nail driven in at an angle. Rafters are connected to plates with a skew nail driven through the bottom section of both faces of the rafter into the plate below.

Skillion
A roof that has only one slope and no centre ridge.

Skirting board
A length of timber joined to the bottom of the wall where it meets the floor.

Skylight
An opening in a roof or ceiling fitted with glass and inclined at the same angle as the roof (See *Roof types*).

Slump
In concrete, an approximate measure of the amount of water in the mix indicated by the 'slump' of a sample released from a truncated cone.

Slurry
A very wet mixture of cement or concrete.

Smoke alarm
A device that triggers an alarm when it detects smoke. Checks should be made with the local fire authority on the compliance of smoke alarm battery replacement and smoke alarm replacement.

Smoke alarm (installation)
Installation of smoke alarms at strategic points in a building is mandatory and highly regulated. It is the landlord's responsibility to maintain the smoke alarms in residential rental properties. For details of a landlord's obligations, website details of all Real Estate Institutes are listed in the appendix.

Soffit
This is the underside of the eaves, normally constructed from cement sheet. Some are vented to provide air circulation in a roof space.

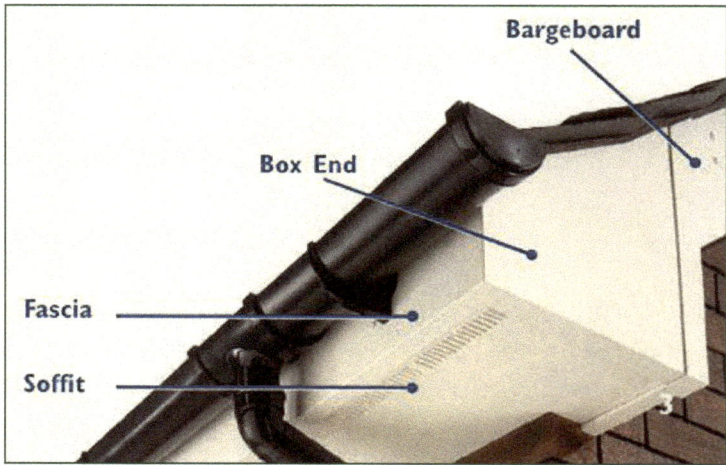

Figure 57: **Photo of a real house showing various components around a gutter**

Soil classification

Following soil testing, the site is classified according to Australian Standard AS2870 as one of the following:

Class	Description
A	little or no ground movement
S	slightly reactive site
M	moderately reactive site
H1	highly reactive site
H2	highly reactive site with greater ground movement than H1
E	Extremely reactive site
P	Problem site

Soil test

One of the first considerations in building is the type of soil underlying the construction. The composition of the soil, the existence of rock or sand, or the possibility of shallow underground streams can be found by a soil test. The results of the soil test will influence the foundations required and therefore the construction costs. Soil tests are undertaken by specialist operators who drill a series of small deep holes, taking soil samples across the proposed building area.

Soldier course
A course of bricks, often used as a finish to a wall or a border to paving, laid with the bricks vertical.

Span
The horizontal distance between the supports of a structural member.

Sparrow pick
A technique which uses a sharp-pointed pick to roughen a concrete surface in order to produce a better surface for other materials to adhere to.

Splashback
A panel attached to the wall above a basin or cooktop that protects the wall from splashes.

Spirit level
A tool for testing vertical and horizontal alignment, consisting of glass tubes containing an oil or spirit.

Split air conditioning system
The system is split into two units: one inside the home mounted on a wall and another (condenser) outside the home. Split air conditioning is not ideal for large spaces. The operating cost of split air conditioning is normally higher than a ducted air conditioning system. Care should be exercised in locating the condenser as it emits forced air, water, noise and vibration.

Spreader
A piece of material or a device for keeping apart and spacing parallel objects.

Stringer
The inner or outer supporting member for staircase treads and risers.

Stop chamfering
The chamfering or planning of the edge of a piece of timber which stops short of the ends.

Straight edge
A bar or strip of wood or metal having at least one edge of sufficiently reliable straightness to test straight lines.

Strap clamp
A device for securing objects together by means of a strap

Stretcher bond
Common brickwork where the vertical joints are staggered by one half-brick on each successive course.

Stucco (modern)
A type of plaster composed of cement, sand and hydrated lime mixed with water which is used as an exterior finish for walls. It may also contain additives which supply strength and stability.

Studs
The upright supports in the walls of a building.

Sub-base
A layer of compacted crushed rock beneath the bedding sand of paving.

Subfloor
This is the open space below an elevated floor.

Sub-grade
The native soil or earth beneath a structure or pavement.

Subsidence

An unexpected movement of a building or structure as a result of the failure of a part of the structure or the soil beneath the structure.

T

Tenon saw

A short, rigid bladed saw, stiffened with a steel top edge, used for accurate joint cutting

Termites

Subterranean insects that bore into a wooden structure and potentially destroy it. There are over 300 species of termite in Australia.

Termite protection

The process of protecting a whole building from termite activity through the use of a physical or chemical barrier. Most companies that install such systems will only provide a warranty against termite damage if the customer undertakes a periodic inspection in subsequent years.

Tiger tails

The black and yellow striped warning covers cupped over existing aerial power lines for the protection of workers on a building site.

Tile resurfacing

Also called tile refinishing or tile reglazing, it is the process of improving the appearance of tiles, including colour change, without going through the time and expense of replacing the tiles.

Tolerance

A specified allowance in determining limits of accuracy.

Tongue-and-groove joint

Two boards joined by the tongue along the edge of one board fitting into the groove along the edge of the other board.

Top plate

The timber plate at the top of a wall frame.

Tradesperson

A person experienced, but not necessarily qualified, in one of the trades. Before engaging a tradesperson, it is wise to ensure that he/she is adequately insured. Some of the tradespeople ('tradies') engaged on a building project might be a carpenter ('chippy'), electrician ('sparky'), bricklayer ('brickie'), scaffolder ('scaff'), etc.

Transom light

A normally fixed window above a door or window.

Tread

The horizontal part of a step or stair.

Triple grip (proprietary Trip-L-Grip)

A metal connector with three 'wings', used to fix together two or three members.

Truss

A structural frame made up wholly of members in tension or compression lying in the same plane for the bridging of long spans and or the support of superimposed loads. Members are usually arranged in a series of triangles to form a rigid framework.

Tumbling

A process by which bricks and paving materials are tossed in a rotating drum to deform the edges and give them an aged look.

Twenty eight (28) day compressive strength of concrete
This is the amount of compressive stress than a sample of concrete can withstand 28 days after pouring. It is considered to be 99% of its full strength and hence is the parameter commonly used for design and evaluation. Read our book entitled *"It's My Time: Successful Residential Investing"* for more information on choosing the correct strength of concrete for your project needs.

U

Underfloor heating
A heating system that is placed inside a floor slab. The embedded pipes or electric heating cables radiate heat steadily upwards from floor level.

Underpinning
The process of propping up cracked and slumped house slabs using jacks and pouring fresh concrete around the jacks. Underpinning stabilises the alignment of the bricks and adds more stability to the structure.

V

Valley gutter
A metal gutter built into the roof valley to carry water to the eaves guttering.

Variation
Variation refers to changes in the scope of work. These may or may not result in changes to the cost of a fixed price contract.

Veneer
This is a thin coating that covers an underlying surface (comprising, usually, a less attractive and less expensive material). Brick veneer is the most common type of house construction in Australia.

Double brick is another common form of construction and is particularly popular in Western Australia.

Verandah
A long covered porch which may extend along one side or in the case of the Queenslander could extend around three sides of the building.

Verge
A wall under the edge of a roof where it tops a gable end. In some areas, the footpath is also known as the verge.

Void
This is a completely empty space and is an integral part of many insulation systems.

W

Waffle pod slab
An engineered slab design featuring a grid of internal beams created around polystyrene pod formers. High strength and thermal efficiency are claimed attributes.

Wall anchor
An expansion device designed to anchor a structural member to a pre-drilled hole in masonry.

Wall cavity
This is the space between the inner and outer walls of a building.

Water/cement ratio
This is the ratio between the water and the cement in a concrete mix. This is the major factor affecting the strength of the concrete.

Water feature
An architectural element involving water such as a pond, waterfall, fountain or stream as part of the overall landscape plan.

Water meter

A water meter is a device that measures and registers the amount of water that flows through a pipe. Residential water meters are usually located in front of a property, often just inside the front fence near a garden tap. There are also commercial and industrial water meters. (Read our book entitled "It's My Time: Introducing Commercial Investing" for more details on water meter charges and other outgoings).

Water proofing

Process of making a structure or an object water resistant so that it will make become impervious to water (does not allow water to pass-through). Bathrooms, shower recesses, laundries, toilets, roofs, balconies, retaining walls, swimming pools are sections of a building that are waterproofed.

Weep holes

These are formed holes or openings placed in the perpend joints of a masonry wall above the level of a flashing or at the bottom of a cavity to permit drainage of any accumulated water. Weep holes are also installed in a retaining wall to drain water from behind the wall to relieve hydrostatic pressure.

Wind loads

These are all the forces on a building or structure caused by or imputed due to wind pressure which have to be taken into account when designing the structure. Most wind loads on dwellings are uplift loads on roofs and are of particular significance in cyclone areas. There is an Australian Housing Standard for wind loading (cyclone rating) which Western Australia, Northern Territory and Queensland follow.

Window furnishings

Material used to cover window to manage sunlight, to give a decorative look and to provide additional shading. Curtains, drape, pall, mantle, blinds, hanging cloth are some examples of window furnishings.

Wind (acting on a building)

The wind acting on the building creates positive pressure on the windward side of the house and negative pressure (suction) on the leeward side. (The spot where dry leaves and other fine green waste gathers indicates the location of least pressure).

The structural design of the house against wind action is affected by many factors including location (cyclonic or non-cyclonic), topography, shape, orientation, roof pitch, number of openings, etc.

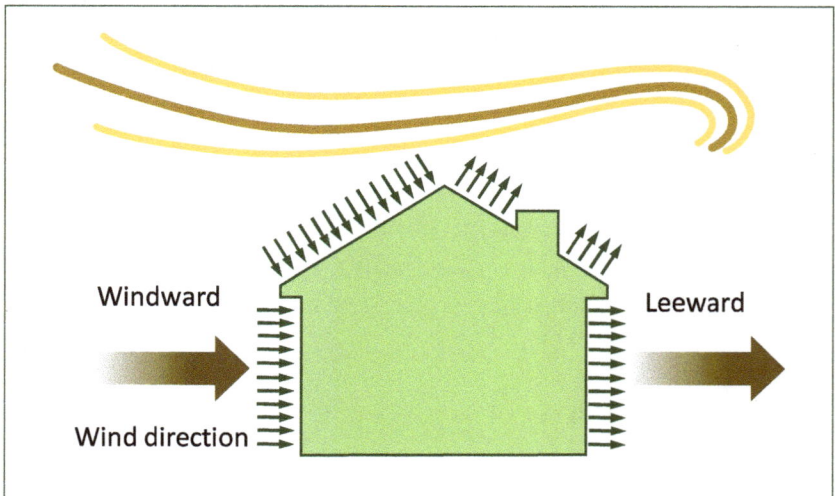

Figure 58: **Image showing windward and leeward (positive and negative pressure areas around a house)**

Weather boarding

This is an exterior cladding attached directly to the frame of a building. Older buildings have timber weatherboards (and high maintenance costs) but many new, synthetic materials are now being used.

Work triangle

Also called a "kitchen triangle" this is a parameter used by kitchen designers in preparing a kitchen layout. It is the total length of sides of a triangle connecting the refrigerator, stovetop and sink in a home kitchen.

Chapter 5

Professional and government bodies

A

Architects Industry Association

The Architects Industry Association is a professional body for architects in Australia. It is the peak body for the Australian architectural profession, and works to improve the Australian built environment by promoting quality, responsible, sustainable design. You can hire a member to inspect a building and to provide reports.

Australian Building and Construction Commission

The Australian Building and Construction Commission (ABCC) promotes an improved workplace relations framework to ensure that building work is carried out fairly, efficiently and productively for the benefit of all building industry participants, without distinction, and for the benefit of the Australian economy as a whole.

Australian Bureau of Statistics (ABS)

The Australian Bureau of Statistics provides statistical information on a wide range of triple bottom line issues (social, economic and environmental) that assists public and all stakeholders to make informed decisions through research and discussions within government and the community. ABS also collects data on populations and supplies, various specific demographic details based on age, gender, marital status, education, age, income, employment details and country of birth.

Australian Property Institute (API)

Australian Property Institute is a professional industry body representing residential, commercial and plant and machinery valuers, analysts, fund managers and property lawyers.

Australian Prudential Regulation Authority (APRA)

Established on 1 July 1998, the Australian Prudential Regulation Authority (APRA) is the regulator of the Australian Financial Services industry. It oversees banks, credit unions, building societies, general insurance and reinsurance companies, life insurance, private health insurance, friendly societies and most members of the superannuation industry. APRA is funded largely by the industries that it supervises and plays an important role in protecting the financial well-being of the Australian community.

In 2017, while the Reserve Bank of Australia has held official interest rates at a record low, APRA has introduced many measures which have forced banks to increase interest rates to customers.

An excerpt of a letter from a bank regarding the connection between a bank's interest rate and APRA.

Dear Customer

Recent announcements by Australia's banking prudential regulator, APRA, have encouraged banks to limit their growth of certain types of loans, for example, loans to investors, and interest only loans more generally. (http://www.apra.gov.au/MediaReleases/Pages/17_11.aspx) This has had the effect of causing banks to review their lending interest rates to achieve this objective.

Figure 59: Excerpt of letter stating the connection between APRA and banks change in policies and procedures

APRA has written to all ADIs today advising, in summary, that APRA expects ADIs to:

- limit the flow of new interest-only lending to 30 per cent of total new residential mortgage lending, and within that:
    - place strict internal limits on the volume of interest-only lending at loan-to-value ratios (LVRs) above 80 per cent; and
    - ensure there is strong scrutiny and justification of any instances of interest-only lending at an LVR above 90 per cent;
- manage lending to investors in such a manner so as to comfortably remain below the previously advised benchmark of 10 per cent growth;
- review and ensure that serviceability metrics, including interest rate and net income buffers, are set at appropriate levels for current conditions; and
- continue to restrain lending growth in higher risk segments of the portfolio (e.g. high loan-to-income loans, high LVR loans, and loans for very long terms).

Figure 60: An excerpt from the APRA website (dated 31ˢᵗ March 2017)

Australian Securities and Investment Commission (ASIC)

The Australian Securities and Investment Commission is a standalone and independent body that acts as a corporate regulator for Australians. ASIC regulates and enforces company and financial services laws to protect consumers, creditors and investors. ASIC provides information about investment advisers, business and company procedures.

Authorised Deposit-Taking Institutions (ADI)

It is an Australian government term for "financial institutions in Australia that are supervised by APRA and authorised under the Banking Act 1959 to take deposits from the public".

B

Banking and Financial Services Ombudsman

The Ombudsman handles disputes involving member banks and can make an award in the consumer's favour to a certain limit. There is no charge for this service.

Building Licensing Authority

A Building Licensing Authority is a state and territory based authority that regulates building and plumbing practitioners to ensure efficiency and competitiveness within the building and plumbing industries.

Building societies and credit unions

Building societies and credit unions are usually focused on a community such as a town or suburb, work place or industry. Regulating bodies are the Australian Association of Permanent Building Societies (AAPBS), the National Credit Union Association (NCUA), and the Credit Union Industry Association (CUIA)). Like banks, they are overseen by the Australian Prudential Regulation Authority (APRA). They are owned by their members and most loans are approved at a board meeting of the directors. They are linked together by one of the largest ATM networks in Australia.

Bylaws
A set of rules (law) that is made by a local authority or body corporate (owner's corporation) that applies in an area under their jurisdiction.

C

Centrelink
Disburses social security payments, provides services for a wide range of the population (retirees, families, carers, parents, people with disabilities, Indigenous Australians). Centrelink and Medicare Australia have been part of the Department of Human services since 1st July 2011. (Read our books entitled "It's My Time: Successful Residential Investing" and "It's My Time: Introducing Commercial Investing" for the economic impact in the suburbs where Centrelink offices are located).

Commonwealth Ombudsman
The ombudsman investigates complaints about Commonwealth government, departments, agencies and officers.

Consult Australia
Consult Australia is the industry association for consulting companies in the built environment sector, including engineers, architects, project managers, planners, environmental scientists and quantity surveyors, among others.

F

Fair Trading Department (or regulatory services or consumer affairs or consumer protection)

This department, in some states, is responsible for the receipt and management of residential tenancy bonds and is the regulatory and licensing body for real estate agents.

J

Justice of the Peace (JP)

A volunteer who provides document witnessing and certification services to the community both during and outside business hours. JPs do not provide legal advice. (See *Affidavit*)

L

Law Council of Australia

This is the peak national representative body of the Australian legal profession.

Each state has a Law Society which helps you find solicitors and can help with disputes and mediation. It is also the body that would investigate complaints against a solicitor.

M

Master Builders Association (MBA)

The Master Builders Association is the organisation representing all sectors of the industry from large national, international, residential and commercial builders and civil contractors, smaller local sub-contractors, suppliers to professional industry advisers.

Master Electricians Australia

This body provides a national approach to industry leadership and development. There is a Electricians Association in each state and territory.

Master Plumbers Australia Ltd (MPA)

The Master Plumbers Australia Ltd is the national body made up of representatives from each state and territory association. The MPA has adopted a unified policy position in the areas of licencing, qualification and regulation and provides a national prospective to governments and industry.

Medibank

This is the primary funding body of health care for Australian citizens and permanent residents including those from Norfolk Island. The residents are entitled to receive free treatment in public hospitals and subsidised treatment from medical and nurse practitioners and other health care professionals that are issued a Medicare provider number. (See *Medibank*). Our books entitled *"It's My Time: Successful Residential Investing"* and *"It's My Time: Introducing Commercial Investing"* for the economic impact in the suburbs where Medicare offices are located).

R

Real Estate Institute of Australia

The Real Estate Institute of Australia (REIA) is the national professional association for Australia's real estate sector. REIA is a political non-aligned organisation that provides research and well informed advice to the government and professional members of the real estate sector and media on a range of issues affecting the property market.

Table 25: Types of property markets

Type	Examples
Residential	Construction of new, and resale of existing, homes
Commercial	Shopping centres, hotels, offices, medical suites, apartment buildings
Industrial	Manufacturing units, warehouses
Land	Vacant land, working farms, acreages

Chapter 6

General terms in Property

A

Affidavit
A written statement, confirmed by oath or affirmation, for use as evidence in a court.

App (mobile or web)
It is an application that is downloadable by a user into a mobile hence called mobile app or mobile application. If the application is web browser based (openable in Google Chrome, Internet explorer), then it is called a web application or web app. (See *appendix for useful websites relevant to the property and related businesses*)

Arborist
This is a specialist in the cultivation and care of trees and shrubs, including tree surgery, the diagnosis, treatment, and prevention of tree diseases, and the control of pests. If undertaking any development which may affect established trees, council is likely to require a report from an arborist before granting any permits for development.

Arm's length transaction
A transaction among parties in which each of them has their own best interest. A transaction between a used car dealer and a needy buyer is an example of an arm's length transaction but one between a husband and wife is not.

Artificial intelligence

The ability of a computer or a network of computers to evaluate information and make decisions based on the some pre-established criteria. (Refer to our book entitled *"It's My Time: Setting Financial and Personal Goals"* on the *Fourth industrial revolution* and *Luddite fallacy*).

Asset protection

When a council is notified, via a building permit application, that construction is about to take place, it will take steps to protect its assets (road, pavement, nature strips). It does this by asking the builder to apply for an Asset Protection Permit (see below).

Asset Protection Permit Application

(For payment in person and via mail only)

Applicant details

Name:
(Name refund is to be made to)

Address:

Suburb: Postcode:

Contact name: Phone Number:

Signature of applicant: Date: / /20

Property address where building activities are occurring

Street no: Lot no:

Street name: Suburb:

Type of construction/works

New ☐ Demolition & removal ☐

Additions/alterations ☐ Swimming pool ☐

Type of building

Residential ☐

Non-residential ☐

Fees

(Please note the Permit fee is non-refundable once Permit is issued. Deposit may be refunded subject to the issue of Occupancy Permit/Final Certificate and the completion of Council's asset inspection)

Asset Protection Permit	☒	$ 162.30	GL Code: 405 (includes GST)	
Security Deposits: (Select as appropriate)	☐	$ 1,000.00	GL Code: 401	**All Demolition Sites**
	☐	$ 500.00	GL Code: 401	**Residential Site** - Single Street allotment
	☐	$ 1,000.00	GL Code: 401	**Residential Site** - Cnr allotment (dual street frontage)
	☐	$ 1,000.00	GL Code: 401	**Non-Residential Site** - Single Street allotment
	☐	$ 1,500.00	GL Code: 401	**Non-Residential Site** - Cnr allotment (dual street frontage)
	☐	$ 1,000.00	GL Code: 401	**Residential Site** - Demolition & New Construction*
	☐	$ 1,500.00	GL Code: 401	**Non-Residential Site** - Demolition & New Construction*
Total Payable:		$		

Privacy Collection Statement
The personal information collected on this form is for the purpose of enabling Council staff to process and assess an application for an Asset Protection Permit and will be solely used for that purpose. This information will not be disclosed to any other person unless required by law. You may apply for access and/or amendment to your personal information if required by contacting Council's Freedom of Information Officer in writing.

Figure 61: Asset protection permit sample application

The permit conditions will require that the builder takes appropriate measures for protection. A common example of this is a timber crossover laid on a footpath over sand (shown below).

Figure 62: **Timber crossover laid on a footpath**

A Team

Professional investors and developers will often refer to their A team. This is their team of professionals that they rely upon for advice and may include professionals such as accountants, solicitors, town planners, surveyors, quantity surveyors and engineers. The makeup of their team will depend upon the type of property work being undertaken. A property investor that buys property as a long term 'buy and hold' may have an A Team comprising of an accountant, solicitor, surveyor and quantity surveyor whereas a property investor who wants to buy property to renovate and 'on sell' for a profit may have an A Team of accountant, solicitor, surveyor and various tradespeople like carpenters, electricians, plumbers and painters.

Figure 63: **A team (leadership team, support and service team)**

Atmosphere
It is the gaseous blanket surrounding the earth.

Australian Business Number
Australian Business Number (ABN) is a unique number that the Australian Tax Office (ATO) issues to identify you and your business dealings you have with the ATO and other stakeholders across Australia.

AWOL
This acronym is a military term meaning 'absent without leave'. It is used in a building sense when the builder or tradesperson whom you engage ceases to work for you, and is uncontactable, without explanation.

B

Baby boomers
This refers to people born after World War 2 between 1946 and 1964 when there was a strong rise in the birth rate. This group is recognised as having attained a reasonable level of wealth.

Bilateral contract
A contract under which each party promises performance.

Bill
This is a draft or proposed law for discussion in parliament. A bill can only become a law if it is passed by a majority vote in the House of Representatives and the Senate. The bill must be agreed to in identical form by both chambers, and given Royal Assent by the Governor-General. It is then known as an Act of Parliament. A bill is no more than a proposal for a law or a change to the law.

Blackwater
Wastewater produced from toilets. It has larger organic loading compared to greywater and is treated through a wastewater system.

Blueprint
Historically it was a set of plans used as a guide for construction of a building. They were blue as a result of the process used in printing them, starting in the 19th century. Today, the term is used more to describe the concept or plan for any project.

Board of directors
A board of directors comprises the individuals elected by the shareholders to oversee the management of a company. The members are paid and meet several times a year, and are accountable by the legal responsibility for the company's activities. (See insurance).

Bona fide
This means in good faith, honesty, without fraud, collusion or participation in wrong doing.

Breach of contract
A violation of the terms of a legal agreement.

Budget deficit
Also called fiscal deficit. It shows how much additional money the government needs to borrow to finance its spending. Governments raise money normally through taxes, borrowing or printing money. (Refer *Taxes in Australia*)

$$budget\ deficit = government's\ tax\ revenue - government\ spending$$

Budget surplus
This is a positive number and it shows how much additional money the government generates from tax revenue over its spending.

$$budget\ surplus = government's\ tax\ revenue - government\ spending$$

Business confidence
The level of optimism that business leaders have about the prospects of the companies they are responsible for. An indicator of the state of the economy and the business cycle.

Business cycle
A business cycle is a predictable long-term pattern of alternating periods of economic growth (recovery) and decline characterised by changing asset prices, industrial productivity, interest rates and employment.

Business day
In Australia, a business day is part of a day when business operates usually from 9 am to 5 pm, Monday to Friday.

Business days in agreements

Various notices required in real estate contracts, leases, or other agreements, may have deadlines based on the passage of a certain number of days, or of business days. Some contracts may specify 21 business days for finance approval which is different from 21 days for finance approval. Business days will exclude Saturday and Sunday and any public holidays that fall during the specified period. If the settlement of a contract, or various conditions of a contract such as building inspection or finance approval, when expressed in a defined number of days falls due on a Saturday or Sunday or a Public Holiday, settlement takes place on the next business day.

Business in Australia

According to the Australian Bureau of Statistics, business is categorised into four categories: (*see Appendix I for more information on business*)

Table 26: Types of business in Australia

Type of business	Number of people	Example	Risk profile
Microbusiness	Less than four people	Local bookkeeper	Unlimited risk (no difference in law between ownership and company)
Small business	Less than 20 people	Local builder	Unlimited risk (no difference in law between ownership and company)
Medium business	Between 20 and 199 people	Local farming business	Limited risk
Large corporations	200 people or more	Mining and oil companies including supermarkets	Reduced risk

C

Cancellation clause
A clause in a contract that gives the right to terminate obligations upon the occurrence of specified events or conditions.

Capillary action
The ability of a liquid to flow through narrow spaces or pores against the action of gravity.

Central Business District (CBD)
The commercial and business centre of a city that has offices, hotels, entertainment, private and public offices with some high density housing.

Certificate of Insurance
Also called a certificate of currency, it is the document provided by an insurance company or broker that confirms the currency of the insurance policy.

Client
This is a term used to describe the person who appoints an agent such as a real estate agent, buyer's agent or other professional to act for them and is responsible to them for fees or commission payable.

Code assessable
This relates to a development application assessment against all the applicable codes in Brisbane City Plan 2014. Code assessable is relatively quick in approval and does not require public notification (see *impact assessable and development approval*).

Common Law
An unwritten body of law based upon the West Minister System.

Company

This is a separate legal entity that can sue and be sued. A company can acquire property but, unlike individuals and trusts, companies are not eligible for the 50% capital gains discount if held for more than twelve months. For 2016-17 income year, the company tax rate is 27.5 %for companies with turnover less than $10 million. The company tax rate remains at 30 % for those companies not classified as small business entities.

Companies have limited liability for shareholders. For this reason, companies are used as corporate trustees for family trusts. The directors of the company and the beneficiaries of the trust may be the same person. A company is any form of business whether it is small or large. Generally, the term 'company' indicates a kind of business dealing in a specific product.

Company title

This is an older form of title (predating strata title) that uses a company structure to subdivide property into separate units. Each property owner actually owns a number of shares in the company. Company title properties are more complicated than strata/unit title properties mainly because there may be restrictive conditions in the company documents and in the agreements between the shareholders. An example of such conditions would be getting the consent of other owners to a prospective purchaser. (See *strata title, joint tenants and tenancy in common* for more details).

Compliance

The procedures and policies a company follows to make sure it abides by company or other legislation. Compliance is a method of doing business according to a set of rules. It is a big no no for non-compliance in any business and that includes your investment business.

Complete replacement cover

Insurance which covers damage or loss to a building for the total amount it would cost to rebuild it.

Conflict of interest

A situation in which a person is faced with a decision in an official capacity from which she or he stands to benefit personally because of another relationship.

Consumer confidence

The level of optimism that consumers have about the state of the economy. High economic growth and low unemployment leads to high consumer confidence.

Consumer Price Index (CPI)

This is a measure of the cost of living and also a measure of the total value of goods and services purchased by consumers. CPI is used to measure inflation and is calculated by measuring the cost of a 'market basket' comprising food, non-alcoholic beverages, clothing, footwear, housing, furnishings, household equipment and services, health, transport, communication, recreation, culture, education, insurance and financial services and other goods and services. The amount of each item to be included in the calculation is determined by interviewing families on which items they purchased. CPI is an index, not a dollar figure, and is the common measure of Australia's inflation rate.

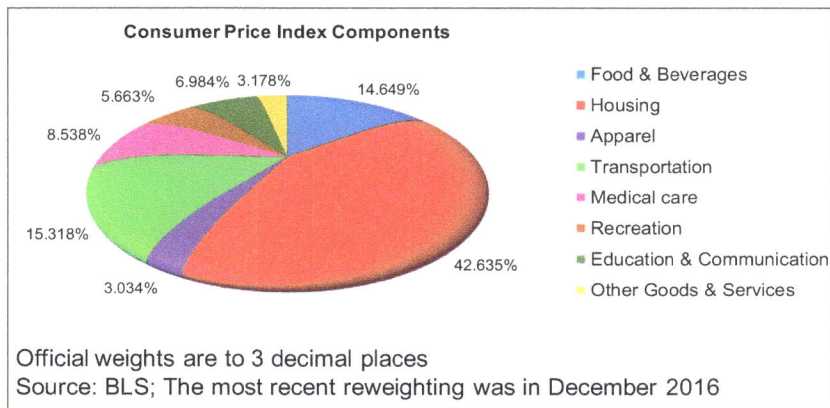

Consumer Price Index Components

6.984% 3.178% 14.649%
5.663%
8.538%
15.318%
3.034%
42.635%

- Food & Beverages
- Housing
- Apparel
- Transportation
- Medical care
- Recreation
- Education & Communication
- Other Goods & Services

Official weights are to 3 decimal places
Source: BLS; The most recent reweighting was in December 2016

Figure 64: Pie chart showing consumer price index components

Contaminant

Any harmful pollutant or material that could cause a deleterious effect on a living organism or biodiversity in general

Contaminated sites

Caution must be exercised when purchasing commercial property in view of the prospect of contamination. That old and improperly bunded petrol tank that is buried underground could bleed hazardous chemicals into the soil and ground water system nearby. If purchasing in the vicinity of recent mining operations, all supporting documents on rehabilitation should be sourced.

The New South Wales Environmental Protection Agency has a public domain that has contaminated site details available for public viewing. A recent incident published in the media concerned hazardous chemicals that had been leaching into the soil for many years. These hazardous chemicals included benzene and other carcinogens (petroleum hydrocarbons, lead and arsenic) and had travelled hundreds of metres under sporting fields, cemeteries and residential areas. (*see Appendix for more website references*) (See BTEX)

Table 27: Websites references to access an Environmental Protection Agency and similar bodies

State/ Territory	Weblink to access (contaminated site land record, contaminated sites notified to EPA....,)
New South Wales	http://www.epa.nsw.gov.au/prclmapp/searchregister.aspx http://www.epa.nsw.gov.au/clm/publiclist.htm
Victoria	http://www.epa.vic.gov.au/your-environment/land-and-groundwater/contaminated-site-management
Tasmania	http://epa.tas.gov.au/regulation/contaminated-sites
South Australia	http://www.epa.sa.gov.au/data_and_publications/site_contamination_index
Western Australia	https://www.der.wa.gov.au/your-environment/contaminated-sites
Northern Territory	https://ntepa.nt.gov.au/waste-pollution/contaminated-land

Contingency

This is an allowance for future events that are not entirely certain but could eventuate.

Corporation

Corporation is a common form of business organisation and is chartered by state or territory. Corporation is given legal rights as an entity separate from its owners and is characterised by limited liability of its owners. The legislations regulating corporations, and the securities and future industries in Australia, are administered by the Australian Securities and Investments Commission.

Counter offer

An offer given in response to the original offer. It implies rejection of the original offer and puts the onus back onto the original offeror who has three options: to (1) accept it, expressly (by replying) or by implication (by not replying), (2) issue another (counter-counter) offer, or (3) reject it expressly. No binding contract can be created until one party accepts the other's offer.

Covenant

A restriction on the legal title to property that either benefits or burdens the land. These restrictions or covenants are imposed by either state government, local government (local councils) and developers. These restrictions serve some of the same functions as Building Code of Australia and zoning standards. The following are some of the restrictions imposed on the land use: type of construction, type of building and materials used, and building dimensions.

There are two main types of covenants: positive and negative. Positive covenants expect the issuer to perform certain tasks and negative covenants forbid the issuer from undertaking certain activities. For commercial property:

Positive covenant	Negative covenant
• pay rent as per the lease agreements • insure the building or reimburse the landlord for the cost of insurance • maintain the premises internally and externally at specified intervals (like lawn mowing) • pay a service charge for services provided by the landlord (if there is more than one tenant)	• not to make alterations to the property • not to use the premises for any purposes other than that mentioned on the lease agreement • not to assign the leasehold interest without the permission of the landlord • not to display an advertisement without permission

Cover note
A note from an insurance cover giving temporary cover until a formal policy is issued.

Cul-de-sac
A street with only one way in and out. It is sometimes signposted as No Through Road. In Australia, it is sometime called a court.

Figure 65: **Realtime photo showing a cul-de-sac (no through road)**

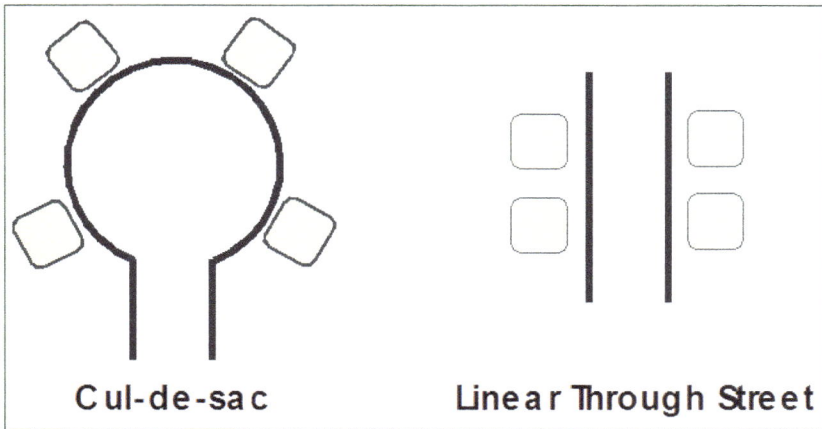

C ul-de-sa c **Line a r Through Stre e t**

Figure 66: **Schematics of cul-de-sac and linear street**

D

Deed
The legal document of title to a property. It is the document that transfers title to real property. (See *real property* and *personal property*).

Demographics
The characteristics of a population: for example, gender, marital status, education and age.

Direct labour
Money paid to employees that are directly involved in the process of creation of goods and provision of services.

Disclaimer
A formal statement denying responsibility. At the start of this book, the authors have inserted a disclaimer stating that they are not legally responsible if the reader misinterprets or misunderstands a topic.

Disclosure statement

A statement, mandatory by law, in which manufacturers or producers of a particular type of goods, including property, must reveal specific information to potential buyers.

Discount

Where the asking price is below the valuation of an asset.

Documentary evidence

Evidence, or proof, in the form of written or printed papers, including electronic copies.

Document management

The process of generation, distribution, storage and archiving of information.

Due Diligence (DD)

It is the process of compilation, appraisal and validation of information about a property or organisation or business, or a process required for assessing accuracy and integrity. It is a specific term that refers to the actions taken to ensure a project meets specific requirements to ensure there is a potential for profit before the purchase of the property goes unconditional.

Due diligence is also about taking all reasonable steps before purchase of a property to avoid committing a tort or offence. For commercial properties due diligence can be exercised after the contract is signed but not so for residential properties. In Queensland, a contract can be subject to due diligence.

E

Economic growth

A significant increase in the total production of goods and services in an economy over a period of time. It can be measured by comparing Gross Domestic Product (GDP) figures over different years.

Economic risk

This is the risk that conditions such as exchange rates, government regulation or political upheaval might affect an investment in a given country.

Electronic signature

A method of confirming identity through the internet for the purpose of 'signing' documents. It is a verification of the sender's intention to sign the document as compared with conventional signing using a pen on a hard copy. (*See appendix 1 for sign now mobile application*)

Emergency home assist

A fee-for-repair service for a person's home (principal place or rental properties) when an emergency occurs. Normally there are limitations on calls every year based on the plan chosen with the insurance provider. The emergency events included varies between insurance providers and may be a blocked toilet, pipe, drain, burst pipe, gas leak, hot water system failure, cooling system failure, gas or electric heating failure, or access into the property.

Encapsulation

The process of containment of hazardous materials usually by covering them. Asbestos may be encapsulated using a type of spray paint. (See Asbestos (*friable and non-friable*)

Enterprise Bargaining Agreement (EBA)

An enterprise bargaining agreement is a collective industrial agreement between both an employer and a trade union acting on behalf of employees, or an employer and employees acting for themselves.

Environmental Impact Statement (EIS)

A process which analyses the potential effects of a project, or a development, on the surrounding environment.

Environmental Impact Study

An investigation designed to assess the comprehensive and long range environmental effects of a proposed project.

Environment protection

The protection of the environment is mostly under the control of state governments and territories. Each government writes and then passes environmental legislation so that it becomes law. The Commonwealth Government can pass laws if the matter is of national environmental significance or if it is a commonwealth responsibility.

Erosion

The gradual wearing away of land through the action of wind and water.

Errors and omissions coverage

Coverage of negligent acts, including errors and omissions, in a contract by professional liability insurance.

et al

An abbreviation of the Latin *et alii*. It literally means "and others"

Executed contract or agreement

This refers to a contract or an agreement where the terms have been completely fulfilled.

Excess

The money that a customer must pay on an insurance premium claim. Example: If John has a building insurance with an excess of $1000, then any repair or claim less than $1,000 must be paid by John. His insurance company would financially contribute only if the repair or replacement cost goes above $1000. (Read our book entitled *"It's My Time: Setting Financial and Personal Goals"* for more details on how to save money by selecting a product appropriate to your needs).

Exclusive dealing
This is when a person trading with another imposes some restrictions on the other's freedom to choose with whom, in what, or where, they deal. (See the *Australian Competition and Consumer Commission (ACCC) website* for more details).

Exports
Any commodities that generate foreign currency through an overseas sale. The top ten exports are shown in the table. (See *"It's My Time: Successful Residential Investing"* and *"It's My Time: Setting Financial and Personal Goals"* on the impact of exports on the Australian economy and property industries).

Table 28: **Table listing the top 10 exports of Australia (as per 2016 data)**

Commodity	AUD (Billion dollars)
Iron ores & concentrates	66
Coal	38
Natural gas	17
Education (international student tuition fees and living expenses)	17
Personal travel (excluding education)	14
Gold	13
Crude petroleum	10
Beef	7
Aluminium ores including alumina	6
Wheat	5.9

F

False or misleading statements
Statements representing goods or services that are false, inaccurate and not able to be substantiated.

First Tuesday of a month
In Australia, the Reserve Bank plays a key role in determining interest rates and holds its regular meeting on the first Tuesday

of the month. If there is to be a change in official interest rates, it is likely that the Reserve Bank will announce the change on the day after its monthly meeting.

Flooding
Water that rises above normal level from a water source or water body (river, creek, stream).

Foreign purchaser
A foreign purchaser is someone who is neither a citizen, nor a permanent resident of Australia, nor a New Zealand citizen with a special category Visa (subclass 444)

G

Gentrification
Gentrification is a process of social mobility and renovation of deteriorated urban neighbourhoods through the influx of more affluent residents.

Going concern
A business that is in good working order and one whereby transfer of ownership would not affect or interrupt the business.

Goods
Items that are purchased, bought, sold or traded. (See GST)

Greywater
Relatively clean wastewater produced from baths, sinks, washing and kitchen appliances. Greywater is domestic wastewater with the exception of sewage.

Gross Domestic Product (GDP)
Gross Domestic Product is calculated from personal consumption expenditures plus business investment plus government spending plus exports minus imports.

Gross Realisation Value

This refers to the end value of a project.

Guarantee

A promise or an assurance especially given in writing. Guarantee attests to the quality or durability of goods or services. Consumer guarantees apply regardless of any warranty and may continue to apply after the warranty period has expired. (See *Australian Competition and Consumer Commission* website and *Warranty* for more details).

H

Heads of Agreement

A list of agreed conditions between vendor and purchaser which is then taken to a solicitor to turn into a legal contract.

Heritage overlay

Heritage overlay is part of a planning scheme and is used to protect sites that have heritage value. It covers individual buildings but may also apply to whole areas. Any work proposed on a building affected by a heritage overlay must be the subject of a planning permit. A heritage overlay is usually denoted as HO on the zoning map.

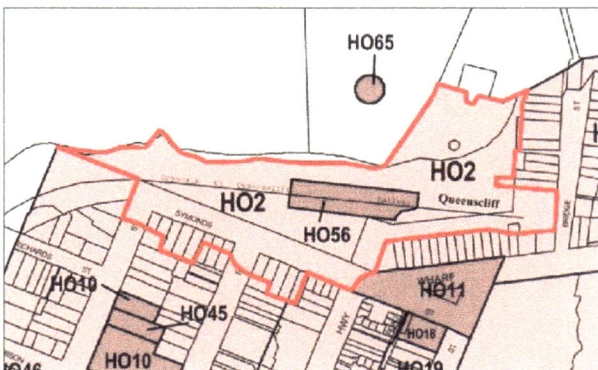

Figure 67: **Schematic showing a heritage overlay on a landscape**

Heritage sites
There are around 1052 world heritage sites of cultural or physical significance. In Australia, there are 19 world heritage sites including the Great Barrier Reef, the Greater Blue Mountains and the Sydney Opera house.

Housing Expenses ratio
The portion of gross income needed to pay housing expenses.

House Price Income ratio
The number of times average income needs to be multiplied to buy the average house.

I

Import
An import refers to goods or services brought into a country from abroad for sale. The top imports to Australia are shown in the table below:

Table 29: Table listing the top 10 imports to Australia (2016 data)

Commodity	AUD (Billion dollars)
Personal travel (exc. education) services	24.60
Crude petroleum	20.05
Refined petroleum	18.58
Passenger motor vehicles	17.56
Telecom equipment & parts	9.85
Freight transport services	9.69
Medicaments (including veterinary)	7.50
Computers	7.31
Passenger transport services	6.14
Goods vehicles	6.01

Indemnity
Indemnity is a legal agreement to compensate a person for a loss. The person is indemnified (See *insurance for types of insurance*).

Industries

The top performing industries in Australia are:

- Finance
- Business Consulting
- Metals and Mining
- Energy and Utilities
- Industrial and Materials
- Healthcare and Pharmaceutical

Australian industry can be broken down into five sectors:

Type	Process	Examples
Primary	Converts natural resources into primary products	Agriculture, fisheries, forestry and mining
Secondary	Changing raw materials produced in the primary industries into usable goods and products	Manufacturing of goods (timber into roof trusses)
Tertiary	Provision of services	Banking, transport, retail
Quaternary	Knowledge sector	Education, information technology, research and innovation
Quinary	Research	Medical and health related research, high level management

Industrial revolution

Industrial revolution is a shift in paradigm in the way the manufacturing process improves. The improvements in process are slowly replacing the number of people involved. The first industrial revolution was notably marked by the invention of the Spinning Gin machine. The second industrial revolution was mechanisation, the assembly line, followed by the invention of electricity. The third industrial revolution was computerisation and automation. The fourth industrial revolution is current and also imminent in the areas of cyber-physical systems. Some of these technology advancements are changing the way the real estate industry operates (See *Luddite fallacy*).

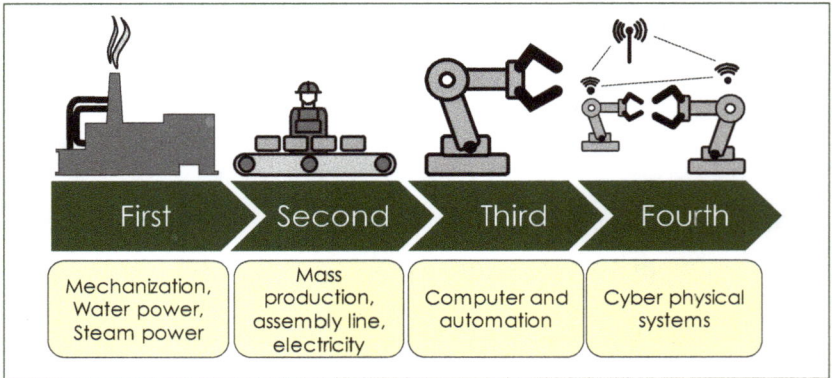

Figure 68: **Image showing various the four industrial revolutions**

Inflation

Inflation is an increase in the price of goods and services over time and fall in the purchasing value of the money. For those on a fixed income it means that there is less money available for non-essentials.

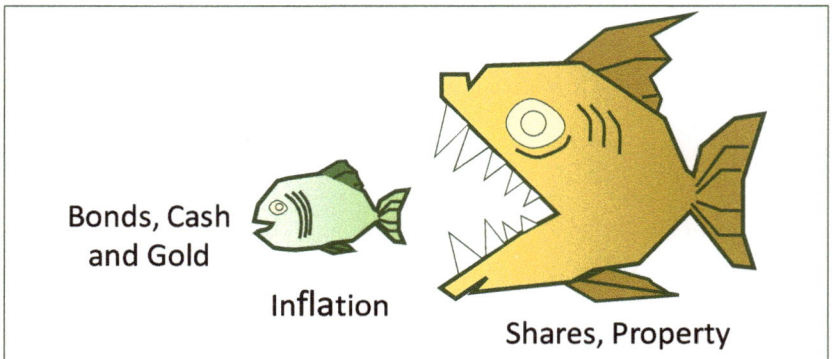

Figure 69: **Correlation among bonds, cash, gold, inflation and other types investments including shares and property**

Infringement notice

This is a way of dealing with common breaches of the law where the impacts are not considered serious enough to warrant prosecution.

Insurance

It mitigates risks that can be anticipated and quantified as potentially or possibly likely to happen or occur. There are many types of insurances: building insurance, landlord insurance, contents insurance (as landlord), contents insurance (as tenant or homeowners), building insurance (during construction), special occupants and class of buildings, public and products liability insurance, life and disability insurance, professional indemnity insurance, landlord insurance – replacement policy, landlord insurance – indemnity policy, fidelity guarantee, motor insurance, boat, caravan or trailer, on-site caravan, veteran, vintage and classic vehicle insurance and so on. (Read our book entitled *"It's My Time: Setting Financial and Personal Goals"* for more details on insurance and how a lack, or absence, of insurance could lead to financial hardship in unforeseen incidents such as death, accident, fire, theft, or bankruptcy).

SCHEDULE OF INSURANCE		
Professional Indemnity		
Limits of Indemnity:		
Any One Claim:	$	5,000,000
In the Aggregate - Combined for the Group	$	10,000,000
Excess: $1,000		
Public & Products Liability		
Limits of Liability:		
Public Liability		
Any one Occurrence	$	20,000,000
Products Liability		
Any One Occurrence and in the Aggregate during the period of Insurance	$	20,000,000
Goods in Care. Custody & Control	$	50,000

Figure 70: Schedule of insurance (professional indemnity, public and products liability insurance)

Insurance policy

A contract between an insurance company and its customers that describes the details of policy cover, value of an insured product, excesses, products, services, a payment schedule, and how to make a claim.

J

Job safety analysis

Job safety analysis is a type of risk assessment. This details, step by step, how a task is to be carried out safely, as opposed to many risk assessments which only consider static conditions such as a machine or chemical storage.

Joint Venture (JV)

A commercial enterprise undertaken jointly by two or more parties which otherwise retain their distinct identities.

L

Land in Australia

Australia has six states and two territories and each of these has a central register of ownership. Of the total land of Australia (7.69 million km^2), the three main categories are: private, public and Aboriginal and Torres Strait Islanders (see table below). Public land (owned by the government) is commonly called Crown land. The different categories are: agricultural, commercial, farming, forest, industrial, manufacturing, natural reserves, residential and water bodies (lakes, rivers, streams).

Table 30: Table listing landownerships

Land ownership	Owners
Public land	23 %
Private land	63 %
Aboriginal and Torres Strait Islander	14 %

L

Laws
These are rules that help maintain stability in a society. A law passed by a government is usually in the form of an Act of Parliament. They are the legal version of 'the rules'.

Law society
The local lawyers' society may offer assistance in locating solicitors and barristers.

Leading indicators
Statistics used to predict economic trends.

Legal entity
An organisation or individual legally permitted to enter into a contract.

Lifetime warranty
Life time warranty means a warranty for:

- the lifetime of the product,
- the owner's lifetime,
- the time he/she owns that product.

In real estate, termite protection usually comes with a lifetime warranty but also with a special condition attached. For this long-term warranty to apply throughout the period, the company must inspect the property every year (for a fee). If an inspection is missed, the lifetime warranty becomes void.

Limited warranty
This means the warranty is limited to some specified parts, or type of defects, or certain conditions.

Liquidation
This is a process where insolvent companies and funds are being wound up, with assets being sold and, as far as possible, liabilities settled.

Local government (or council)

There are over 547 local governments (councils or shires) in Australia. They are responsible for the provision and maintenance of local infrastructure and for the collection of funds (rates) to fund it.

M

Machinery breakdown

A machinery breakdown insurance policy can protect a business owner from financial loss when machines break down or are accidentally damaged.

Main street

This is a term that refers to individual investors, small business, employees and the overall economy.

Mean

Another term for average (but not to be confused with median).

Median

The middle value as opposed to the average value or mode value.

Memorandum of Understanding (MOU)

Also called gentlemen's agreement, it is a non-legally binding agreement that sets out the proposed terms at the negotiation stage.

Meridian

A longitudinal reference line that traverses the earth in a north-south direction through both poles. In the past 22 years the entire continent of Australia has moved 1.5 metres to the North. To maintain accuracy with the GPS system the government has updated the continents latitude and longitude bearings.

Mining industry

The mining industry is part of a large commodity chain of fundamental forces: population, urbanisation, and income growth. The Australian mining and mineral industry, a critical part of the Australian economy, produces a wide range of commodities including bauxite, coal, copper, diamond, gold, iron ore, rutile, unrefined lead, unrefined zinc, uranium, unrefined nickel, and zircon.

Minority interest

This is the equity in a partly owned subsidiary that is not held by the parent company or its subsidiary companies.

N

Net

In financial terms, net is the total after subtracting any deductions. A person's net income is what an employer pays after deducting tax and any other negotiated amounts such as salary sacrifices and union fees.

Net current assets

This refers to the net assets of a company minus any liabilities due within a year. Also known as working capital.

Net metering

Net metering refers to a billing system where the owner of a solar energy system get credits for providing surplus power to the grid. (See back to grid).

No fault indemnity

This means that, if a claim arises, it is not necessary to prove negligence on the part of a third party. Just to show that the policy holder has suffered a loss is enough to activate (trigger) a claim.

No liability company

This is a public company whose shareholders are not liable for the debts of the company.

Nominee

A person or company acting on behalf of another.

Notice of default

A formal notice to a borrower that they have defaulted and may face legal action.

Null and void

Something that cannot be legally enforced.

O

Operating profit, operating loss

This refers to the profit/loss for the relevant period resulting from the operations of a company.

Organisation

A company is an organisation but the latter may be defined as a collection of people with a common goal. As such, an organisation is not just a company.

Overland flow

The movement of water over the land after rainfall before it enters a water body or after it leaves a water body as floodwater. Measurement of overland flow is very critical so that habitable areas (residential or commercial) are not constructed in an area where concentrated overland flow occurs (usually low points and gullies). (See *Contour map and Flooding*. Read our book entitled *"It's My Time: Successful Residential Investing"* regarding the relationship between stormwater pipes, gullies and contour map reading).

P

Partnership

In a business sense, this is a group of like-minded people who put their money, time and other resources together towards an investment, or business, that generates income. Similar to a joint venture, a carefully planned agreement is necessary for success: details of outcomes of the project, decision making stages, the role of each partner involved, the type of structure involved, payment of bills, managing finance, workflow method, mode of communication, dispute resolution, exit strategy. (See also *joint tenants, tenancy in common, non-disclosure agreement, information memorandum, joint venture* for more details).

Pawnbrokers

Provide secured loans to people who put up an asset (usually movable assets like jewellery, car, and electronics) as collateral on the debt.

Pension

A regular payment made by the Australian government to its people after their official retirement age and to people with special needs. Payments to pensioners is a liability to the government balance sheet and, as the pensioners' population increases, the government liability also increases (due to a shortfall between tax income and pension payouts). Read our book entitled *"It's My Time: Strategies in Action"* on the positive effect of migration on Australian economy and ways to offset the ageing population.

Pension funds

These are part of a retirement plan provided by an employer for the benefit of employees after retirement. In Australia, the term also refers to that part of a superannuation scheme from which earlier deposits are withdrawn after retirement for subsistence.

Photovoltaic

Photovoltaics is a method of generating electricity from solar cells. A PV sticker on the power meter door indicates that solar photovoltaic panels are on the roof.

Power grid

The network of cables that carry electricity.

PPP

Public private partnership is an arrangement where public sector enters into an agreement with a private sector to create an asset and or service for public benefit such as school, hospital, road, bridge. CityLink in Melbourne is an example of a public private partnership model. Transurban City Link Limited works under this model for CityLink roads in Melbourne. Transurban build - own-operate-transfer (BOOT), levy tolls and maintain the system from 1995 to June 2034, after which CityLink will be transferred to the State Government (Victoria).

Preservation age

This is the age at which superannuation funds can be withdrawn and depends upon the year in which a person is born.

Premium

The amount of money that is charged to a customer by an insurance company to provide the cover stated in the insurance policy.

Pro-rata

A proportion or part of the whole amount, calculated as a ratio, is commonly used in the adjustments at settlement where council rates and taxes are calculated on a pro-rata basis.

Proxy

This is a person that represents another person. For example, it might be a written authorisation given by a shareholder for

someone else, usually the company's management, to cast his/
her vote at a shareholder meeting.

Public trustee

Public trustee was established by state/territory governments to
provide professional, affordable and accessible trustee services
to their respective communities and in some cases to their
governments. *Public trustee Australia* expects that everyone
in the community has access to affordable estate and trust
administration services.

R

Realise

To sell an asset.

Recession

A downswing becomes a recession when the economy's Gross
National Product (GDP) declines for at least two consecutive
quarters.

Regulations

These are guidelines that dictate how the legal provisions of
the act should be applied. Examples of some regulations are
Occupational Health and Safety Regulations 2007, garbage
regulations, noise pollution regulations, building regulations, fire
brigade and health regulations.

Replacement cost

Often associated with insurance policies, it is the cost required to
build an equivalent dwelling in today's dollars.

Restrictive trade practices

Also called an anti-trust practice. This is aimed at deterring practices
by companies that are anti-competitive in that they restrict

free competition. (See *Australian Competition and Consumer Commission* for more details).

Revenue

This is also referred to as turnover and is a measure of how much product or service a company is able to sell. Profits are calculated as a percentage of revenue after all expenses have been deducted.

Risk assessment

Risk assessment ensures the ongoing safety of the public that will access a facility once it has been constructed. It is a process of assessing the risks, identifying hazards and placing suitable controls before an operation starts. (See *job safety analysis*).

S

Scam

A fraudulent scheme performed by a dishonest individual, group, or company in an attempt obtain money or something else of value. Scams traditionally resided in confidence tricks, where an individual would misrepresent themselves as someone with skill or authority that is a doctor, lawyer, or investor. After the internet became widely used, new forms of scams emerged such as lottery scams, scam baiting, email spoofing, phishing, or request for help. In terms of property, scams can be associated with investment seminars, rent-to-buy house purchases, selling house and land packages, selling off the plan apartments and providing rental guarantees. Each of these are legal in their own right; it is the people behind some of these that make it a scam.

An example could be in regards to a rental guarantee provided as an inducement to purchase an apartment. The developer or selling agent may offer a twelve month guarantee of $500 per week rent but the developer has normally built this guarantee into the sale price of the property. Some rental guarantees finish when a tenant is found regardless of what rent the tenant is willing to pay. If the property is a high rise apartment block, and in an area where there are a number of other apartment blocks being built around the same time, then it may be very difficult to find a tenant after the rental guarantee has finished. At the end of a twelve month period, if the owner has not found a tenant then he/she will have an apartment with no rental income to meet loan repayments and possibly a poor prospect of finding a tenant unless the asking rental is lowered dramatically to compete with possibly hundreds of other investors or speculators also seeking tenants.

Seasonally adjusted
A term for statistics adjusted for seasonal differences such as the varying number of working days in a quarter.

Sensitivity analysis
An analysis of the relationship between input and output variables in a system or a model. It is a method of using historical data to predict the future impact of current decisions.

Settling dispute
If one party breaches a contract unilaterally then they would be liable to the other party for any loss caused by the breach. Settlement of the breach can be potentially resolved in 3 ways:

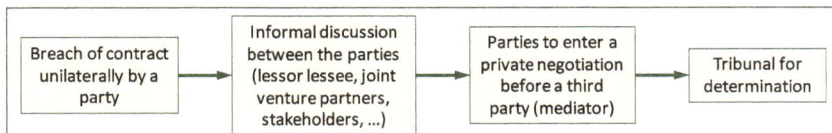

Figure 71: **Steps involved in dispute resolution**

Silk Road (One Belt One Road)
China is looking to expand infrastructure and service-based projects outside its borders under the name called One Belt One Road. This megaproject deals with 65 countries throughout Eurasia

and Africa to construct ports, power stations, rail lines, roads and all the tunnels and bridges needed to connect them back to mainland China. This project is tagged at a price of over 1 trillion dollars due to its size and scope. Further details about Australia's major export partner, China, can be found in our book entitled *"It's My Time: Setting Financial and Personal Goals"*.

Six Sigma
A standard that focuses on ways to improve business processes by greatly reducing the probability that an error or defect will occur. For a company to achieve Six Sigma, it cannot produce more than 3.4 defects per million opportunities. For example, if McDonald's makes one million burgers, and have made only 3 defective burgers in a particular time frame, then that particular store, or chain of stores, can claim to have reached Six Sigma standard.

Social capital
Social capital can be measured by the level of trust and reciprocity in a community, or between the individuals. It is a proven fact that people with greater social capital close more deals, are better respected and get higher ranking positions in the business and community as a whole.

Social network
Social network is a web and mobile application that enable users to communicate with each other by posting information, sharing information, sending messages, images, etc. It is a network of social interactions and personal relationships. (See *mobile application*)

Service level agreement
This is a statement of intentions existing between the service provider and the customer (recipient of service) which sets out a specified level of service. (A template of service level agreement is in our book titled *"It's My Time: Introducing Commercial Investing"*).

Smart devices

Smart device (radio frequency identification) tags are prevalent in many sectors of property and allied industries including smart meters for electricity and water usage.

Smart meters

A smart meter is a digital meter located at a property that measures the amount of electricity used in real time. It enables two-way communication between the meter and the electricity provider.

Stagflation or moderation

This is when economic growth stagnates but inflation rises along with unemployment. It is an uncommon situation because inflation does not normally occur when the economy is weak. It is also associated with a decline in the Gross Domestic Product (GDP). A classic example of this occurred in Zimbabwe in 2004 when the government printed too much money and stagflation turned into hyperinflation.

Strict liability

The legal liability for an act or omission.

Surveyor's report

This is a report required to determine the value of a property and suitability for numerous purposes. It may be for the purpose of land purchase, building certificates, development applications, subdivision, or monitoring of movement.

Sovereign debt

This is a total debt owned by a government - also called public or national debt. Australia's net government debt as a percentage is the amount owned by the Australian Federal Government. As of April 2017, the gross Australian Government debt was $551.75 billion. Australia's net government debt as a percentage of GDP is lower than most developed countries. Australia's bond credit rating was rated AAA by all three major credit rating agencies as of May 2017 (See *Credit rating*).

T

The great Australian dream

The Great Australian dream is a strong belief that "owning a detached house on a fenced block of land" can lead to a better life. The dream became reality during the Post-World War II era mainly due to the expansion of Australian manufacturing, low unemployment rates, baby boomers and removal of rent controls.

Table 31: **Table showing the percentage of howeownership in Australia**

Year	Percentage of home ownership in Australia
1947	53 %
1954	63 %
1961	70 %
2011	67 %

Two-Factor Authentication (2FA)

Two factor authentication is an added layer of online protection and involves entering a system-generated random passcode (sent to you via an SMS or phone call) when logging into an online account or making a transaction. (See *blockchain, cryptocurrency*)

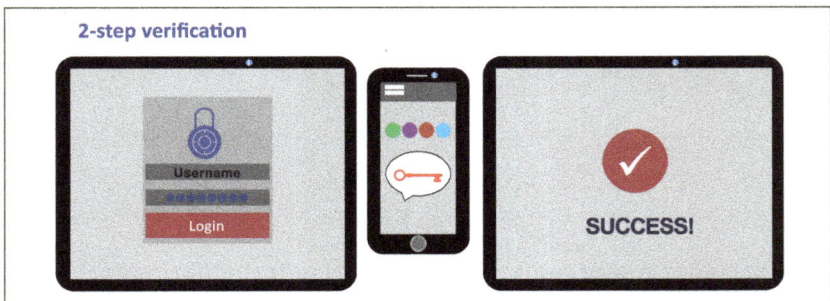

Figure 72: **The working principle of a two step verification process**

Tasman line

This is an imaginary line that divides Australia geologically. The right side of the Tasman line constitutes roughly the easternmost quarter of Australia (includes the Lachlan, New England and Kanmantoo fold belts). Read our book entitled *"It's My Time: Setting Financial and Personal Goals"* for details on the Australian population in 2050, how it is aligned towards the left and right-hand side of the Tasman line, and what the driving forces behind the future economy are.

Timeline

A line that marks time and the order in which important events happened.

V

Void

This means to have no legal standing. For example, if a drunk driver had an accident and tried to claim on his insurance policy, his claim would be void (See *terms and conditions*).

W

Warranty

This is a voluntary promise (either written or implied) offered by the person or business who sold goods, product or a service to a customer. Property is considered as a product or good and hence the warranty promised by the supplier (builder, developer) becomes a right that can be enforced under Australian Consumer Law. Structural and non-structural warranty periods differ from builder to builder. (See *Guarantee*)

Water restrictions

Applicable to customers on a piped water (reticulated) supply. The level of water restrictions is different in each state and territory but they generally do not apply to the use of recycled, reclaimed, rain or grey water. Restrictions are based on the location and include watering lawns, washing vehicles, refilling swimming pools and using sprinkler systems in gardens.

Water treatment plant
A plant where wastewater from residential and commercial properties is sent for further treatment before it is discharged into the ocean or nearby tailings dams

White elephant
A property that is too expensive to maintain and generates too little rent to pay for the outgoings (heavily negatively geared). Ownership of such a property is normally the result of lack of due diligence and proper market analysis.

Will
Also called testament, it is a document that serves as a sign or evidence of the disposition of one's property that take effect after one's death. (See *Testator*)

Workers compensation insurance
This insurance covers an owner against claims by tradespeople and others injured while working on the property.

Appendices

Appendix I: Useful websites

A to Z of Government Services

www.australia.gov.au/information-and-services/a-z-of-government-services

www.australia.gov.au

Australian Building and Construction Commission:

www.abcc.gov.au

Australian Bureau of Statistics:

www.abs.gov.au

Australian Competition and Consumer Commission:

www.accc.gov.au

Australian Institute of Criminology (Property Crime: Arson, Burglary, Drug use, Property Crime, Graffiti and Vandalism, Vehicle Theft)

www.aic.gov.au

Australian Investment Research Services:

www.airs.com.au

Banking and Financial Services ombudsman:

www.fos.org.au

Banks (Australian big four):

www.commbank.com.au

www.anz.com.au

www.nab.com.au

www.westpac.com.au

Banks in Australia other than the Big Four:

www.suncorpgroup.com.au

www.amp.com.au

www.australianmilitarybank.com.au

www.asl.com.au

www.auswidebank.com.au

www.bankofmelbourne.com.au

www.boq.com.au

www.banksa.com.au

www.bankwest.com.au

www.bankvic.com.au

www.beyondbank.com.au

www.greater.com.au

www.heritage.com.au

www.humebank.com.au

www.imb.com.au

www.bankaust.com.au/personal

www.gcmutualbank.com.au

www.macquarie.com/au/personal

www.mebank.com.au

www.pnbank.com.au

www.policebank.com.au

www.qudosbank.com.au

www.racq.com.au/banking_

www.stgeorge.com.au

www.suncorpgroup.com.au

www.tyro.com

www.ubank.com.au

www.tmbank.com.au

www.bendigobank.com.au/public

Builder licencing authorities:

www.fairtrading.nsw.gov.au

 www.planning.act.gov.au

www.bpb.nt.gov.au

www.qbcc.qld.gov.au

www.sa.gov.au/topics/business-and-trade/licensing/
construction/building-work-contractor-s-licence

www.justice.tas.gov.au/licensing_and_accreditation/builder

www.commerce.wa.gov.au/building-commission

www.vba.vic.gov.au

Commonwealth Ombudsman:

www.ombudsman.gov.au

Company information:

www.afr.com.au

www.asx.com.au

Consulting professionals:

www.consultaustralia.com.au

Consumer protection websites:

www.australia.gov.au/information-and-services/public-safety-and-law/consumer-protection

www.accc.gov.au/consumers/consumer-protection

www.consumer.vic.gov.au

www.consumer.tas.gov.au

www.fairtrading.nsw.gov.au/ftw/Consumers.page

www.accesscanberra.act.gov.au/app/answers/detail/a_id/2269

www.consumeraffairs.nt.gov.au/Pages/default.aspx

www.qld.gov.au/law/fair-trading

www.cbs.sa.gov.au

www.commerce.wa.gov.au/consumer-protection

Consumer rights:

www.consumer.gov.au

www.scamwatch.gov.au

www.fido.asic.gov.au

www.asic.gov.au

Conveyancers:

www.aicnational.com.au

Crime statistics by suburbs:

www.crimestatistics.vic.gov.au/

www.bocsar.nsw.gov.au/Pages/bocsar_crime_stats/bocsar_crime_stats.aspx

www.police.tas.gov.au/about-us/corporate-documents/crime-statistics-supplement/

www.policenews.act.gov.au/crime-statistics-and-data/crime-statistics

www.police.sa.gov.au/about-us/crime-statistics-map

https://data.police.qld.gov.au/CrimeStatsMobile/#/map

www.pfes.nt.gov.au/Police/Community-safety/Northern-Territory-crime-statistics.aspx

www.police.wa.gov.au/Crime/Crime-Statistics-Portal/Statistics

Credit records:

www.mycreditfile.com.au

www.dnb.com.au

www.tascol.com.au

www.equifax.com.au

Credit reporting agencies:

www.mycreditfile.com.au

www.dnb.com.au

www.getcreditscore.com.au

www.foxsymes.com.au

www.freecreditreport.com.au/

www.moneyhelp.org.au/tools-tips/credit-ratings/

www.checkyourcredit.com.au/

www.canstar.com.au/credit-cards/how-do-you-check-your-credit-rating

www.creditsmart.org.au/getting-free-credit-report

www.cvcheck.com/credit-financial-business/australia/australia-credit-history

www.checkmyfile.com.au

www.finder.com.au/credit-check/free-credit-report

www.creditsimple.com.au

www.creditcounsellorsaustralia.com.au

www.getcreditscore.com.au

www.experian.com.au

Cyber Safety:

www.esafety.gov.au

www.acorn.gov.au

www.staysmartonline.gov.au

www.thinkuknow.org.au

Delisted companies:

www.delisted.com.au

Design and drawing web applications:

www.magic-plan.com/magicplan/

www.sketchup.com

www.paintmyplace.mobi

Discount sites:

www.entertainmentbook.com.au

www.lastminute.com.au

Education:

www.iloverealestate.tv

www.jimrohn.com

www.propertydevelopersuccess.com.au

www.knowledgesource.com.au

Electronic signature web application:

www.signnow.com

Electronic recycling:

www.abs.gov.au

www.tradingeconomics.com/australia/employment-rate

Emergency services:

www.esa.act.gov.au/actses/

www.ses.nsw.gov.au

www.pfes.nt.gov.au/Emergency-Service.aspx

www.ses.qld.gov.au/Pages/default.aspx

www.ses.sa.gov.au/site/home.jsp

www.ses.tas.gov.au

www.ses.vic.gov.au

www.dfes.wa.gov.au/aboutus/operationalinformation/Pages/stateemergencyservice.aspx

www.emergency.wa.gov.au

Employment statistics Australia:

www.abs.gov.au/Employment-and-Unemployment

Employment sites:

www.adzuna.com.au

www.mycareer.com.au

www.seek.com.au

Environment Protection Agency:

www.epa.tas.gov.au

www.ehp.qld.gov.au

www.ntepa.nt.gov.au

www.epa.wa.gov.au

www.epa.vic.gov.au

www.epa.nsw.gov.au

www.epa.sa.gov.au

www.environment.gov.au

Fair trading, consumer affairs:

www.ors.act.gov.au

www.fairtrading.nsw.gov.au

www.consumeraffairs.nt.gov.au

www.fairtrading.qld.gov.au

www.cbs.sa.gov.au

www.consumer.tas.gov.au

www.vic.gov.au

www.commerce.wa.gov.au

Financial counselling:

www.fido.asic.gov.au

Financial Planning Association:

www.fpa.com.au

Financial product comparisons:

www.infochoice.com.au

Finding a suitable product online:

www.finder.com.au

www.iselect.com.au

Fire authorities:

http://www.mfb.vic.gov.au/

https://www.afac.com.au/

http://www.fpaa.com.au

https://www.qfes.qld.gov.au/Pages/default.aspx

http://www.pfes.nt.gov.au/Fire-and-Rescue.aspx

https://www.emergency.wa.gov.au

https://www.fire.tas.gov.au

https://www.dfes.wa.gov.au/newsandmedia/Pages/
NewsHome.aspx

https://www.cfs.sa.gov.au/site/home.jsp

http://www.cfa.vic.gov.au

https://www.fire.nsw.gov.au

http://www.mfs.sa.gov.au/site/home.jsp

Foreign financial institutions:

www.arabbank.com

www.banksyd.com.au

www.boc.cn

www.citibank.com.au

www.db.com

www.hsbc.com.au

www.ingdirect.com.au

www.investec.com.au

www.rabobank.com/en/home/index.html

Graffiti:

http://kab.org.au/graffiti/

www.crimeprevention.vic.gov.au/resources/graffiti-in-victoria

www.crimeprevention.nsw.gov.au/Pages/cpd/
protectcommunity/graffitivandalism/graffitivandalism.aspx

www.police.tas.gov.au/services-online/pamphlets-publications/
graffiti-aerosol-paint-laws/

Heritage listing / Heritage Commission:

http://www.environment.gov.au/heritage

https://www.heritage.vic.gov.au/about-heritage-in-victoria/
heritage-in-victoria

http://www.environment.nsw.gov.au/topics/heritage

http://heritage.tas.gov.au

https://www.qld.gov.au/environment/land/heritage/register

https://dtc.nt.gov.au/nt-heritage-council

https://www.environment.sa.gov.au/our-places/heritage/sa-
heritage-register

http://www.stateheritage.wa.gov.au

Housing Industry Association:

www.hia.com.au

Income tax and GST:

www.ato.gov.au

Inflation:

www.rba.gov.au/calculator/

www.rba.gov.au/calculator/annualPreDecimal.html

Institute of Architects:

www.architecture.com.au

Insurance:

www.insurancewatch.com.au

www.choosewell.com.au

www.apra.gov.au

Insurance calculators:

www.canstar.com.au/calculators/life-insurance

www.iselect.com.au/life/calculators

Keep Australia Beautiful:

http://kab.org.au/

www.kabc.wa.gov.au

http://knswb.org.au

www.keepqueenslandbeautiful.org.au

www.kvb.org.au

kesab.asn.au

www.kabtas.com

http://kabcnt.org.au

Land Titles Office (national, state and territories):

www.propertyandlandtitles.vic.gov.au

www.landgate.wa.gov.au/titles-and-surveys

www.dpipwe.tas.gov.au/land-tasmania/land-titles-office

www.sa.gov.au/topics/planning-and-property/land-services

www.dnrm.qld.gov.au/land/titles-valuations/titles-professionals

www.nt.gov.au/law/processes/power-of-attorney/land-titles-office-contacts

www.lpi.nsw.gov.au/land_titles

www.accesscanberra.act.gov.au/app/answers/detail/a_id/2108/kw/2108

Land title offices in states and territories:

www.landata.vic.gov.au

www.lpi.nsw.gov.au

www.nt.gov.au/property/land/contact-a-land-titles-office

www.dnrm.qld.gov.au/land/titles-valuations

www.sa.gov.au/topics/planning-and-property/certificates-of-title

www.dpipwe.tas.gov.au/land-tasmania/land-titles-office

www.accesscanberra.act.gov.au/app/answers/detail/a_id/2108/kw/title

www.landgate.wa.gov.au

Lawyers and solicitors:

www.lawsociety.com.au/community/findingalawyer/australianlegalpractitioners/index.htm

Lender's mortgage:

www.yourmortgage.com.au/calculators/mortgage_insurance

Master Builders Australia:

www.masterbuilders.com.au/Home

www.mbav.com.au/MbavLeadin.aspx

www.mbansw.asn.au

www.mbasa.com.au

www.mba.org.au/home

www.mbawa.com

www.mbasa.com.au

www.mbatas.org.au

Mortgage calculators:

www.yourmortgage.com.au/calculators

www.moneysmart.gov.au/tools-and-resources/calculators-and-apps/mortgage-calculator

Mortgage calculators of big four banks:

www.anz.com.au/personal/home-loans/calculators-tools/calculate-repayments

www.nab.com.au/personal/loans/home-loans/home-loan-calculators

www.westpac.com.au/personal-banking/home-loans/calculator/mortgage-repayment

www.commbank.com.au/digital/home-buying/calculator/home-loan-repayments

Mortgage providers and brokers:

www.finder.com.au/mortgage-brokers

www.ratecity.com.au/home-loans/compare-mortgage-brokers

www.mortgagechoice.com.au

www.choice.com.au/money/property/buying/articles/mortgage-brokers

www.iselect.com.au/home-loans/mortgage-broker

www.aussie.com.au/mortgage-broker1.htm

www.yourmortgage.com.au/brokers

www.smartline.com.au/home-loans/our-lenders

www.rams.com.au

Neighbourhood difficulties:

www.legalaid.wa.gov.au/InformationAboutTheLaw/Homes/neighbours/Pages/NeighboursCommonProblems.aspx

www.legalaid.vic.gov.au/find-legal-answers/disputes-with-neighbours

www.tas.relationships.org.au/services/family-dispute-resolution-mediation

www.act.gov.au/browse/topics/land-building-and-housing/property-disputes-and-issues

www.localcourt.justice.nsw.gov.au/Pages/legal_problem/neighbours_housing/neighbours_housing.aspx

www.legalaid.tas.gov.au/factsheets/neighbourhood-issues-fact-sheet/

www.sa.gov.au/topics/housing/resolving-problems-and-disputes/disruptive-and-noisy-neighbours/report-disruptive-neighbours

https://nt.gov.au/law/processes/resolving-disputes-without-going-to-court

Online comparison of interest rates offered by various banks in Australia:

www.mozo.com.au/interest-rates

www.canstar.com.au

www.infochoice.com.au/banking

www.bankaust.com.au/tools/rates

https://www.ruralbank.com.au/our-rates

http://www.beyondbank.com.au/interest-rates.html

https://www.moneysmart.gov.au/borrowing-and-credit/home-loans/interest-rates

Online product sales:

www.gumtree.com.au

www.ebay.com.au

www.amazon.com.au

Pension calculator:

www.humanservices.gov.au/customer/services/centrelink/age-pension

www.finder.com.au/australian-age-pension-eligibility-requirements

www.yourlifechoices.com.au/age-pension/pension-eligibility

www.industrysuper.com/retirement-info/age-pension/

www.canstar.com.au/superannuation/how-does-the-australian-age-pension-work/

Planning permission:

www.planningalerts.org.au

Australian Bureau of Statistics:

www.abs.gov.au

Professional bodies:

www.archicentre.com.au

www.aiqs.com.au

Property:

www.propertyupdate.com.au

www.realestate.com.au

www.commercialrealestate.com.au

www.domain.com.au

www.archicentreaustralia.com.au

www.apm.com.au

www.realestateview.com.au

www.rent.com.au

www.rentfind.com.au

www.squiiz.com.au

www.allhomes.com.au

www.homepass.com.au

www.apm.com.au

www.property.com.au

www.residex.com.au

www.househuntingaustralia.com.au

www.rpdata.com

www.corelogic.com.au

Property Council of Australia:

www.propertycouncil.com.au

Property Investors Association of Australia:

www.piaa.asn.au

www.pipa.asn.au

Property magazines publishers:

www.afr.com/afr-magazine

www.apimagazine.com.au

www.yourmortgage.com.au

www.choice.com.au

Property Owners Association of Australia:

www.poaa.asn.au

Property Valuers Institute:

www.api.org.au

Public trustee sites:

www.pt.nsw.gov.au

www.pt.qld.gov.au

www.publictrustee.sa.gov.au

www.publictrustee.tas.gov.au

www.publictrustee.act.gov.au

www.nt.gov.au/justice/pubtrust/index.shtml

www.publictrustee.wa.gov.au

Rainfall and flood maps:

www.bom.gov.au/australia/flood/additional_notes.shtml

(Always check local council websites for flood maps).

Real Estate Institute office (national, state and territories):

www.reia.asn.au

www.reiact.com.au

www.reit.com.au

www.reiwa.com.au/home

www.reisa.com.au

www.reiv.com.au

www.reint.com.au

www.reinsw.com.au

www.reiq.com

School term in Australia:

www.australia.gov.au/about-australia/special-dates-and-events/school-term-dates

Schools zone maps (metropolitan cities):

www.schoolzones.net.au/nsw/

www.melbourneschoolzones.com

www.qgso.qld.gov.au/maps/edmap

www.schoolcatchment.com.au/?page_id=1148

www.sa.gov.au/topics/education-and-learning/schools/choosing-a-school/school-zones

www.schoolcatchment.com.au/?p=1302

www.findschoolzones.com.au/school-zone-list.php?state=TAS&region=All

Solicitors and lawyers associations:

www.lawcouncil.asn.au

www.lawsociety.com.au/community/findingalawyer/australianlegalpractitioners/index.htm

Stamp duty calculation for states and territories:

www.stampduty.calculatorsaustralia.com.au

www.moneybuddy.com.au/home-loans/guide-stamp-duty.html

www.realestate.com.au/calculators/stamp-duty-calculator

State Revenue Office in states and territories (stamp duty, land tax):

www.sro.vic.gov.au

www.osr.nsw.gov.au

www.osr.qld.gov.au

www.osr.wa.gov.au

www.treasury.nt.gov.au

www.sro.tas.gov.au

www.revenuesa.sa.gov.au

Superannuation Complaints Tribunal:

www.sct.gov.au

Superannuation information:

www.asfa.asn.au

www.apra.gov.au

www.abs.gov.au

www.ato.gov.au/Super/

Taxation information:

www.ato.gov.au

Telecommunication comparisons:

www.phonechoice.com.au

www.cheapphonedeals.com.au

Tenancy advice:

www.tica.com.au

Time zones and daylight saving

http://www.australia.gov.au/about-australia/facts-and-figures/
time-zones-and-daylight-saving

Tribunals in states and territories:

www.qcat.qld.gov.au

www.vcat.vic.gov.au

www.ncat.nsw.gov.au

www.sat.justice.wa.gov.au

www.nt.gov.au/law/courts-and-tribunals/northern-territory-civil-
and-administrative-tribunal-ntcat

www.sacat.sa.gov.au

www.justice.tas.gov.au/tribunals

www.tenantsact.org.au/renting-advice/tenancy-factsheets/tribunal-acat-general-information/

Waste disposal:

www.environment.gov.au/protection/national-waste-policy

www.sustainability.vic.gov.au/services-and-advice/households/waste-and-recycling

www.vic.gov.au/environment-water/recycling-waste/waste-management.html

http://epa.tas.gov.au/regulation/waste-management

http://rethinkwaste.com.au

www.lgnsw.org.au/policy/waste-and-recycling

www.environment.nsw.gov.au/sustainabilityadvantage/

www.ehp.qld.gov.au/waste/

www.tccs.act.gov.au/recycling-and-waste

www.sa.gov.au/topics/energy-and-environment/recycling-and-waste

www.zerowaste.sa.gov.au

https://ntepa.nt.gov.au/waste-pollution

www.wasteauthority.wa.gov.au

Working With Children Check and Working With Vulnerable People (states and territories):

www.workingwithchildren.vic.gov.au

www.kidsguardian.nsw.gov.au/working-with-children/working-with-children-check

www.nt.gov.au/emergency/community-safety/apply-for-a-working-with-children-clearance

www.bluecard.qld.gov.au

www.workingwithchildren.wa.gov.au

www.accesscanberra.act.gov.au/app/answers/detail/a_id/1804

www.families.sa.gov.au/pages/protectingchildren/CSEHome

www.justice.tas.gov.au/working_with_children

www.form.act.gov.au/smartforms/landing.htm?formCode=1318

Appendix II: Questions to ask a lender

The following appendices give a list of questions that you might ask various professionals involved in your real estate journey. It is recommended you ask 'what, how, when' type questions instead of 'why' questions because the latter make people uneasy and less willing to assist.

1. What type of loan products are available for investors ?
2. What are the interest rates, monthly payments and period of loan (25 or 30 years)?
3. Are there any repayment penalties?
4. Is there any mortgage insurance payable on the loan?
5. On what date is the interest rate debited to my account?
6. Will the loan be available before the settlement date on the property?
7. How will I be advised in advance of any increases in rates and do I have the option to extend my loan, should the repayments increase?
8. How long would it take to obtain approval of my application from the date of submission of my loan application?
9. What ratio do you use of my gross income towards the debt service ratio?
10. What ratio do you use of the rental income towards the debt service ratio?
11. What is the maximum period of investment loan?
12. Can weekly, fortnightly or monthly repayments be made?
13. Are there any penalties for early repayments or lump sum reductions?
14. Is there any lenders mortgage insurance payable on the loan?
15. When is the loan interest debited to the account?
16. Can the underlying security change to another property should the current property be sold and another one bought?

17. If so, what is the maximum period between selling of one property and buying the next?

18. Is there the option to extend my loan should the repayments increase?

19. How long would it take to obtain approval of the application from the date of submission of the application?

20. What percentage do you use of rental income towards the debt servicing ratio?

21. What other fees and charges are applicable to the loan?

22. Is there a requirement to take out a credit card with the loan?

23. Is any discounted home and contents insurance offered?

24. Are credit card annual fees waived if an investment loan is taken out?

25. Is there any offset facility available?

26. How are changes in interest rates advised and how long before they take effect?

27. Are there any special packages offered with loans such as:
    - Credit card annual fees waived?
    - Cheque transaction fees waived?
    - Increased credit card limits?
    - Reduced interest rates on credit cards?
    - Discounted home and contents insurance?
    - Free financial advice?

Appendix III: Questions to ask a mortgage broker

1. Do you consider all the major banks and lenders?
2. Do you evaluate several loan products from each institution including budget and premium loans?
3. How do you calculate the impact of fees?
4. Do you apply weightings to various parts of the deals?
5. Does your commission vary according to which loan you recommend?
6. How many lenders do you represent?
7. How long have you been in the industry?
8. Are you affiliated with any major banks?
9. What are your fees or do you get paid a commission by the lender?
10. Does the commission paid vary across lenders?
11. What types of products are available to investors?
12. Do you present two or three choices to choose from or just one loan product that you have chosen?
13. Do you take into account the various fees and charges as well as interest rates when recommending a loan product?
14. Why use a finance broker rather go directly to the bank?
15. What is the maximum period of investment loan?
16. Can weekly, fortnightly or monthly repayments be made?
17. Are there any penalties for early repayments or lump sum reductions?
18. Is there any lenders mortgage insurance payable on the loan?
19. When is the loan interest debited to the account?
20. Can the underlying security change to another property should the current property be sold and another one bought?
21. If so, what is the maximum period between selling of one property and buying the next?

22. Is there the option to extend my loan should the repayments increase?

23. How long would it take to obtain approval of the application from the date of submission of the application?

24. What percentage do you use of gross income towards the debt servicing ratio?

25. What percentage do you use of rental income towards the debt servicing ratio?

26. What other fees and charges are applicable to the loan?

27. Is there a requirement to take out a credit card with the loan?

28. Is there any professional package offering reduced interest and annual fees?

29. Is any discounted home and contents insurance offered?

30. Are credit card annual fees waived if an investment loan is taken out?

31. Is there any offset facility available?

Appendix IV: Questions to ask yourself before finalising an investment property for renting

1. How many bedrooms, bathrooms?
2. How many cars can be parked in the garage?
3. How close is the property to the amenities (shopping centre, school, university, public transport, childcare or hospitals)?
4. Does the property have a balcony if it is an apartment?
5. Are the rooms located in the direction of sunlight?
6. What is the crime rate in the neighbourhood?
7. What is the yield and rental return?
8. What is the market rent for similar properties?
9. What is the vacancy rate for this suburb?
10. Is the property double or single brick, timber or steel frame structure?
11. What kind of foundation is the building placed on?
12. Are the termite protection and warranties still in place?
13. Are there any cracks in either internal or external walls?
14. What is the type of roof - tile, colorbond or galvanised steel?
15. Are there any renovations or extensions? Were these notified to the council and was there a planning permit applied for this before construction?
16. Are all permits in place ?
17. What are the risks involved regarding construction completed without a planning permit?
18. Is there a compliance certificate for any electrical or plumbing work recently completed?
19. How big is the hot water system and is it adequate for the size of occupants in this building?
20. What is the current zoning of the property?
21. What is the minimum lot size for this suburb?

22. What are the new plans in the council's master plan for this area – any new house developments, amenities (shopping centre, new schools and train stations)?
23. Does the building have a view of a park or garden? Would it be noisy during weekend if the park is very close to an open basketball court?
24. Are the gardens and backyards low maintenance?
25. Are there any trees very close to gutters and roofs? What kind of canopy does the tree create?
26. What kind of fencing is around the property and what condition is it in?
27. Is the property in a good location?
28. Does the property have any 'wow' features?
29. Will this property be tenanted at all times?
30. Will the property generate enough cash flow so that I can buy another property?
31. Is this a part of town that people want to live in?
32. How does it fit in with local schools?
33. Will it attract tenants?
34. Is there likelihood that this area could be rezoned?
35. If it is an apartment, is it next to a lift well or high traffic area that may be noisy?
36. Does the Body Corporate allow Airbnb tenants?
37. Does the body corporate specify limits on the number of occupants per unit?

Appendix V: Questions to ask before purchasing a property in a mining town

1. What is the population of the town?
2. Which is the closest city?
3. Has the population increased, decreased or remained steady over the past 10 – 15 years?
4. Is the town subject to flooding?
5. What other industries are in the town?
6. What schools and hospitals are available in the town?
7. What supermarkets and banks are available in the town?
8. Is the council pro-development and does it have a 10 – 15 year plan?
9. How many houses are on the market for sale?
10. What is the median price?
11. What has been the median price over the last 1,3,5,7 and 10 years?
12. What are the average number of days on the market when selling?
13. How many houses are on the market for rent?
14. What is the median rent?
15. What has been the median rent over the last 1,3,5,7 and 10 years?
16. If the current rent was to drop by 50%, how does that affect the feasibility of owning the property?
17. If the property value dropped by 50% and the rent dropped by 50%, how would that impact on moving forward with future property purchases?
18. How many mines does this town service?
19. How many mining companies are represented?
20. What is the expected life of the mine?
21. Does the mining company employ fly-in/fly-out workers? If the answer is yes to the above question, then local infrastructure spending and residential rental would be lower).

22. Is there a mining camp for workers and who owns the camp?
23. Does the council allow Airbnb and rooming house style accommodation?
24. Is there a demand for this style of accommodation?
25. Is there a need for executive style leasing?
26. Is the mining company happy to sign a corporate lease?
27. What other infrastructure development is happening?
28. At what stage is this and how many workers are employed?
29. What is the rental return for the property?
30. What is the phase of the mining project in that area?
31. What type of mining is involved? How long is the mine scoped for full scale operation?
32. What is the proposed infrastructure funding in and around that area?

Appendix VI: Questions to ask yourself to assess the value of the property based on internal factors

1. Air conditioning and other fixtures
2. Architecture style
3. Building / land ratio
4. Construction materials
5. Date of construction
6. Dimensions and floor area
7. Floor plans
8. Heating
9. Interior utilities
10. Placement of building
11. Plumbing
12. Special equipment such as elevators
13. Utilities

Appendix VII: Questions to ask yourself to assess the value of the property based on external factors

1. Climate
2. Educational institutions
3. Employers
4. Hazards and nuisances
5. Industries
6. Level of business activity
7. Location in block
8. Location of facilities: schools, shopping, recreational, cultural
9. Natural resources
10. Restrictions on the property
11. Population density
12. Population trends
13. Public transport
14. Topography
15. Water bodies (ravines, rivers, lakes) and other attractions
16. Zoning
17. Location

Appendix VIII: Questions to ask your local town planner before you plan to develop or to invest

1. What is the size of the business – sole practitioner or larger company with multiple offices?
2. How long have they been practising?
3. What experience do they have with local council?
4. Do they have a multi-disciplined team?
5. Do they specialise in any particular area – residential, industrial, sub division?
6. Do they 'push the envelope' or are they conservative?
7. Are they accredited with the local Council eg Risksmart Development Assessment for Brisbane City Council?
8. What councils do they work with?
9. Do they have experience with similar projects?
10. Do they have the necessary insurances and certifications?
11. Do they understand your time constraints and can you work with them?
12. Are they easy to communicate with and are hey readily contactable?
13. Do they respond promptly?
14. Can they supply references?
15. Can they provide an estimate of costs for this project?
16. What are their hourly rates?
17. Do they charge a fee for pre lodgement meetings?
18. Do they handle public notifications?
19. What sub consultants and contractors do they use?
20. How supportive is council towards development?
21. What is the estimated timeframe for a development application?
22. What is the minimum lot size in the suburb (you are looking for)?

23. What is the processing time for development applications in the local council or shire?
24. Are subdivisions allowed in the street or suburb you are looking for?
25. How supportive is the council towards developers?

Appendix IX: Questions to ask a rental manager – residential properties

1. What geographical areas do you cover with your rental properties?
2. What is happening in the local market and where is it likely to go in the next 12 months?
3. What types of property do you rent?
4. What is the average time a similar property will remain vacant?
5. Does the agency have a dedicated property manager?
6. Is the agency a member of the Real Estate Institute in that state?
7. What is the staff to rental ratio?
8. How experienced are the property managers?
9. How long have they worked for this company?
10. Is there a dedicated staff to a landlord or is it based on geographic location?
11. How often to do undertake property inspections?
12. Can you provide a sample copy of a property inspection report?
13. How are the inspection reports provided to the landlord?
14. How often and when do you remit rental income?
15. Do you provide monthly and annual statements via email and mail? (Sample required).
16. What are your rental arrears?
17. How soon do you take action on rental arrears?
18. How do you deal with rental arrears and maintenance issues?
19. Will you go to the tribunal if needed and what is your success rate from previous appearances?
20. How do you minimise vacancies between tenants?
21. How is the market rent determined?
22. What advertising is undertaken for tenants and who pays?

23. Do you have a database of prospective tenants?
24. What methods are used to check prospective tenants regarding credit worthiness, rental history and current employment?
25. What processes are used to show prospective tenants the property?
26. Do you attend inspections required by valuers, building inspectors, pest control and contractors?
27. Do you have reliable tradespeople you use on a regular basis?
28. How often do you compare these tradespeople prices with their competitors to ensure competitive pricing?
29. Do you organise quotes for any repairs and cleaning as required? (Three quotes required for work estimated at over $500).
30. Do you obtain water meter reading as required?
31. Do you organise repairs to any item which may be claimed within the warranty period?
32. What commission do you charge?
33. Are there any additional charges apart from commission?
34. What companies do they earn commissions from?
35. Will the property manager offer suggestions on ways to improve the rental and value of property?
36. Do you provide a written proposal?
37. Can you supply references including phone numbers from current landlords?

Appendix X: Questions to ask a rental manager – commercial properties

1. What geographical areas do you cover with your rental properties?
2. What is happening in the local market and where is it likely to go in the next 12 months?
3. What types of property do you lease?
4. What is the average time a similar property will remain vacant?
5. Does the agency have a dedicated property manager?
6. Is the agency a member of the Real Estate Institute in that state?
7. What is the staff to rental ratio?
8. How experienced are the property managers?
9. How long have they worked for this company?
10. Is there a dedicated staff member to a landlord or is it based on geographic location?
11. How often to do undertake property inspections?
12. Can you provide a sample copy of a property inspection report?
13. How are the inspection reports provided to the landlord?
14. How often, and when, do you remit rental income?
15. Do you provide monthly and annual statements via email and mail? (Sample required).
16. What are your rental arrears?
17. How soon do you take action on rental arrears?
18. How do you deal with rental arrears and maintenance issues?
19. Will you go to the tribunal if needed and what is your success rate from previous appearance?
20. How do you minimise vacancies between tenants?
21. How is market rent determined?
22. What advertising is undertaken for tenants and who pays?

23. Do you have a database of prospective tenants?
24. What methods are used to check prospective tenants regarding credit worthiness, rental history and current employment?
25. What processes are used to show prospective tenants the property?
26. Do you attend inspections required by valuers, building inspectors, pest control and contractors?
27. Do you have reliable tradespeople you use on a regular basis?
28. How often do you compare these tradespeople's prices with their competitors to ensure competitive pricing?
29. Do you organise quotes for any repairs and cleaning as required? (Three quotes required for work estimated at over $500).
30. Do you obtain water meter readings as required?
31. Do you organise repairs to any item which may be claimed within the warranty period?
32. What commission do you charge?
33. Are there any additional charges apart from commission?
34. What companies do you earn commissions from?
35. Will the property manager offer suggestions on ways to improve the rental and value of property?
36. Do you provide a written proposal?
37. Can you supply references including phone numbers from current landlords?
38. Can you assist with negotiating leases?
39. Can you organise fire safety and asbestos reports and air conditioning servicing?
40. Are you up to date with legislation such as retail shops?
41. What experience have you had with negotiating 'make-good' requirements?
42. How experienced are you with managing government tenants?

Appendix XI: Questions to ask a real estate agent (or the vendor)

1. How long the vendor has owned the property?
2. What is the vendor's plan after selling the property (interstate, retirement)?
3. What is the reason for selling?
4. How long has the vendor owned the property?
5. Is the property vacant or tenanted?
6. If leased, when was the last time the rent was reviewed?
7. Who manages the property? Are they doing a good job?
8. What are the outgoings, taxes, maintenance, management fees, rates and water, electricity, land tax, strata management fees?
9. How long is the settlement time?
10. Are there any encumbrances, caveats or a second mortgage on the property?
11. Will the owner offer vendor financing?
12. Will the owner accept a trade-in deal with another higher value asset?
13. Does the owner have any other property for sale?
14. Would I be able to renovate before settlement?
15. Who was the last owner and how long did he/she own the property?
16. If strata title, could I get a copy of the strata management rules?
17. What is the vendor's asking price?
18. How and why did they reach that figure?
19. How long has the property been on the market?
20. Has there been any previous offer made on this property?
21. How motivated is the vendor?
22. How do you see this type of property growth over the next 5 years?
23. What could be done to enhance the property's value?

24. Have you sold any other or similar houses nearby recently?
25. Do you know of any encumbrances, caveats or second mortgage over the property?
26. Does the owner have any other property for sale?
27. Is the vendor flexible on sale terms?
28. Will the vendor look at a long settlement?
29. Will the vendor look at an option to purchase?
30. Would the vendor allow early access prior to settlement?
31. Will the vendor offer any vendor financing?
32. If the property was rented, what is the expected rent?
33. Who would be the ideal tenant for this property?
34. If property is already rented – what date is it rented to?
35. What are the outgoings – rates, water rates, maintenance, property management fees, strata fees if applicable
36. How long have tenants lived here?
37. When was the last rent review and what was the increase?
38. Who manages the property?
39. What is the minimum expectation of the vendor?
40. What are the vendor's plans after selling the property?

Appendix XII: Sample forms – budget, property inspection checklist, feasibility, quotation form for repairs, record of telephone conversation, telephone call log

Typical costs for a landlord on a residential investment property

Property address: Total loan value: Monthly repayment:	
Land value: Rent: Vacancy rate:	
Items	
Managing agent Commission Reletting fee Advertising cost Document fee End-of-financial year statement Tribunal fee Order of possession Postage Statement fee (monthly)	
Insurance Landlord combined policy premium (house and contents, workers' compensation, public liability, rent)	
Rates (council, water, land tax)	
Strata levy – body corporate fee	
Maintenance Cleaning gutters Cleaning carpet Other repairs AC and heater duct cleaning Fire alarm maintenance	
Pest inspection	
Total	

Appendix XIII: Types of fees and charges to be paid on or before settlement

Costs	$
Legal costs Conveyancing fees Registration fees Other fees	
Finance Loan application fee Property valuation	
Tax Stamp duty on purchase Stamp duty on mortgage	
Inspections Pre-purchase building inspection Pest inspection Mortgage insurance Insurance (building and contents)	
Total	

Appendix XIV: Property file notes

Address of property:		
Date of discussion / Email:		
Description of matters discussed:		
By Phone? Yes		No
They rang me I rang them		Contact phone number:
By Email? Yes		No
They emailed me I emailed them		
In Person? Yes		No
Discussions/email with:		
Tenant Property Manager		Other
Summary of discussion /email:		
Matter resolved Yes		No
Follow-up needed Yes		No
By whom?		
By when?		
Signed and dated:		

Appendix XV: Correspondence register

Project Date	Portfolio Number	Subject	Action Required	Action taken	Date completed

It's My Time: The A to Z of Property and Financial Terms

Appendix XVI: Inspection times

Time	Location	Map Ref	Description	Land Area	Price	Agent
9.00 –10.00						
10.00 –11.00						
11.00 – 12.00						
12.00 – 1.00						
1.00 – 2.00						
2.00 – 3.00						

Appendix XVII: Property inspection checklist

Area	Condition – Exterior							
	Type	Good	Fair	Poor	Repair	Replace	N/A	Commence
Exterior								
Front fence								
Right hand side fence								
Left hand side fence								
Rear fence								
Front path								
Driveway								
Gardens								
Outdoor entertaining								
Decking								
Stairs								
Exterior walls								
Windows								
Roofing								
Guttering and downpipes								
Foundations								
Rubbish								
Street appeal								
	Condition – Interior							
Internal								
Front door								
Entry - floor								
Entry - ceiling								
Entry - walls								
Entry - light fittings								
Living - floor								

Appendix XVII: Property inspection checklist

Area	Type	Condition – Exterior						Commence
		Good	Fair	Poor	Repair	Replace	N/A	
Living - ceiling								
Living - walls								
Living - light fittings								
Dining - floor								
Dining - ceiling								
Dining - walls								
Dining - light fittings								
Kitchen - floor								
Kitchen - ceiling								
Kitchen - walls								
Kitchen - cupboards								
Kitchen – tapware (including water hammering)								
Kitchen -appliance								
Kitchen - light fittings								
Bathroom - floor								
Bathroom- ceiling								
Bathroom - walls								
Bathroom - vanity								
Bathroom - shower								
Bathroom- towel rails								
Bathroom light fittings								
Toilet - floor								
Toilet - ceiling								
Toilet- walls								
Toilet- cistern								
Toilet - light fittings								
Ensuite - floor								
Ensuite- ceiling								

Appendix XVII: Property inspection checklist

Area	Condition – Exterior							
	Type	Good	Fair	Poor	Repair	Replace	N/A	Commence
Ensuite - walls								
Ensuite - vanity								
Ensuite - shower								
Ensuite- towel rails								
Ensuite - light fittings								
Ensuite - toilet								
Bedrooms (all) - floors								
Bedroom (all) - ceiling								
Bedroom (all) - floor								
Bedroom (all) - walls								
Bedroom (all) - wardrobes								
Bedroom (all) - light fittings								
Laundry - floor								
Laundry - ceiling								
Laundry - walls								
Laundry - vanity								
Laundry - light fittings								
Plumbing general								
Electrical general (check for residual current circuit breaker)								
Pest								

Bibliography

1. Whittaker, N., 1998. Getting it Together: To the Young People of the World, Our Future Depends on You. Simon & Schuster Australia.
2. Davis, L.M., 2010. The Facebook Era: Tapping Online Social Networks to Build Better Products, Reach New Audiences, and Sell More Stuff.
3. Atkin, B. and Brooks, A., 2014. Total facility management. John Wiley & Sons.
4. Friedman, J.P. and Lindeman, J.B., 2013. Dictionary of real estate terms. Barron's Educational Series.
5. Zeller, D. 2007. The Champion Real Estate Team: A Proven Plan for Executing High Performance and Increasing Profits, McGraw-Hill Companies, Incorporated.
6. Poorvu, W.J., 2008. Creating and growing real estate wealth: the 4 stages to a lifetime of success. FT Press.
7. Anderson, P.J., 2009. The Secret Life of Real Estate and Banking. Shepheard-Walwyn Limited.
8. Ventolo, W.L. and Williams, M.R., 2001. Fundamentals of real estate appraisal. Dearborn Real Estate.
9. Armatys, J., Askham, P. and Green, M., 2013. Principles of valuation. Taylor & Francis.
10. Dureu, B., 2011. Raw and finished materials: a concise guide to properties and applications. Momentum Press.
11. Banks, E., 2015. Finance: the basics. Routledge.
12. Warren, Tony. & Real Estate Institute of Australia. 1991, Managing residential property / Tony Warren Real Estate Institute of Australia Canberra
13. Lomas, M. 2013. How to Achieve Property Success, Major Street Publishing.
14. Lomas, M. 2011. How to Maximise Your Property Portfolio, Wiley.
15. Martin, D.M., 2006. The AZ of facilities and property management. Thorogood Publishing.

16. Leopold, L., 2012. How to Make a Million Dollars an Hour: Why Hedge Funds Get Away with Siphoning Off America's Wealth. John Wiley & Sons.

17. Huston, S. and Elliott, P., 2012. Property valuation and investment. Cengage Learning.

18. Greer, G.E. and Kolbe, P.T., 2003. Investment analysis for real estate decisions (Vol. 1). Dearborn Real Estate.

19. Geltner, D., Miller, N.G., Clayton, J. and Eichholtz, P., 2001. Commercial real estate analysis and investments (Vol. 1, p. 642). Cincinnati, OH: South-western.

20. Wilkinson, S., Reed, R. and Cadman, D., 2008. Property development (Vol. 2). London: Routledge.

21. Cisneros, H. & Institute, U. L. 2015. Urban Real Estate Investment: A New Era of Opportunity, Urban Land Institute.

22. Airey, G. J. 2003. The Property Investor's Handbook, John Wiley & Sons Australia, Limited.

23. Barrett, P. and Finch, E., 2013. Facilities management: The dynamics of excellence. John Wiley & Sons.

24. Binkley, A., 2013. The Real Estate Solar Investment Handbook: A Commercial Property Guide to Managing Risks and Maximizing Returns. Routledge.

25. Breitenmoser, K. & Ahmed, A. & Bastiaenz, R. & Video Education Australasia 2012, The nature of business in Australia, VEA, Bendigo, Vic.

26. Greene, G., 2004. The end of suburbia: Oil depletion and the collapse of the American dream. Electric Wallpaper Company.

27. Brian-Wheatley, C., 2015, Building wealth in a self-managed super fund, Global Publishing Group.

28. Cerexhe, P. 2004. Smarter Property Investment: Ways to Make More Out of Residential Property Investment, Allen & Unwin.

29. Falkson, A. J. 1991. Investing in Real Estate on a Budget, Elephas.

30. Dunstan, B. & Review, A. F. 1991. Understanding Finance with the Australian Financial Review, Wrightbooks.
31. Newell, G. & Sieracki, K. 2009. Global Trends in Real Estate Finance, Wiley.
32. Berlatsky, N. 2015. Bankruptcy, Greenhaven Press, A part of Gale, Cengage Learning.
33. Partnoy, F. 1997. F.I.A.S.C.O.: Blood in the Water on Wall Street, Profile Books Limited
34. Davis, S. 1997. The Architecture of Affordable Housing, University of California Press.
35. Clauretie, T. M. & Sirmans, G. S. 2010. Real Estate Finance: Theory & Practice: Theory and Practice (with CD-ROM), Cengage Learning.
36. Taylor, L. 2003. Tax and You, Pascal Press.
37. Gans, J., King, S., Stonecash, R., Libich, J., Byford, M. & Mankiw, N. G. 2014. Principles of Economics, Cengage Learning Australia
38. D.K., 2017, How Money Works: The Facts Visually Explained, Dorling Kindersley Ltd
39. Australian Taxation Office, Accessed 1 Nov 2017 www.ato.gov.au
40. Australian Securities and Investments Commission, accessed on 1 Nov 2017 www.moneysmart.gov.au
41. Australian Government, accessed on 1 Nov 2017 www.australia.gov.au
42. Australian Building Codes Board, accessed on 1 Nov 2017 www.abcb.gov.au/Resources/Publications/Education-Training/Building-classifications
43. First Home Owner Grant, accessed on 1 Nov 2017 www.firsthome.gov.au
44. The Australian Property Institute, accessed on 1 Nov 2017 www.api.org.au
45. The Reserve Bank of Australia, accessed on 1 Nov 2017 www.rba.gov.au

46. Department of Infrastructure, Local Government and Planning, Queensland Government, accessed on 1 Nov 2017 www.dilgp.qld.gov.au
47. Commonwealth of Australia Constitution Act, accessed on 1 Nov 2017 www.aph.gov.au
48. Smith, A., 1827. An Inquiry into the Nature and Causes of the Wealth of Nations (No. 25202). Printed at the University Press for T. Nelson and P. Brown.

Index (selective keywords)

Index (selective keywords)

Awning window, 181
AWOL, 251

B
Baby boomers, 252
Backfill, 182
Bad debt, 84
Bad vacancy rate, 73
Bagging, 182
Balance sheet, 84
Balcony, 182
Balloon payment, 85
Balustrade, 182
Bank deposits, 144
Bank guarantee, 86
Banking and Financial Services
    ombudsman, 287
Banking and Financial Services
    Ombudsman, 244
Bankruptcy, 86
Banks (Australian big four), 287
Bare trust, 87
Barge board, 182
BAS, 92
Base rent, 144
Basic home loan, 87
Basic renovation, 168
BASIX, 182
BASIX Certificate, 183
Bat, 183
Batten, 183
Batter boards, 183
Battle-axe block, 16
Bay window, 183
Beam, 183
Bearers, 183
Bearing wall, 184
Bear market, 145
Bedrock, 184
Benchmark, 145, 184
Beneficiary, 87
Benzene, toluene, ethylbenzene and
    xylene, 184
Bequeathment, 20
Betterment statement, 87
Betterment tax, 87
Bevel, 185
Bifold door, 185
'Big four' banks, 88
Bilateral contract, 252
Bill, 252
Bill of Quantities, 185
Bill of Sale, 17

Binding offer, 88
Birdsmouth notch, 185
Bitcoin, 88
Blackwater, 252
Blanket mortgage, 88
Bleeding, 185
Blockchain, 17
Block splitter, 185
Blue board, 185
Blue chip, 145
Blueprint, 252
Board of directors, 252
Body Corporate, 18
Body corporate fee, 19
Body corporate insurance, 19
Bolster, 185
Bona fide, 253
Bond, 19, 145
Bond (brick pattern), 185
Bond (government), 88
Bonds, 89
Bookkeeping, 89
Book value, 89
Boom phase, 145
BOOT, 89
Borrower qualification and loan
    underwriting, 89
Borrowing costs, 89
Bottom plate, 186
Box gutter, 186
Brace, 186
Bracket, 186
Breach of contract, 253
Break-even point, 89
Bretton Wood system, 90
Brick construction, 186
Brick paving, 186
Bricks, 186
Bricks and mortar, 146
Brick ties, 187
Brick veneer construction, 187
Bridging loan, 90
Brokerage, 91
BTEX, 184
Budget, 91
Budget deficit, 92, 253
Budget surplus, 92, 253
Builder licencing authorities, 289
Builders' sand, 187
Building agreement or contract, 187
Building Application, 187
Building certificate, 188

340   It's My Time: The A to Z of Property and Financial Terms

Index (selective keywords)

Index (selective keywords)

It's My Time: The A to Z of Property and Financial Terms

Index (selective keywords)

Vault cash, 139
Vendee, 76
Vendor, 76
Vendor finance, 139
Vendor terms, 76
Veneer, 237
Venture capital, 140
Verandah, 238
Verge, 238
Very low density house, 76
Villa, 76
Void, 238, 285
Volatility, 175

W

Waffle pod slab, 238
WALE, 175
Walk up flats, 76
Wall anchor, 238
Wall cavity, 238
Wall Street, 175
Warranty, 285
Waste disposal, 307
Water/cement ratio, 238
Water feature, 238
Water meter, 239
Water proofing, 239
Water restrictions, 285
Water treatment plant, 286
Weak currency, 105

Wealth, 140
Wear and tear, 140
Weather boarding, 240
Weep holes, 239
Weighted Average Lease Expiry, 175
Wetlands, 77
White elephant, 286
Will, 286
Wind (acting on a building), 240
Wind load, 239
Window furnishings, 239
wine equalisation tax, 92
Work Cover insurance, 77
Workers compensation insurance, 286
Working capital, 140
Working With Children Check, 307
Working With Vulnerable People, 307
Work triangle, 241
Write down, 140
Write-off, 140
Written down value, 140

Y

Yield, 177
Yield increase, 178

Z

Zone, 77
Zoning, 77

Reference and copyright credits

The authors and the publisher (*Arthur Phillip Books*) have made every effort to credit and refer to the images, graphs, tables, and other statistics mentioned in this book. If any attribution is incorrect, the publisher will correct the factual and reference error(s) once it has been brought to their attention on the next print. Kindly contact the publishers at apbooks2020@gmail.com.

About the authors

Brian McNicol has been happily married for over 40 years and has three married sons. He followed his father into the accounting profession and was exposed to the stock market at an early age purchasing shares in companies that his father worked for or on recommendations from his father's stockbroking advisers. Brian dabbled in the share market for many years having a portfolio of shares ranging from *blue chip to penny dreadful* but it was the property market that held his interest.

Brian's first purchase in 1975 was a vacant block of land which was soon to become his principal place of residence being completed just after their return from the honeymoon. On moving in, there was no internal painting, no floor coverings, batten holders only for light fittings and no landscaping. Every spare hour and dollar then went into completing that house.

Since that time, Brian has lived in different parts of Australia and overseas, purchased off-the-plan investment apartments, lived on acreage and subdivided property. Brian has renovated houses and designed and built a number of new houses. He has obtained development approvals for one into two, two into four and high rise apartments.

Over the years, Brian has spent thousands of dollars on books and hundreds of thousands of dollars on education and mentoring. He has learnt, sometimes costly lessons, to be wary of new 'gurus' with little long term experience, new schemes that are not tested over time and things that are too good to be true. Brian has a wealth of experience and has made mistakes along the way. Ask him about negative gearing and interest rates of 18 %. He has spoken at a number of large events but prefers talking to small groups or one on one with other investors. This book and the others that will follow in this series is one way that Brian can give back to the community.

Today Brian focuses mainly on commercial property both as an investor and as a buyer's agent through his company *Commercial Property Buyers Agency Australia*.

Brian has spoken to hundreds of people about commercial property and has mentored students who wish to learn more about commercial property.

Muthu Pannirselvam has had a varied international career that has included university teaching, industry consulting, strategic advising and property investment. Muthu's family was involved in the silk business for over 6 generations. Muthu's father was an accountant who worked in a financial institution and his mother was an economics and commerce teacher. Muthu had business acumen from a very young age that sharpened further during the time he helped his family business in various areas: bookkeeping, accounting, purchasing bonds, shares and bullion. His businesses at an early age included: leasing a local cafe as sole owner, profit-sharing model with a larger restaurant and improving sales strategies of a few local businesses. After reaching America in his early 20s, he started to learn more about western economics and business. His knowledge on western economics has grown exponentially after his mentor in the financial world suggested that he read books like *The Wealth of Nations* where *Adam Smith* discusses labour, capital, land and technology. From an early age, Muthu was very conscious that he had to work hard before venturing into entrepreneurship later in life. In the past 12 years, he has lectured over 500 students, has completed over 150 small to large industrial projects and has organised some 25 seminars that have attracted at least 1000 industries in the past 12 years. Now he joins hands with his mentor and co-author Brian McNicol to extend his property journey through books and coaching, mainly in the areas of commercial properties.

Muthu was always curious of knowing "how things work" from atoms to space. His curiosity has helped him to sharpen his skills in research and development. He has developed a few products in the USA and in Australia and writes programs and codes during the weekends for mobile and web applications. He is an author and an editor of various technical articles for trades teaching, book chapters and a recent book focused on technology and smart cities. Muthu lives happily with family in Melbourne West.

Commercial Property Buyers Agency

Commercial Property Buyers Agency is a boutique company specialising in the purchase of commercial property, primarily in Queensland and New South Wales, on behalf of its clients. The company is very active in the commercial property real estate market and in regular contact with many commercial real estate agents.

As such, we can save you time (and ultimately money) by finding the right commercial property for you. People will waste hundreds of hours looking at commercial properties without having the clarity of what they want to purchase, no strategy nor sequence of steps to find what they want. Through our comprehensive buying service, we will establish your property requirements and buying criteria, and develop a property brief with you. We then research and shortlist properties both on and off market that meet your criteria, evaluate them and then, if you wish, negotiate on your behalf to secure your commercial property.

We will, as your buyer's agent, always work in the best interest of you, the buyer, and always look to secure the property at the lowest possible price and best terms. We understand your time and budget constraints and will work within those to secure a property at a price and terms favourable to you.

Our aim is to purchase a commercial property that meets our client's requirements, will attract and retain quality tenants, have good long-term leases and provide strong rental yield. Above all, we aim to save our clients time, money and stress. We are committed to always acting with integrity and honesty and in our client's best interest. If you would like to find out more about how *Commercial Property Buyers Agency* can find the right commercial property for you, or more about mentoring, contact cpbuyersagency@gmail.com

Auction Bidding 4 U

Auctions are designed to play on people's emotions and create a competitive atmosphere. How many stories have you heard of auctions of properties being sold thousands of dollars over the reserve price? We have also seen the same thing on some episodes of *The Block* when the apartments go to auction and achieve well over the reserve.

Why? Because people's emotions are involved and a good auctioneer can create an atmosphere of fear and frenzy – "it will be sold today, you don't want to miss out" is commonly heard at auction. The potential purchaser is generally at a distinct disadvantage when it comes to buying at auction. You can be in hostile territory and surrounded by 'the enemy'. Let's have a quick look at who might be in attendance at an auction and who is likely to create this environment:

Firstly, the selling agent whose primary responsibility is to their client, the vendor. The agent's role is to promote and attract as many people to the auction as possible; not what you as a buyer want.

Secondly, associates of the agent who attend to boost the numbers at auctions and will 'work the room' by finding potential bidders and then provide encouragement during the auction to bid higher. They are also working for the vendor and will try to encourage attendees to keep bidding as the more people that bid, the better the result for the vendor.

Thirdly, the auctioneer is specifically aiming for a successful result – reaching reserve and selling for the highest price. The auctioneer aims to achieve this by creating an atmosphere of excitement, fear, greed and confidence as they seek multiple bids.

Fourthly, the 'rent a crowd' invited to the auction – neighbours, friends and maybe the genuine buyer/s who wish to purchase the property. They are the ones that are nervous or supremely overconfident until reality sets in.

In such a hostile environment, an inexperienced bidder can easily end up paying far more than the property is worth. A buyer's agent is a licensed real estate agent working solely on behalf of his/her client. By engaging the services of a professional buyer's agent, (or *buyer's advocate*) the chances of securing the property at a realistic price are greatly increased. Furthermore, the bidder might not be available at the time of the auction and he/she might wish to maintain anonymity regardless. The money saved using an experienced professional is nearly always far more than the commission paid.

To find out more contact Brian at auctionbidding4u@gmail.com

Real Estate Investor or Gambler!

Which do you want to be?
Written by John Bone
(ISBN: 978-0-646-97111-7 (Paperback)

A Guide to Financial Feasibility Studies for Australian Real Estate Investments and Developments is a book for every one of the two million investors in Australia who own at least one investment property. The purpose of the book is to help real estate investors and developers understand the reason for, and the process of undertaking and/or evaluating, a financial feasibility study into real estate investment opportunities. Much of it is just plain common sense but, unfortunately, this is something that is often lacking in our fast-paced lifestyle.

Financial feasibility studies aim to objectively and rationally uncover the strengths and weaknesses of an existing business or proposed venture, opportunities and threats present in the environment, the resources required to carry through, and ultimately the prospects for success. In its simplest terms, the two criteria to judge feasibility are costs required and value to be attained. Unfortunately, these simple rules are often overlooked and/or misinterpreted leading to financial failures and lost opportunities.

The author's intention from the outset has been to write a book that would appeal to all people who have an interest in real estate. There is something here for everyone, whether you are a developer or investor, experienced or beginner. It is also intended to be brutally honest with the good intention to educate the beginner and to improve the understanding of investors with some experience. In pointing out the problems, the author has also proposed some solutions.

Website address:

http://realestateinvestingsoftware.com.au/about/australia-property-investor-john-bone/john-bone/

Keep on reading

We hope that you have found the information in this book useful. If you have any questions, or if you would like to provide a testimonial, please email us at apbooks2020@gmail.com.

This book is the first of six books that we are writing. It was designed as a resource, a useful reference for terminology, providing reference websites and some basic forms. It is designed to complement our next books. A key to success is to continually improve your financial competence and this series of books is designed to assist with improving your competency in property investment.

The second book titled "*It's My Time: Setting Financial and Personal Goals*" is about planning and developing a blueprint for the rest of your life, regardless of what age you are. Most people have no financial plan, nor a belief that they can be financially free. Most people have little or no understanding of their current financial position and even less understanding of their projected financial situation. Many invest in shares and/or property with little thought as to why they are doing so, or how it will fit into their current or future lifestyle. We therefore need to look at our attitude to money and our psychology of spending. Our second book provides a framework for self-evaluation, of where you are now financially, and then moving on to goal setting. We also look at risk profile, structures, finance, insurance and taxation. Expected publication date is April 2020.

The third book titled "*It's My Time: Successful Residential Investing*" in the series then builds upon the first two and focuses on residential property investment. Yes, there are a lot of residential books currently in the market but we have attempted to make ours relevant with information that is for today's investors. Yes, we will cover the basics but we will also delve into aspects of being a landlord that aren't included in most books, for example abandoned goods and meth labs. We have purposely tried to make this book different and we hope that you will find it a useful resource on your property investment journey. Expected publication date is March 2020.

The fourth book titled *"It's My Time: Introducing Commercial Investing"* is about commercial real estate. Commercial real estate in the last couple of years has seen an increase in popularity as the yield from residential property declines. As property prices particularly in Sydney and Melbourne have increased, residential rents have not kept pace and investors are looking for alternatives. Some investors have sold their Sydney and Melbourne properties and looked at commercial property to provide better yields. Many Self-Managed Superannuation Funds are also looking at commercial property because of the returns and the long-term leases. Generally, there is less legislation around commercial property than retail and we will look at the legislative requirements for retail shop investors. Expected publication date is March 2020.

The fifth book is about how to retire with peace and security. It covers planning for retirement; not only financially but also how to transition from work life to retirement – where you may live, friendships outside of work, and what you will do to fill in your day without going to work: travel, volunteering, part time work etc. The book is entitled "It's My Time: Planning a Holistic Retirement". Expected publication date is Dec 2019.

The sixth and last book in this series is about planning and developing a blueprint for the rest of your life, regardless of what age you are. Having learnt the basics of residential and commercial investment in books three and four, our fifth book is about planning and developing a blueprint for the rest of your life, regardless of what age you are. It is about taking what you have learnt in the other four books and creating a strategy. (There are many strategies, whether it be for shares or property, and we will have touched on a number of these in books two, three and four). You may decide to follow one strategy, or you may decide to follow a number of strategies which complement each other. One of the important things with establishing your strategy is that you follow your strategy and repeat it...... and keep repeating it. This is the secret to financial success: becoming a master at those things that make up your strategy and staying focused. The book is entitled *"It's My Time: Strategies in Action"*. Expected publication date is June 2020.

We have some combined 50 years of investment experience and we are happy to impart our knowledge through these books. We hope that you enjoy reading them and that they provide you with new understandings on your investment and wealth creation journey. All pre-ordered books or additional copies purchased through our website receive a 10% discount off the listed price. If you would like to pre-order any of these books, visit our website www.arthurphillipbooks.com or email us at apbooks2020@gmail.com.

Other books in the series

Book 2

It's My Time: Setting Financial and Personal Goals

Book 3

It's My Time: Successful Residential Investing

Book 4

It's My Time: Introducing Commercial Investing

Book 5

It's My Time: Planning a Holistic Retirement

Book 6

It's My Time: Strategies in Action

Notes

Notes

Notes

Notes

www.ingramcontent.com/pod-product-compliance
Lightning Source LLC
Chambersburg PA
CBHW041207220326
41597CB00030BA/5070